THE BEST OF
Out of my Treasure

THE BEST OF
Out of my
Treasure

Edited By
DON EARL BOATMAN

COLLEGE PRESS PUBLISHING CO., Joplin, Missouri

Copyright © 1990
College Press Publishing Company

Printed and Bound in the
United States of America
All Rights Reserved

Library of Congress Catalog Card Number: 90-55861
International Standard Book Number: 0-89900-358-3

DEDICATION

This book is dedicated to Don and Elsie DeWelt. Their vision for College Press has been a phenomenal development and furthered Restoration Movement reading beyond the greatest imagination and hopeful dreams.

College Press has majored in home Bible Studies therefore this volume is not a typical production. The five previous volumes have been out of print for several years. This volume is a compilation of the five which have been very popular among their readers.

FOREWORD

"Clipped" and "Copied" are two of the most famous of all authors. I have done both in order to prepare these volumes. It is impossible to trace the source of some material, since it has evidently been treated with the scissors through several generations of church papers. Perhaps it is just as wll that the ideas rest on their own merit without giving them the added blessing of truths from famous men.

Only the Word of God is inspired of God and these "treasures" in this book are to be received and used of men as the words of man and not always as the best wisdom of man.

Table of Contents

Things Divine

God	12
The Christ	19
The Bible	27
Death	39
Eternal Life	41
Heaven	44
Hell	49

The Church

The Church	52
Attendance	72
Elders and Deacons	77
Preachers	82
Teachers	95
Missions	100

The Home

Home, Marriage	110
Father, Man	119
Mother, Woman	124
Parents, Grandparents	135
Children, Teenagers	145
Aged	151

The Christian Life

Accomplishment	158
Goals	162
Determination	165
Stewardship	170
Prayer	180
Salvation	190
Forgiveness	193
Evangelism	195
Lord's Supper	200
Service	201
Christian Living	209
Repentance	221
Trials and Tribulations	227
Influence	234

Fruits of the Spirit

Faith	242
Hope	249
Love	250
Joy	256
Peace	258
Goodness	260
Kindness	261
Patience	267
Humility	269
Mercy	270
Honesty	272
Knowledge	274

Blessings

America	282
Freedom	285
Friends	289
Opportunity	294
Blessings	299

National Evils

War	310
Worldliness	312
Alcohol	329
Tongue	340

Special Days

Thanksgiving	348
Christmas	352
Fourth of July	358
New Year's	360
Easter	365

THINGS DIVINE

God

UNDERSTANDING

Who is he with understanding . . .
  Who can know the ways of God—
He, who laid the earth's foundation;
  And brought abundance from the sod?

Who can understand the saying
  Of the ocean's restless wave?
How our God has set its boundary?
  Who can see into the grave?

What mortal man controls the morning?
  Or makes the dayspring know its place?
Who understands the veil of darkness?
  The way of light, what man can trace?

The Lord's abundant treasure hides
  The rain and hail, in wind and snow.
What man is there, the stars can count;
  The ordinances of heaven know?

'Tis God alone, Who hold the earth
  And heaven firmly in His hand
Who gives, in wisdom, more than man
  Can ever know or understand.
                    —K.B. Hoschourer

God is satisfied with Christ's work as settling the sin question. We should be satisfied with what satisfies God!

GOD'S WILL

God is working out His purpose
He has planned for you and me;
Tho' from us it may be hidden
Someday we will plainly see
How He stands behind the shadows,
Waiting to perform His will
Whisp'ring, "Child, be of good courage,
Ev'ry promise I'll fulfill."

God is working out His purpose,
Even tho' we go alone;
It may take us from our loved ones,
Lead us far away from home.
It will be the greatest pleasure,
Just to feel His presence near,
And to know that God is working
Out the purpose to Him dear.

God is working out His purpose,
Tho' it lead thro' desert bare;
He'll go with us on life's journey,
And our heavy burdens share;
Thro' the weary years of waiting,
When the heart cries, "Lord, how long?"
God is working out His purpose,
Right will triumph over wrong.

God is working out His purpose,
Never murmur or repine;
For our future's in His keeping,
Gladly to His will resign.
When the veil at last is lifted
And the shadows flee away,
We shall understand His purpose
Thro' one glad eternal day.

—Mrs. F.W. Suffield

THE BEST OF OUT OF MY TREASURE

GOD IS IN EVERY TOMORROW

God is in every tomorrow,
   Therefore I live for today,
Certain of finding at sunrise,
   Guidance and strength for the way;
Power for each moment of weakness,
   Hope for each moment of pain,
Comfort for every sorrow,
   Sunshine and joy and rain.

God is in every tomorrow,
   Planning for you and for me;
E'en in the dark will I follow,
   Trust where my eyes cannot see.
Stilled by His promise of blessing,
   Soothed by the touch of His hand.
Confident in His protection,
   Knowing my life-path is planned.

GOD'S LOVE

Earth is but a borrowed place
That God has sent to man;
He expects us to take care of it
And mend it now and then.

I pray that you will help me
Keep this earthly place
A place without God's sorrow;
A place that He'll be glad to share
And proud He let us borrow.

                —Connie Hines

YOU NEVER WALK ALONE

You never walk alone my friend,
Though you may think you do,
For in your sorrow and despair
God always walks with you.
There is no hour, no passing day
He is not by your side;
And though unseen he still is there
To be your friend and guide.
So, when you think you walk alone,
Reach out and you will find
The hand of God to show the way
And bring you peace of mind.

—Harold Mohn

GOD CALLS HIS CHILDREN:

Saints because of their character.
Disciples because they are learners.
Believers because of their Faith.
Brethren because of their relationship.
Christians because of their birth in Christ.

I am weak; Satan is mighty; God is almighty.

Fear God for His powers.
Trust Him for His wisdom.
Love Him for His greatness.
Praise Him for His faithfulness.
Adore Him for His holiness.

—Mason

WHERE AIN'T GOD

He was just a little lad, and on the Lord's Day, was wand'ring home from Sunday School, and dawdling on the way.

He scuffed his shoes into the grass; he found a caterpillar; he found a fluffy milk-weed pod, and blew out all the "filler." A bird's nest in a tree o'head, so wisely placed on high, was just another wonder that caught his eager eye.

A neighbor watched his zig-zag course, and hailed him from the lawn; asked him, where he'd been that day, and what was going on.

"Oh, I've been to Sunday School." (He carefully turned the sod, and found a snail inside.) "I've learned a lot of God."

"M'm a very fine way," the neighbor said, "For a boy to spend his time; if you'll tell me where God is, I'll give you a brand new dime."

Quick as a flash his answer came, nor were his accents faint; "I'll give you a dollar mister, if you'll tell me where God ain't."

EACH IN THEIR OWN TONGUE

> The haze on the far horizon,
> The infinite, tender sky,
> The ripe, rich tint of corn fields,
> The wild geese sailing high;
> And all over upland and lowland
> The color of Goldenrod;
> Some of us call it Autumn,
> And others call it God.

The atheist wrote, "God is nowhere." His little daughter read it, "God is now here," and thus the matter was straightened out.

EVIDENCE OF GOD

1. Creation declares the POWER of God.
2. Providence the BENEVOLENCE of God.
3. Redemption the GRACE of God.
4. Judgment the JUSTICE of God.

GOD'S PRESENCE DESIRED

God be in my head and in my understanding;
God be in mine eyes and in my looking;
God be in my mouth and in my speaking;
God be in my heart and in my thinking;
God be at mine end and at my departing.

THE MYSTERY OF GOD

"I'm not so much of a farmer as some people claim," said William Jennings Bryon, with a twinkle, "But I have observed the watermelon seed. It has the power of drawing from the ground through itself 200,000 times its weight and when you can tell me how it takes this material and out of it, colors an outside surface beyond the imitation of art, and then forms inside it a white rind and within that a red heart thickly inlaid with black seeds, each of which in turn is capable of drawing through itself 200,000 times its own weight — then you can explain to me the mystery of God."

"The world is like a symphony orchestra," Madame Galli-Curci observed. "God is the conductor. When nations turn to Him for direction, there is harmony; but when they turn away, then there is confusion and strife."

> Matthew 5:44-45
> To render evil for good is devil-like.
> To render evil for evil is beast-like.
> To render good for good is man-like.
> To render good for evil is God-like.

"All I have seen teaches me to trust the Creator for all I have not seen."
—*Ralph Waldo Emerson*

PEOPLE ARE THE GREATEST INVENTION

"People are the greatest invention yet," read an advertisement of the Bell Telephone System. After viewing an exhibit of the amazing modern equipment now used in telephones, a visitor wrote, "The man of the house came out with a new reverence for people." Yes, greater than any invention is its inventor; greater than any engineering project is its engineer. And greater than any man is his creator.

GOD AND MAN

There is a story about an old woman who was in distress because she had lost her sense of God. A friend who was with her one day said, "Pray to God. Ask Him to touch you. He will put His hand on you."

The old woman began to pray and suddenly felt a hand touching her. She cried out in joy, "He has touched me!" Then she added, "But do you know, it felt just like your hand!"

Her friend said, "Sure, what do you think God would be doing? Did you think He'd reach a long arm out of heaven to touch you? He just took the hand that was nearest and used that."

> *I sought to hear the voice of God*
> *And climbed the topmost steeple*
> *But God declared, "Go down again,*
> *I live among the people."*
>
> —Newman

Man can take the atom apart. It takes God to hold it together.

Life's greatest tragedy is to lose God and not miss Him.

"The only real way to prepare to meet thy God is to live with thy God, so that to meet Him shall be nothing strange."
— Phillips Brooks

"I cannot believe that a power without moral sense could have created beings with a moral sense. I believe that the absolute eternally existent, self-sustaining power is not an 'it' but a He."
— E. Frank Salmon

The Christ

A man may go to heaven ... without health, without fame, without great learning, without a great name, without big earnings, without culture and without friends, without a thousand other things, but he can never get to heaven without Christ.
— Western Hills Messenger

THE LOCATION OF THE CROSS

A place called Golgotha is a most famous place on earth. It is more famous than Valley Forge or the Grand Canyon. Golgotha is both famous and infamous. The place had not a will of its own, the hillside called the skull could not complain. It was the infamy of man that made the place famous.

Man hated his lover at the cross and the Christ of the cross loved His HATERS. Man tried to kill his Saviour to prove that He was not the Saviour. Christ walked to the cross to prove that He was the Son of God and that He could not be destroyed. He was crucified but He consented to it.

God had to allow man to use every means and method to disprove Christ's Deity in order that God could prove it conclusively by the Resurrection.

—Don Earl Boatman

MOMENT BY MOMENT

Never a trial that He is not there,
  Never a burden that He doth not bear;
Never a sorrow that He doth not share,
  Moment by moment, I am under His care.

Never a heart ache, and never a groan,
  Never a tear drop, and never a moan,
Never a danger but there, on the throne,
  Moment by moment, He thinks of His own.

Never a weakness that He doth not feel;
  Never a sickness that He cannot heal.
Moment by moment, in woe or in weal
  Jesus, my Saviour, abides with me still.

—Daniel W. Whittle

WHAT CHRIST LOOKED LIKE . . .

The only reliable pen picture of Christ as he was in natural life is taken from a manuscript in the Library of Lord Kelley. It was copied from an original letter of Publius Lentulus, a procurator of Judea, and written to the Roman senate, as it was the custom in those days for the Roman governors to advise the senate concerning newcomers to the city. Publius Lentulus says:
"There appeared in these, our days, a man of great virtues named 'Jesus Christ,' who is yet living amongst us, and, of the Gentiles is accepted as the prophet of Truth. He raises the dead and cures all manner of diseases. A man of stature somewhat tall and comely such as the beholder may both love and fear. His hair is the color of chestnut, fully ripe; plain to his ears, whence downward it is more orient and curling, waving about his shoulders.

In the midst of his head is a seam, a partition in the hair, after the manner of the Nazarites. His forehead plain, his face without spot or wrinkle, beautiful with a lovely red. His nose and mouth so formed so that nothing can be reprehended. His beard is in color like his hair, not very long, but forked, his look innocent and mature.

His eyes, gray, clear and quick and luminous. In reproving he is terrible, his eyes piercing — as with two-edged sword — the greedy, the selfish and the oppressor, but look with tenderest pity on the weak, the erring and the sinful . . . Courteous and fair spoken; pleasant in conversation, mixed with gravity. It cannot be remembered that any have seen him laugh, but many have seen him weep. In proportion of body most excellent — a man of his singular beauty surpassing the children of man."

CHRIST

Christ is not valued at all unless He be valued above all.
—Augustine

FIRST AND SECOND COMING

In His humanity He was crowned with thorns;
In His exhaltation He is crowned with diadems,
He came the first time meek, lowly riding on a beast;
He will come again in power, glory riding the clouds of triumph.

He came the first time as the suffering Messiah;
To His own who received Him not;
He will come again as the Bridegroom for this bride.

Those who have been redeemed by His blood
Out of every kindred and tongue, people and nation
He comes the first time as the sin-bearer;
He will come again as the conquering King
To rule the nations with a rod of iron.

He came to you, for in His gentle voice
He'd much that He would say.
Your ears were turned to earth's discordant sounds,
And so — He went away.

He came; and in His hand He had a task
That He would have you do,
But you were occupied with other things,
And so you missed that too.

He would have touched you; and His touch could thrill,
And give you quickening power;
But earthly things enveloped, and you could
Not feel Him in that hour.

Jesus is not only a very present help in trouble, but also is help in preventing trouble.

THE GREATEST

When Jesus walked upon the earth
He didn't talk with kings,
He talked with simple people
Of doing friendly things.

He didn't praise the conquerors
And all their hero host,
He said the very greatest
Were those who loved the most.

He didn't speak of mighty deeds
And victories. He spoke
Of feeding hungry people
And cheering lonely folk.

I'm glad His words were simple words
Just meant for me and you,
The things He asked were simple things
That even I can do!
—Marion Brown Shelton

CHRIST, THE ONE

The Redeeming One — Galatians 3:13
The Reconciling One — Romans 5:10
The Risen One — Romans 4:25; 8:34
The Residing One — Colossians 1:27; Galatians 2:20
The Returning One — I Thessalonians 1:9-10; Titus 2:12-13
The Receiving One — John 14:1-3; I Thessalonians 4:15-18
The Rewarding One — II Corinthians 5:10; James 1:12
The Rejoicing One — Psalm 104:31; Luke 10:21

MY MASTER DIED AT THIRTY-THREE

My Master died at thirty-three
Burdened with love and care,
He should have lived a long, long time,
He was so young and fair.

Yet who can say how long Christ lived?
He lived so strangely well
That he put more into three brief years
Than the Four Gospels tell.

They nailed him to a Roman Cross
But His life had such a drive
That he'd done more at thirty-three
Than others at seventy-five.
—Charles Hannibal Voss

IN CHRIST WE HAVE

A love that can never be fathomed;
A life that can never die
A righteousness that can never be tarnished;
A peace that can never be understood;
A rest that can never be disturbed;
A joy that can never be diminished;
A hope that can never be disappointed;
A glory that can never be clouded;
A light that can never be darkened;
A happiness that can never be interrupted;
A strength that can never be enfeebled;
A purity that can never be defiled;
A beauty that can never be marred;
A wisdom that can never be baffled;
A resource that can never be exhausted.

BEHOLD THE CHRIST

Look backward, see Christ dying for you.
Look inward, see Christ living in you.
Look upward, see Christ pleading for you.
Look FORWARD, see Christ COMING for you.

WAYS

Philosophy — Think your way out.
Indulgence — Drink your way out.
Science — Invent your way out.
Industry — Work your way out.
Communism — Submit your way out.
Fascism — Bluff your way out.
Militarism — Fight your way out.
Christ — "I am the way" out.

Life is short, death is sure. Sin's the curse, Christ the cure.

WHY CHRIST DIED

That we might become righteous — II Corinthians 5:21
That we might die to sin in Him — I Peter 2:24
That we might no longer live to self — II Corinthians 5:15
That we might be delivered from the world — Galatians 1:4
That we might become the Sons of God — Galatians 4:4-5
That we might be sanctified unto Him — Ephesians 5:25-27
That we might become His possessions — Titus 2:14
That we might receive His Holy Spirit — Galatians 3:13-14
That we might be taken back to God — I Peter 3:18

I have a Friend unseen to me,
Who follows close where'er I go,
And everything I do or say
This Friend of mine is sure to know.

When Satan tempts with things so vain
And tries his best to catch my eye,
Somehow, someway, new strength I gain,
My unseen Friend is standing by.

Though I should stoop to depths so low,
My feet held fast by Satan's snare,
And all my earthly friends forsake,
My unseen Friend would follow there.

This love so great I can't define
Will follow me on through the end,
What would I do, where would I go
If I should lose my unseen Friend?

REVEALMENT

They planned for Christ a cruel death;
  Steel pierced His hand, His feet and side;
They mocked His last expiring breath,
  And thought then hate was satisfied.
They wagged their heads and said, "Lo, He
  would crush our temple and in three days
Restore its beauty. Come and see
  This boaster gone death's quiet ways."
They did not know that on that hill
  Eternal love was satisfied;
That Christ who hung there, triumphed still.
. . . And only cruel death had died.

MY UNSEEN FRIEND

Lonely I'd be without Him,
So long He's been my friend;
Never has He faltered,
My Saviour, Brother, Friend.

He has been my rare Companion
Through the years that are gone,
Just the same dear, loving Saviour
As when first our walk began.

A steadfast stay in every trouble,
His strength has been my plea;
With all my faults so patient,
My unseen Friend is He.

—A.P. Walker

Our God is the only God with wounded hands and a pierced side.

The Bible

Blessed Bible, how I love it!
  How it doth my bosom cheer.
What hath earth like this to covet,
  What stores of wealth are hidden here!

Yes, dear Bible, I will hide thee,
  Hide thee richly in my heart;
Thou, through all my life will guide me,
  And in death we will not part.

YOUR BIBLE

Know it in the head;
Stow it in the heart;
Show it in the life;
Read it to be wise;
Believe it to be safe;
Practice it to be holy.
If you know the Author, you will love His Book.

SHE KNEW TOO MUCH BIBLE

A little girl, being asked by a priest to attend religious instruction, refused, saying it was against her father's wishes. The priest said she should obey him, not her father. "Oh! Sir! We are taught in the Bible to 'Honor thy father and thy mother,' " she replied. "But you are to call me, Father," was his answer. To which she replied, "No, for the scriptures say, 'Call no man your father upon the earth for one is your father, which is in heaven.' "

The priest was not anxious to lose a religious discussion to one so young and he said, "You have no business reading the Bible." "Then why did Jesus tell me to 'Search the Scriptures'?" she asked. He replied by saying, "But that is only to the clergy. You understand that a little child cannot know the scriptures." "Then why," she asked, "did Paul write to Timothy: 'From a child thou hast known the holy scriptures'?"

Surely there was some way to get the best of this young upstart. Said the priest: "Timothy was being trained to be a Bishop and he was taught by the church authorities." "No sir," said the little girl, "He was taught by his mother and his grandmother. At least that's what Paul wrote."

The priest turned away and someone said they heard him mumbling something about "she knew enough Bible to poision a whole parish."

THE ANVIL OF GOD'S WORD

Last eve I paused beside the blacksmith's door,
  And heard the anvil ring the vesper chime;
Then looking in, I saw upon the floor,
  Old hammers worn with the beating years of time.

"How many anvils have you had," said I
  "To wear and batter all these hammers so?"
"Just one," said he, and then with twinkling eye,
  "The anvil wears the hammers out, you know."

"And so" I thought, "The anvils of God's Word
  For ages sceptic blows have beat upon
Yet though the noise of falling blows was heard,
  The anvil is unharmed, the hammers gone."
                                        —John Clifford, D.D.

NOT DEPENDENT ON FEELINGS

Someone asked Luther, "Do you feel that you have been forgiven?" He answered, "No, but I am as sure as there is a God in Heaven. For feelings come and feelings go, and feelings are deceiving. My warrant is the Word of God. Nought else is worth believing."

GOD'S WORD

Condemns — Galatians 3:10
Convicts — Acts 2:37
Converts — Ephesians 5:23
Cleanses — Ephesians 5:26
Commands — Matthew 28:20
Comforts — Romans 15:4
Consoles — John 14:1

THE BOOK OUR MOTHERS READ

*We search the world for truth, we cull
The good, the pure, the beautiful,
From graven stone and written scroll,
From all old flower-fields of the soul,
And weary seekers for the best,
We come back laden from our quest,
To find that all the sages said
Is in the Book our Mothers read.*
—John Greenleaf Whittier

A BIBLE NOT READ

"Mother, I've found an old dusty thing,
High on the shelf, just look!"
"Why, that's a Bible, Tommy dear;
Be careful that's God's Book!"
"Then, Mother, before we lose it
We'd better send it back to God,
For you know we never use it!"

THE BOOK OF BOOKS

*Within this ample volume lies,
The mystery of mysteries,
Happiest they of human race
To whom their God has given grace
To read, to fear, to hope, to pray,
To lift the latch, to force the way;
But better had they ne'er been born
That read to doubt or read to scorn.*
—Sir Walter Scott

Thy Word, O Lord, is my delight,
　'Tis manna to my hungry soul;
It is a never failing light
　That marks the reef and rocky shoal.

Its pages teem with sacred lore,
　From which all wisdom is conferred;
It grows in splendor more and more,
　This Book of Books, God's Holy Word.

It guards me from the tempter's snare,
　And counsels wiser than a friend;
It comforts grief and lightens care,
　Its yield of riches has no end.

It is a treasure house of gold,
　From whose supplies I would not part;
It gives return a thousand fold,
　When planted in the human heart.

O Book of Life, of Love and Truth,
　My hope of heaven I find in thee;
The only guide of age and youth
　The Word of God — His gift to me.

Holy Bible, Book divine,
　Precious treasure, thou art mine.
　　　　　　　　　—Charles Gabriel

There is nothing in the Bible that benefits you unless it is transmitted into life, unless it becomes a part of yourself, just like your food. Unless you assimilate it and it becomes body and bone and muscle, it does you no good.

　　　　　　　　　—Henry Weston

Your newspaper will tell you how men and women are living — your Bible will tell you how they ought to live.

> The doctor stopped reading his Medical Journal —
> He lost out.
> The teacher stopped reading his works on pedagogy —
> He lost out.
> The farmer stopped reading his agricultural journals —
> He lost out.
> The church member stopped reading his Bible —
> He lost out worst of all!

"I urge you to be present on the floor in time for the opening prayer by our Chaplains at 12:00 noon. He always has some helpful, encouraging, inspiring thoughts. I also suggest you read the Holy Bible, for if you do, you will find out that almost all of the smart things which are now being said have already been said in that Great Book."

—Sam Rayburn

IT WORKS

A skeptic in London in speaking of the Bible said it was quite impossible in these days to believe in any book whose authority is unknown.

A Christian asked him if the compiler of the multiplication table was known. "No," he answered. "Then, of course, you do not believe in it" the preacher replied. "Oh, yes I believe in it because it works well." "So does the Bible," was the rejoinder, and the skeptic had no answer.

Men do not reject the Bible because it contradicts itself but because it contradicts them.

BIBLE READING A GOOD TONIC

Some years ago a lady went to consult a famous physican about her health. She was a woman of temperament. She gave the doctor a list of her symptoms, and answered his questions only to be astonished at his brief prescription after the consultation. "Go home and read your Bible an hour a day, and then come back to see me a month from today." And he bowed her out before she could protest.

At first she was inclined to be angry; then she reflected that at least the prescription was not an expensive one. She went home determined to read conscientiously her neglected Bible. In one month she went back to the doctor's office. She was an entirely different person, and then she asked the doctor how he knew what she needed.

In answer the doctor turned to his desk and there worn and marked, lay an open Bible. "Madam," said the doctor, "If I were to omit my daily reading of this Book, I would lose my greatest force of strength and skill."

READ THE BIBLE THROUGH

"I supposed I knew my Bible, reading piece-meal, hit or miss;
Now a bit of John or Matthew, now a snatch of Genesis,
Certain chapters of Isaiah, certain Psalms — the twenty third,
Twelfth of Romans, first of Proverbs, Yes, I thought I knew the Word;
But I found a thorough reading was a different thing to do,
And the way was unfamiliar when I read the Bible through!
You who treat the Crown of Writings as you treat no other book —
Just a paragraph, disjointed, just a crude, impatient look,
Try a worthier procedure, try a broad and steady view;
You will kneel in very rapture, when you read the Bible
 THROUGH!"

—Amos R. Wells

I have known 95 of the world's greatest men in my time and of these 87 were followers of the Bible. The Bible is stamped with a speciality of origin and an immeasureable distance separates it from all competitiors.

—W.E. Gladstone

TRIBUTES TO THE BIBLE

George Washington: ". . . above all the pure and benign light of Revelation has had a meliorating influence on mankind and increased the blessings of society."

Thomas Jefferson: "I always have said and always will say that the studious perusal of the sacred volume will make better citizens, better fathers and better husbands."

Calvin Coolidge: "The foundations of our society and of our government rest so much on the teachings of the Bible, that it would be difficult to support them if faith in these teachings should cease to be practically universal in our country."

There is a big difference in the books that men make and the Book that makes men.

It is impossible to mentally or socially enslave a Bible reading people.

—Horace Greely

The reason people are down on the Bible is that they are not up on the Bible.

—W.W. Ayer

The Bible not *Read* is a Christian not *Fed*.

THE BIBLE

The Bible is shallow enough that the most timid swimmer may enjoy its waters without fear.

It is deep enough for the most expert swimmer to enjoy without touching bottom.

Its critics have been legion but it is still here . . . . They are gone.

It has comforted millions as no other book can comfort and still continues to do so.

When nations ignored its teachings, they fell.

It is God's vital and inviolate Word, and can never be set aside.

God takes us just as we are "without one plea," but he does not intend for us to stay that way. On the contrary, the Holy Bible has much to say about increases of various kinds.

DOES YOUR BIBLE NEED OILING?

Fred W. Cropp, President of the American Bible Society, received a letter asking a question: "What do you recommend for keeping the leather on the back of Bibles from getting stiff, cracking and peeling?"

The reply was, "There is one oil that is especially good for treatment of leather on Bibles. In fact, it will insure your Bible to stay in good condition. It is not sold, but may be found IN THE PALM OF THE HUMAN HAND."

An Irish boy, under threats, was commanded to burn his Bible. He replied, "I thank God that you cannot take away the twenty chapters that I know by heart." If your Bible were taken away from you, would you have part of it hidden in your heart?

MY BIBLE

*Whene'er my soul is torn with grief
Upon my shelf I find
A little volume, torn and thumbed,
For comfort just designed.*

*I take my little Bible down
And read its pages o'er
And when I part from it I find
I'm stronger than before.*

GOD'S WORD

*Where is comfort for your sorrow,
 Wounded heart that peace would know?
Where is help to aid and strengthen,
 Weary pilgrim here below?
Where is wisdom that will guide you,
 Puzzled youth with questioning plea?
Where is cleansing for transgression,
 Sinner longing to be free?
All is answered, all provided,
 In God's Word to you and me.*
—Della Adams Leitner

The devil is not afraid of the Bible that has dust on it.

BIBLE AND COLLEGE DEGREE

"I believe a knowledge of the Bible without a college course is more valuable than a college course without the Bible."
—Professor Phelps, Yale University

THINGS DIVINE

THE BIBLE

Despised and torn in pieces,
　By infidels decried,
The thunderbolts of hatred
　The haughty cynic's pride —
All these have railed against it
　In this and other lands;
Yet dynasties have fallen, and
　Still the Bible stands!

What is a home without a Bible?
'Tis a home where daily bread
For the body is provided
But the soul is never fed.

—C.D. Meigs

Those who find the most difficulties in the Bible are those who seldom read it.

Dust on your Bible is not evidence it is a dry book.

　　　Put it first — the Great Commission.
　　　Put it first — the Great Command.
　　　Put it first — our Standing Orders.
　　　Put it first — on sea and land.
　　　Put it first — in every parish
　　　Put it first — in every heart
　　　Put it first — don't put it second.
　　　God's own Bible is our chart.

ANSWERING AN INFIDEL

Replying to an atheist who had mailed him some infidel literature, one Christian gave the following excellent answer: "My dear sir, if you have anything better than the Sermon on the Mount, the story of the Prodigal Son and that of the Good Samaritan, or if you have any code of morals superior to the Ten Commandments, or if you can suggest anything more consoling and beautiful than the 23rd Psalm, or if you can supply anything that will throw more light on the future and reveal to me a Father more merciful and kind than the New Testament does, please send it along." There was no answer.

—Preacher's Magazine

> To do God's work
>   We must have God's power
> To have God's power
>   We must know God's will
> To know God's will
>   We must study God's Word.
>
> —John R. Matt

No book that prepares one for tomorrow can ever be out of date or old fashioned.

Someone has said, "If all Christians were to dust their Bibles at the same time, we would have the greatest dust storm in our history!"

The family Bible can be passed from generation to generation because it gets so little wear.

The great question is not what you make of the Bible, but what the Bible makes of you.

A man may memorize the Bible and never really know the author.

Death

IF I DID . . . THEN WHAT???

Did you ever think as the hearse goes by, that someday both you and I will take a ride in that big black hack, and shall never remember coming back. Rake, scrape, borrow, and save. You lose it all when you go to the grave. Money, a dead man's hand won't hold. Nor can life be purchased with silver or gold; the rich would live, but the poor would die! "For what shall it profit a man if he shall gain the whole world and lose his own soul?" (Mark 8:36).

The world has forgotten in its concern with left and right that there is an above and below.

Die when I may, I want it said of me by those who know me best that I always plucked a thistle and planted a flower where I thought a flower would grow.
—Abraham Lincoln

When we die we leave behind all we have and take with us all we are.

WAITING

We went one day at eventide,
  To stroll where fancy led,
My son with restless dancing steps,
  And I with slower tread.
He loosed his hand from mine
  And looking up he said,
"You walk so slowly, Mother dear,
  I'll just run on ahead."
And soon his eager rushing feet
  Had carried him from view,
Around the bend far down the land
  Where wild flowers grew.
And when with measured steps I came,
  And made the turning too,
He called to me, amid the flowers,
  I'm waiting here for you."
And now those restless feet are still,
  The eager spirit, free
Has gone ahead to be with God
  Through all eternity.
And though my heart is heavy
  For the days that cannot be,
I know, among God's fragrant flowers,
  He's waiting there for me.

Dying men have said, "I am sorry that I have been an atheist, infidel, agnostic, skeptic, or sinner." But Christians on their death bed never say," I am sorry I am a Christian."

Why should we be forlorn? Death only husks the corn. Why should we fear to meet the thresher of the wheat?

DEATH IN LIFE

He always said he would retire
  When he had made a million clear;
And so he toiled into the dusk
  From day to day, from year to year.
At last, he put his ledgers up,
  And laid his stock reports aside.
But when he started out to live
  He found he had already died.

Death is like a ship on this shore. We say, "She is gone." On the shore of heaven they will say, "Arriving."

Death is not so much an exit but it is an entrance.

Death is not a termination for the Christian but a transfer.

Eternal Life

"Eternity is not a country beyond the grave, a land over which the sun never sets and the tale of the years is endless. Eternal life is a state of a man's soul; it is life's deepest realilty unfolding itself before his astonished eyes."
—J. Anker Larsen

He who provides for this life, but takes no care for eternity, is wise for a moment, but a fool forever.

ETERNITY

Once upon a time I heard a preacher say;
  "Suppose an angel were to start today
From some far star ten trillion miles
  away:

And wing his way to earth through trackless
  space,
And pick one grain of sand, and then
  retrace
His weary journey to its starting place.

Each trip eons of time! So on and on,
  'Til earth's last tiny grain of sand
was gone,
  And still eternity has just begun!"

The mind reels back from such immensity
  Of time! . . . Undying soul, where will
you be,
Where will you spend your long eternity?
—Martha Snell Nicholson

WHERE

How brittle is the thread of life,
  How short is earthly time;
How carelessly amidst the strife
  We deal with things sublime.
Today we're here, tomorrow where?
  Eternity — how long!
In it, will we, with others share
  Heaven's love, its joy, its song?
—Margaret Locke

If you expect to be a crown wearer you should be a cross bearer on earth.

The future belongs to those who prepare for it!

A SURE GUARANTEE

"*Whosoever believeth in Him should not perish but have eternal life*" (John 3:15).
The following poem was written on a Lb. note with indelible pencil:

This scrap of paper in your hand,
Declares to you that on demand,
Twenty shillings you shall receive.
This simple promise you believe,
It puts your mind as much at rest,
As if the silver you possessed.
So Christ that died and now does live,
Did unto you this promise give,
That if in His Name you believe,
Eternal life you shall receive.
Upon the first you calmly rest,
Which is the surest — and the best?
Banks may break — Heaven never can,
'Tis safer trusting God than man!

The closer we draw to the mountain the greater we see it to be. The closer we draw to eternity, the greater we see it will be, whether for our blessing or our condemnation.

The Books are balanced in heaven — not here.

—Shaw

Heaven

When you get to heaven,
  You will likely view
Many folks whose presence there
Will be a shock to you.
Be very quiet; do not even stare;
  Doubtless there will be many folks
Surprised to see you there!

To reach the port of heaven, we must sail sometimes with the wind and sometimes against it. But we must sail and not drift or lie at anchor.

—O.W. Holmes

HOMES HERE AND THERE

On earth our houses are in constant need of repair. I look forward to my eternal home because there will not be termites, floods, or winds. It is built upon the rock of ages. No vicious people will be lurking to break in so I will not need lock or dead bolts.

Heaven would be Hell to an unspiritual man. One who cannot stand a prayer meeting here would find no satisfaction There.

Going to heaven when we die is first of all a matter of becoming something while we live.

IF I AM WRONG

If I am wrong and you are right,
   If death is nothing but a flight
To endless nowhere, and beyond it
   No spirit ever stands upon it —
It is nothing, just a void of space,
   And no one needs redeeming grace —
Just nothing: death the final end,
   Should you be right in that, my friend;

If you are right and I am wrong
   In thinking that the "Glory song"
Will only be for those in Christ,
   Who, trusting His great sacrifice,
Are saved by Him — but should it be
   That this is wrong, and we should see
Everyone in heaven's bliss
   And no one has a chance to miss —

Well, my friend, I have no care;
   For if no eternal life is there,
If it is all a dream, then all I say
   Is, "Thank the Lord for joy today."
And if it should be that everyone
   Is there when heaven is begun,
I'll be there, too, to share delight —
   So if I'm wrong, I still am right.

But if you are wrong, and I am right,
   If the Bible is the only light
By which we know of God's great plan
   To save the lost and sinful man
Through faith in Christ, and thus provide
   A heaven on death's farther side;
If I am right, to God be praise!
   If you are wrong, you're wrong both ways.

—Louis Paul Lehman

"Mother," said Johnny, "Is dad going to leave?"
"Why, Son?"
"Well," Johnny replied, "In all the pictures of angels I have ever seen they don't have a beard and daddy has one."
"Well," said Mother, "If your father gets there it will be by a close shave."

People will be allowed in heaven because they allowed God to be their God.
—Seth Wilson

Better grades just don't come
   By bringing an apple to the teacher.
Nor will you get to Heaven because
   You happen to know the preacher.

ENTRANCE REQUIREMENTS

Passport Sign
   Persons seeking entry will not be permitted past the gates without having proper credentials and having their names registered with the ruling authority.

Bible Sign
   There shall in no wise enter into it anything that defileth. . . . But they which are written in the Lamb's Book of Life (Rev. 21:27).

A man may go to heaven on half of what it costs to go to perdition.

If some men get to heaven the way they are facing, they will have to do a lot of running backward.

AN AIRPORT LOBBY IS LONELY

You missed your flight. Trials come and we face an unfriendly world. The ticket agent is so busy. Remember we are strangers and exiles on this earth. (Heb. 11:13). This world is not our home — our citizenship is in heaven. (Phil. 3:20).

"A lot of people, from the way they live, make you think they've got a ticket to Heaven on a pullman parlor car and have ordered the porter to wake'em when they get there. But they'll get sidetracked before they've started."
—Billy Sunday

The truest end of life is to know that life never ends.

A just God will not prepare the same place for both good and bad people.

The more of heaven there is in our lives, the less of earth we shall covet.

It is not the fact that a man has riches which keeps him from the kingdom of heaven, but the fact that riches have him!

If a hypocrite is between you and heaven then he is closer to heaven than you are.

To get to heaven — turn right and keep Straight.

Heaven must be begun below in all those who shall enjoy its perfections above.

You can't steal quietly to heaven in Christ's company without a cross to bear.

Some people are trying to get to heaven with their compass in reverse.

The train on the railway to heaven carries no baggage cars.

I dreamed death came the other night and heaven's gate swung wide; with kindly grace an angel ushered me inside, and there, to my astonishment — stood folks I'd known on earth; some I had judged and labeled, 'unfit, of little worth.' Indignant words rose to my lips, but were never set free — for every face showed stunned surprise, not one expected me!

He who is on the road to Heaven will not be content to go there alone.

If there were no future life, your soul would not thirst for it.

Let "Deserved" be written on the door of Hell, but on the door of Heaven, "The Free Gift."

If you ever get to heaven, it will be on purpose.

Hell

WHICH DISTURBS YOU MOST?

A soul lost in hell — or a scratch on your new car?
Your missing the worship service — or missing a day's work?
A sermon ten minutes too long — or lunch a half hour late?
A church not growing — or a garden not growing?
Your Bible being unopened — or your newspaper unread?
Your contribution decreasing — or your income decreasing?
Your children late for Bible School — or late for school?
The church work being neglected — or your own work being neglected?
Missing a good Bible lesson — or missing your favorite TV program?
Low attendance at worship — or low attendance at the club meeting?

There is only one way to keep out of Hell, but there is no way to get out.

Hell is for two classes of people: Those who will do anything, and those who won't do anything.

The rich man goes to Hell not for making all the money he can, but for canning all the money he makes.

If you're going to Heaven, try to take a group. If you are going to Hell, be an individual about it.

"But cowards who turn back from following Me, and those who are unfaithful to Me, and murderers, and those conversing with demons, and idol worshipers and all liars — their doom is in the Lake that burns with fire and sulphur. This is the Second Death." (Revelation 21:8 from Living Prophecies.)

PACKING TO MOVE

". . . I know that the putting off of my body will be soon . . . " (II Peter 1:14.

Before Columbus made his trip across the Atlantic, the motto on the Spanish coat of arms read: *Ne Plus Ultra* — "nothing more beyond." They thought they had discovered all of the earth's land area. When Columbus returned, reporting a new world across the sea, *Ne* was dropped from the motto, leaving *Plus Ultra* — "more beyond."

A new world awaits the Christian on the other side of the grave. There is "more beyond." Peter didn't consider death the end, just a transfer.

Chambers of Commerce do a brisk business corresponding with people who are being transferred. They are anxious to know about the town's industries, shops, schools, churches, climate. They want to do as much preparation as possible before the move.

Even a two-week vacation sends us scurrying for maps and books about the places we intend to visit. And every conversation probes for information about these places.

It does seem that a place which is to be our *eternal* home would draw our interest and investigation. Peter gives some "packing hints" if you're interested. You'll need a good supply of faith, virtue, knowledge, self-control, steadfastness, godliness, brotherly affection, and love. If you have these things "there will be richly provided for you an entrance into the eternal kingdom . . ." (II Peter 1:5-11).

THE CHURCH

The Church

JUST SUPPOSE

JUST SUPPOSE the Lord should begin tomorrow to make people as sick as they claim to be on Sunday.
JUST SUPPOSE the Lord should take away the child whom the parents use as an excuse for staying away from the church.
JUST SUPPOSE the Lord should make some people as poor as they say they are when asked to help finance His program.
JUST SUPPOSE the Lord should have everyone stoned who is covetous as He did Achan.
JUST SUPPOSE the Lord should strike dead all who lie about their giving as He did Ananias and Sapphira.
JUST SUPPOSE the Lord let some parents look into the future and see what their examples and lax control are doing to their children.

It is never "my Church" as long as it is "those people" who are keeping it going.

A member never belongs to the Church unless he feels that the work of the Church belongs to him.

Too many people who depend on the Church can not be depended on by the Church.

The Church that is not a missionary Church will soon be a missing Church.

THE CHURCH

The non-church-goer cannot be reached by the non-going Church.

One must be a live, wide-awake Christian before he can fall "asleep in Jesus."

THE CHURCH IS NOT:

... a refrigerator for preserving perishable piety.
... a store to furnish hammocks for the lazy. It is rather a place that offers well-fitting yokes for drawing life's loads.
... a place to dodge difficulties, but rather a place that furnishes strength and courage to meet them.

WHY CHURCHES FAIL

I'll go where you want me to go, dear Lord,
Real service is what I desire.
I'll say what you want me to say, dear Lord.
But don't ask me to sing in the choir.

I'll say what you want me to say, dear Lord,
I like to see things come to pass
But don't ask me to teach the boys and girls, dear Lord,
I'd rather just stay in my class.

I'll do what you want me to do, dear Lord,
I yearn for the Kingdom to thrive.
I'll give you my nickels and dimes, dear Lord,
But please don't ask me to tithe.

I'll go where you want me to go, dear Lord,
I'll say what you want me to say,
I'm busy just now with myself, dear Lord,
I'll help you some other day.

CHRIST NEEDS IN HIS CHURCH:

More workers and fewer shirkers.
More backers and fewer slackers.
More praying and less straying.
More actions and fewer factions.
More burden bearers and fewer tale bearers.
More working squads and fewer tightwads.
More tithes and fewer drives.

THIS IS MY CHURCH

A DOOR
into an opportunity for service,
into the most useful life,
into the best experience
into the most hopeful future,
my church gives me a start.

AN ARMORY
to get power to fight evil,
to get inspiration to keep going right,
to get an uplifting influence,
to learn how to use spiritual weapons,
to get a vision of Christ,
my church keeps me moving.

AN ANCHOR
to steady me in the storm,
to keep me from the breakers,
to guide me in the strenuous life,
to hold me lest I drift away from God,
to save me in the hour of temptation,
and lead me into the harbor.

Is This Your Church?

THE CHURCH

SEVEN PROBLEMS OF THE CHURCH

1. Unbended knees
2. Unread Bibles
3. Unattended Church services
4. Unpaid tithes and offerings
5. Unrealized Cross of Christ
6. Unpassionate hearts
7. Unconcern for the lost

AN IDEAL CHURCH

No strangers . . . shall remain ungreeted.
No unfortunate . . . member shall go unfriended.
No invalid . . . shall be unvisited.
No needy . . . person shall be unassisted.
No bewildered . . . person shall go unadvised.
No home . . . of mourning shall be neglected.
No act . . . of mercy shall be omitted.

If a Church doesn't reach out it passes out!

The church should not seek to bring Christ down to men's level but to bring men up to Christ's level.

"Cowards in the pulpit" explains sin in the Church.

A cold church is like butter, it will not spread.

The church gives people what they need, but the theatre gives them what they want.

If students went to school like some of us go to church, THEY WOULD FAIL.

If an employee went about his work like some of us go about the task of soul winning, THEY WOULD BE FIRED.

If a person ate his meals like some of us partake of the Lord's Supper, THEY WOULD STARVE.

If a person paid his bills like some of us support the church, THEY WOULD GET NO CREDIT.

If a person neglected his family as much as some of us do the Lord and His Church, THEY WOULD BE CHARGED WITH DESERTION.

If a person spoke to others as seldom as some of us pray to God, THEY WOULD BE BRANDED ANTI-SOCIAL.

The Church is God's workhouse where His jewels are being polished for His palace.

Wake up, sing up, preach up, pray up, pay up, stand up and never give up, let up, back up, or shut up until the cause of Christ in the Church and in the world is built up.

LOYALTY TO THE CHURCH

I will be loyal to the Church:
  because I love its Founder
  because I love its purpose
  because I love its message
  because I love its principles
  because I love its people
  because I love its security
  because I love its achievements
  because I love its goal

CHURCHES are hospitals for sinners — not clubs for saints.

You do not make a Church of Christ by putting His name upon it, but by putting His Spirit into it.
—Raymond C. Brooks

HOW TO BUILD UP A CHURCH

ATTEND IT UP:
  Hebrews 10:25 — "Not forsaking the assembling . . . "
TALK IT UP:
  Acts 8:4 — ". . . They went everywhere preaching."
  I Peter 3:15 — ". . . be ready . . . to give answer . . ."
PRAY IT UP:
  I Thessalonians 5:17 — "Pray without ceasing. . . ."
  James 5:16 — ". . . prayer availeth . . . "
WORK IT UP
  Ephesians 2:10 — ". . . We are . . . unto good works . . ."
LIVE IT UP:
  Romans 12:1 — ". . . a living sacrifice . . . "
PAY IT UP:
  Malachi 3:10 — Whole tithe
  Hebrews 7:8 — receive tithe

WHICH CHURCH?

It does not make any difference what church one belongs to:
PROVIDED
That Church belongs to Christ.
PROVIDED
The Church is not ashamed of Him, His commands and His Name.
PROVIDED
That Church teaches and practices all things whatsoever He commanded.
PROVIDED
One belongs to it and not merely attends its services.

DISAPPOINTED!

"I came to your church last Lord's Day,
I walked up and down the aisle.
I noticed your seat was vacant,"
Said the Master, with a kindly smile.

"Yes, I was at home" I answered.
"Some folk from up St. Louis way
Drove down for a week-end visit,
So we stayed in the house all day.

Or, I had an awful headache;
I had a roast in the pan
Or we overslept that morning;
But I go whenever I can.

I went to the morning service
Not over two months ago,
So much work must wait till Sunday,
I've no time for church, you know."

The Master gazed at me sadly,
As he was about to speak,
"My child," he replied, "are there not
Six other days in the week?"

"If all of my other children
Should treat me the same as you;
My house would be closed — deserted!
Then what would lost sinners do?"

I saw I had grieved my Master,
As slowly he turned away,
And I vowed He'd not find me absent
Again on His Holy Day.

THE CHURCH

THE MAN WITH THE CONSECRATED CAR

He couldn't speak before a crowd;
  He couldn't teach a class . . .
But when he came to Sunday School,
  He brought the folks "enmasse."

He couldn't sing to save his life;
  In public couldn't pray . . .
But always his "jalopy" was
  Just crammed on each Lord's Day.

And although he could not sing,
  Nor teach, nor lead in prayer,
He listened well, he had a smile,
  And he was always there . . .

While all the others whom he brought,
  Who lived both near and far . . .
And God's work prospered . . . for he had
  A consecrated car.

ONE CHURCH AS GOOD AS ANOTHER

Is one church as good as another? I met a man who said that it really didn't matter what we believe as long as we were sincere. He was a denominalist, and was unaware of New Testament truth. He said "One church is as good as another." He did not believe it. I asked him if one church was as bad as another. "Oh no," he said. Then he began to tell me what he disliked about some churches.

Good logic says if one church is as good as another then one church is as bad as another.

Good logic says that no church created by man can be as good as the church which Christ established.

Let us not be lazy religionist but seekers for truth. The church that is closest to the Church of the Lord is the best church.

—Don Earl Boatman

WHAT A POWER THE CHURCH WOULD BE:

If all of the sleeping folk would wake up
And all of the lukewarm folk would fire up
And all the dishonest folk would confess up
And all the disgruntled folk would sweeten up
And all the discouraged folk would cheer up
And all the estranged folk would make up
And all the gossipers would shut up
And all the true soldiers would stand up
And all the church members would pray up
And all that are in debt would pay up!

—Frank Knox

BETTER THAN BIRDS

A group of birds decided to form a church. They called a meeting. As the birds flocked around and fluffed-up their feathers to look important — one long-billed Duck quacked out, "Let's begin! The first thing for this church is to require baptism. It should be by immersion in water." A squatty little Rooster crowed loudly against this. He said, "No! That's too old fashioned and complicated. It is quicker and less embarrassing if we just sprinkle water on the members."

Comments chirped and chimed from this side and that. One great green parrot said, "Listen, what we need first of all is a good program." This brought lots of cheers from the birds. Any wise bird knows that a church cannot build a reputation for itself without a rousing program.

A sleek looking black Mocking Bird said, "Don't forget — We need a good choir."

"And we need good organ music too," said a red-faced Robin.

"Oh," objected a brown-skinned Thrush, "We can't afford an organ, besides I think a piano is much better." Then a grey Sparrow said, "It would be just as well if they threw out music altogether."

The birds hushed a minute as a long-legged Goose stood up and motioned — "What we really need is a Preacher who is good with the young birds. If we don't attract the young birds the other churches in town will gobble them up for sure."

A little Starling said, "It seems to me that it's more important for the preacher to be just a good mixer."

A blue-faced Jay said, "If the preacher would lay off sin, and didn't get so dogmatic on the Bible, almost anyone would come — as long as he was popular with the rest of the birds in town."

The real wrangle came over the budget. Some thought everyone should tithe — providing they could afford it. Others thought they should do away with the offering and just have faith . . . .

So finally, the Owl arose, smoothed his feathers, and everything went quiet . . . for they knew he had great wisdom. "Brothers and Sister," he said, "All these things are secondary . . . I'll tell you what we need . . . What we need is SINCERITY!"

All the birds applauded, stomped, and whistled — "Yes, Sir!" repeated the Owl, pleased with himself, "Above all, we want to be SINCERE!"

And so, they formed a church . . . AND it was FOR THE BIRDS!

Enter to worship; depart to serve.

ALL GOD'S CREATION PRAISES HIM

The Bible is rich in the thought of the Psalmists, prophets, and other writers, who declare *the simple acts of worship* even among "inanimate" objects.

The trees "clap," the seas "roar," the birds "sing," the hills "dance," etc.

All summer, while enjoying the great out of doors . . . observe this worship. Each sigh of the wind in the cedars, a sigh of love. Each song of the bird, a carol of joy. Each lap of the water, or slap of a leaf — a sound of adoration. Even the sound of animals becomes a "hymn of praise."

A certain man moved into our community. He didn't fall among robbers who beat him, and left him half-dead. He just moved in. And by chance a certain neighbor was going down that way, and when he saw him, passed by on the other side, saying to himself, "I'll just wait until the subject comes up some day, and then I'll say: 'Pardon me, I hope you don't get the impression that I am a fanatic on religion, but if you might like to visit our church some Sunday, we would be glad to have you; that is, if you feel like it.' "

But a certain member, as he journeyed, came where he was and when he saw him, he was moved with compassion, and came to him, and courteously welcomed him to the community. During the conversation, he invited him to services, told him how much he would enjoy the service of worship, and that for him to get acquainted, he should come for Bible Study. He left, saying, "I'll come by and pick you up next Sunday about 10 o'clock." And he did, bringing him to the building and introducing him to the preacher and other friends. Then he took the stranger to the proper Bible class and told the teacher, "Take good care of him, and after I get out of my class, I'll come by and get him and sit with him during worship, and if I can render any further service, I'll be glad to do it."

THE CHURCH IS DIVINE

The Church could not stand if it were not of God. I has enemies within and without. Satan invades her membership. The Church is like a great net that gathers all manner of fishes. They are from many cultures, some are ignorant, some educated, some are weak, some are strong, some rich, some poor. To mold them into one peaceful body requires the Spirit of God.

—Don Earl Boatman

The Church that compromises truth today will compromise morals tomorrow.

THE CHURCH

GOD BUILDS NO CHURCHES

God builds no Churches! By His plan
  That labor has been left to man.
No spires miraculously rise
  No little missions from the skies
Falls on a bleak and barren place
  To be a source of strength and grace
The humblest church demands its price
  In human toil and sacrifice
The humblest spire in mortal kin
  Where Christ abides, was built by men
And if the Church is still to grow
  Is still the light of hope to throw
Across the valley of despair
  Men must still build God's House of Prayer
God sends no Churches from the skies
  Out of our hearts they must arise!

GOD BLESS THE CHURCH

God bless the church on the avenue that hears
  the city's cry;
The church that sows the seed of the Word where the masses of
  men go by
The church that makes, midst the city's roar, a place for an
  Altar of Prayer.
With a heart for the rich and a heart for the poor, and rejoices in
  their burdens to share.
The church that's true to the call of Christ who wept o'er
  the city's need,
And who sent his disciples to labor for Him where the forces
  of evil breed.
The church that gives and the church that lives, as seen by the
  Master's eye.
God bless the church on the avenue that answers the
  city's cry.

I WAS LOST, BUT YOU WERE IN A HURRY!

I attended your church this morning. You wouldn't remember me . . . I may be one who is eleven or eighty . . . but I was there . . . and I was hunting for something. I think I would have found it if you hadn't been in such a hurry. The choir . . . even you in the congregation . . . sang hymns about a living Lord that made my heart beat faster. I felt a tight, choking sensation in my throat as your minister described the condition of a lost person.

"I am lost. He is talking to me," I said to myself. "From the way he is speaking, being saved must be very important." I looked about at you in the pews near me. You were listening; you seemed to think that the preacher's words were important. "All these people are so concerned," I thought. "They want me to be saved, too." At the last the minister finished his appeal and asked you to stand and sing another of the beautiful songs you know so well. I swallowed a lump in my throat and wished I knew the joy with which you sang. Then your pastor looked at me and started telling me once again how I could have this joy but his words were drowned in a buzzing beside me.

When I glanced around, you were putting on your little girl's coat and telling her to get her things. I looked on my other side and saw you touching up your lipstick and rearranging your hair.

Looking in front of me, I saw you frown at your watch as if time were running out. Suddenly, I didn't want to look at any more of you . . . my eyes burned, and my throat hurt . . . my feet were so tired I couldn't have walked toward the pleading minister.

You really didn't care. This salvation the minister had been telling me about was not important. You didn't care that I was lost . . . you only wanted to get away. I wanted to get away too. I wanted to run, but I was afraid if I did, you would wonder what I was hunting for. I waited until the service was over and walked out among you . . .alone . . . lost!

A Church unlike a lodge is the only fellowship which exists for the non-members.

"Some elders want the best preacher in the land to be in their pulpit, but constantly encourage the youth of the church to avoid Bible College where preachers are made.

Some Bible School teachers want their pupils to learn, but discourage them from going to Bible College where they can really learn.

Some Churches want an effective Choir director but turn their young people away from Bible College where they are trained.

Some Churches want a young man to be a great leader of the youth, but they have discouraged every young man who wanted to go to Bible College.

Some Churches expect to use up preachers until Christ comes, but it never occurs to them that they ought to recruit some from their own congregation.

Some Churches want a great musician to lead them in a revival but every talented youth in the congregation has been encouraged to be a concert singer.

Some Churches desire a great evangelist to lead them in soul winning, but they have led their most talented young men to be doctors, lawyers, etc.

The Lord needs the best in the Church. Let us wake up. Money or fame must not be the deciding factor for choosing a life's work. Let us upgrade Christian service."

—Don Earl Boatman

WHY SOME GO TO CHURCH

Some go to church to take a walk;
Some go to church to laugh and talk;
Some go there to meet a friend;
Some go there their time to spend;
Some go there to meet a lover;
Some go there a fault to cover;
Some go there for speculation;
Some go there for observation;
Some go there to doze and nob;
The wise go there to worship God.

OFF DUTY FOR GOD UNTIL FALL
(Are you in the picture in the summertime?)

I forgot my Lord in the summertime,
Just the time when I was needed most
I was not away, but on each Lord's Day,
I just failed to be at my post.

I forgot my church in the summertime,
As I lazily lay in bed,
While the faithful few had my work to do,
And I was spiritually dead.

I forgot my offering in the summertime,
When He needed it most of all,
While my cash was spent, I was pleasure bent,
Just off duty for God until fall.

I forgot my class in the summertime,
But the Devil did not forget,
Working day and night, he kept up the fight,
He's a go-getter, you can bet.

I forgot my soul in the summertime
Got along without spiritual food-
While my Lord on high sent me blessings,
I showed Him naught but ingratitude.

If my Lord should come in the summer time,
When from my duty to God I am free
Wonder what I'll do, when my life is through,
If by chance, He should forget me?

Regular family worship proves to the children that the spiritual convictions of their parents are real and deep — not shallow or hypocritical.

THE CHURCH

PHRASES THAT STIFLE AND KILL

It isn't in the budget.
It will not work in our church.
We have tried it before.
It is too radical a change.
We haven't time to.
It cost too much.
It is not practical.
We're too large for that.
We are too small to try it.
Some of our members would scream.
We have never done it that way.
You are years too far ahead.
You are three years behind time.
Why change? It still works.
They will never go for it.
We will be the laughing stock.
We are doing alright without it.
Let us shelve it for the present.
Has anyone else ever tried it?
Let us form a committee.

Heaven's gates are wide enough to admit sinners saved by grace, but too narrow to admit any sin.

EIGHT WAYS TO HELP THE CHURCH:

1. Know what it stands for.
2. Live what it teaches.
3. Pray for it daily.
4. Tell others about it.
5. Give regularly and generously.
6. Attend its services faithfully.
7. Win others to Christ.
8. Speak highly of the leadership.

HYPOCRITES IN THE CHURCH

I make no apology to the critics of the Church. A hypocrite is a counterfeit Christian and that proves the great value of the Church. No one counterfeits pennies but look out if you are given a $100 bill.

The hypocrite is in the right place to get help. Where else could they get help? Sick people go to the hospitals. Do we criticize the Alcoholic Anonymous organization for being full of alcoholics?

Churches are in existence to help sinners. The Church is not made up of perfect people, but people in various stages of spiritual growth striving to be perfect.

The critic is really giving us an opportunity to tell of the value of the Church.

—Don Earl Boatman

THE CHURCH TODAY

The church should be a lighthouse in the storm;
A beacon flung against the blackened sky,
A white, unfailing, steadfast light that shines
For men to steer them by.
The church should be a home through these strange days
Where the Bread of Life is served, and we can find
The Father waiting there to soothe our ills,
And give us peace of mind.
The church should be a school where we may learn
The holy truth these hours before the dawn,
That we may go equipped to meet the days
And pass the learned truth on.
The church should be a church forevermore:
A sure foundation and a true reward
To all whose feet are planted on the rock
Of Jesus Christ, our Lord.

—Grace Noll Crowell

CHRIST AND THE CHURCH

He loved the Church — Ephesians 5:25
He bled for the Church — Acts 20:28
He established the Church — Matthew 16:18
He adds members to the Church — Acts 2:47
He is the head of the Church — Colossians 1:18
He is the bridegroom of the Church — II Corinthians 11:2
He will save the Church — Ephesians 5:23

WE CLEANED OUR CHURCH

We cleaned our little church today;
  Wiped all the dirt and dust away.
We straightened papers, washed the floors;
  Wiped off the lights and painted the doors
We brushed the dirt stains from the books;
  And whisked the cobwebs from the nooks.
We polished windows so we'd see
  The newly greening shrub and tree.
The menfolks too raked up the yard,
  They laughed and said it wasn't so hard.
And oh, it felt so very good
  To have the place look as it should.
We said, "How wonderful 'twould be,
  If we cleaned out what we can't see."
Such things as grudges, hates and lies
  And musty thoughts much worse than flies.
If all would let God's Spirit in,
  To cleanse each heart from soiling sin.
Oh, then our church would really shine;
  Our fellowship would be divine.

If just any Church is good as another, then disobedience is as good as obedience.

The business of the Church is not to furnish hammocks for the lazy; it is rather to offer well fitting yokes for carrying of life's loads.

AN OLD QUESTION

QUESTION: Can I be a Christian without joining the Church?
ANSWER: Yes, it is possible. It is something like being:
  A student who will not go to school.
  A soldier who will not join the army.
  A citizen who pays no taxes and does not vote.
  A salesman with no customers.
  A businessman on a deserted island.
  A seaman on a ship without a crew.
  An author without readers.
  A tuba player without an orchestra.
  A parent without a family.
  A football player without a team.
  A politician who is a hermit.
  A scientist who does not share his research.
  A bee without a hive.

MY CHURCH

My Church is not a masterpiece
In architectural design.
It is the place where I meet God,
To me it is a shrine.
Its portals bid me enter
When other folk are there;
To lift my voice with theirs in praise
And with them bow my head in prayer.
We place our offering on the plate;
We hear the Holy Scripture read;
We hear the preacher preach the word.
It's there our hungry souls are fed.
                Amy Cochran Gettles

THE CHURCH

GOING TO CHURCH

*I reckon if my mother looked
Across the distant view,
She'd like to see me sitting there
In our old family pew.
I reckon that her angel soul
Would thrill, if she could see
Me sitting in the old time spot
Where oft we used to be.*

*I haven't gone as often as
I did when she was here;
I've sort of passed the Church door by
Through many a busy year.
I've sort of heedlessly forgot
The place we used to pray
And kneel together in, since God
Has taken her away.*

*But, oh, I know 'twould be her wish,
Whatever else I do,
On Sunday mornings, that her boy
Should occupy that pew.
And that I'm doing that for her
I think she'd like to know;
And so on Sunday to the Church
Once more I'm going to go.*

      Edgar A. Guest

"If a man is too busy to worship God twice on Sunday and on Prayer Meeting night, he has more business than God intended that he should have."

—J.C. Penney

There will never be a church built that will suit the man who does not want to be better.

STRANGE EXCUSES

Who ever heard of a man . . .
Who complained that the ball game was too long?
Who preferred to drown rather than get into a boat with a hypocrite?
Who quit going to the movies because the manager or usher did not speak to him?
Who refused to eat because he couldn't understand how it could give him the needed physical strength?
Who refused to obey the law of his nation because his parents might object?
Who, on bleeding to death, asked that blood be given to him at a more convenient time?
Who was too busy to breathe?

If everyone put Christ first as you did Sunday night, how many would we have had?

Attendance

ATTEND — It Will Bless You

You need to attend for yourself. Paul writing to Timothy spoke of some who "concerning the faith have made shipwreck." Many a person has started the voyage only to be washed ashore, spiritually waterlogged and lost. Any Christian who says, "It can't happen to me" is deceiving himself. Paul told the Corinthians, "Wherefore let him that thinketh he standeth take heed lest he fall." We as an individual need every Sunday to examine ourself to ask if we are all that He wants us to be.

—Roger Boatman

BEHOLD, A BALL TEAM went forth to play a game of ball. Just as the umpire was saying, "Batter up!" the catcher for the home team arrived and took his place. The center fielder and the second baseman didn't arrive until the second inning. The first baseman didn't come at all, but later sent his regrets saying he had to go to a chicken dinner at Aunt Mary's. The third baseman likewise failed to show up having been up late the night before and he preferred to spend the day in bed. The left fielder was away visiting another ball game across town. The shortstop was present, but left his glove at home.

VERILY, when the pitcher entered the box, he looked around to see his team mates and lo, his heart was heavy when he saw so many empty places in the lineup. The game had been announced and the visitors were already in the stands to see the game. There was nothing left for him to do but go ahead and pitch and hope for the best. So the pitcher tightened up his belt, stepped into the box and did his level best to put one over the plate. But for some strange reason he just couldn't find the groove. Some of his team mates began to ride him for wild pitches and loud "Boos" began to come from the stands. At the close of the game, the home team (what there was of it) was mercilessly beaten. After hearing of the disgraceful defeat, the rest of the team decided that a new pitcher should be hired. It must have been the poor pitching that had lost the game.

BEHOLD, A PREACHER went forth to preach . . . but that's another story . . . .

Christians should go to church each Lord's Day to pray, to pay, to say.

SOME FOLKS ARE LOST IN THE "WOULDS"

1. I WOULD go to church, but it is my day off.
2. I WOULD go to church, but I am too busy.
3. I WOULD go to church, but I am too tired.
4. I WOULD go to church, but . . . you can fill in a lot of other reasons you might have heard.

I love thy Church, O God,
  Her walls before Thee stand;
But please excuse my absence, Lord
  This bed is simply grand.

A charge to keep I have,
  A God to glorify.
But, Lord, no cash from me,
  Thy glory comes too high.

Am I a soldier of the Cross,
  A follower of the Lamb?
Yes. Though I seldom pray or pay,
  I still insist, I am.

Must Jesus bear the cross alone,
  And all the world go free?
No! Others, Lord, should do their part;
  But please don't count on me.

Praise God from whom all blessings flow;
  Praise Him all creatures here below.
Oh, loud my hymns of praise, I bring,
  Because it doesn't cost to sing!

THE EMPTY SEAT

It never helps with the singing, never responds to the invitation. It just sits there. It robs the preacher, takes the joy out of the song. It chills the saint and cheers Satan. It doesn't squirm, never looks at the clock. It is mute. It never gives a smile of encouragement or a nod of appreciation. It is that visible, telling testimony that someone doesn't care.

It is the most expensive thing in the church. It is where the people who are "there in Spirit" sit. It is a stabbing pain to the Son of God, and a source of delight to Satan. LET'S FILL IT!

PECULIAR PEOPLE

A schoolboard hired a teacher, paid him a substantial salary to teach school, filled the coal cellar with coal; everything was in readiness in September to begin school. The taxpayers paid the taxes, which were used to pay the teacher's salary. School opened; a week went by, and there were no students. Upon making inquiry, the teacher was informed that he had the building, and was paid a salary to teach school, and it was up to him to get the pupils there. Would you regard that as a peculiar community?

A young woman was hired as a servant in the home. Plenty of food was purchased; she was a good cook and prepared excellent meals. The first day she prepared breakfast, dinner and supper. However, the father, mother and nine children stayed away from the table. The cook stood it fairly well the first day, but the second morning she inquired why the meals were untouched. The family replied, "We furnish the house and the food and pay you a salary; now it's up to you to persuade us to eat." Would that be regarded as a peculiar family?

A church hired a preacher, gave him a building, paid a fair salary. He prepared messages, went to church each Sunday, but no people. He made inquiry and was informed that he was furnished a building and a salary; it was up to him to go around and induce those paying him to come and worship. Would you regard that as a peculiar church?

ATTEND TO BLESS OTHERS

You need to faithfully attend to encourage your brother or sister in Christ. It was the murderer Cain who asked, "Am I my brother's keeper?"

Sometimes we who are concerned and love each other as a brother commit spiritual murder for our lack of compassion and interest for those in Christ who have problems and need a word of encouragement. The early church met for fellowship. They shared each other's burdens and had all things common.

—Roger Boatman

BUILDING THE CHURCH IN LOVE

1. Build up in love as each part does its work — Ephesians 4:16
2. Build up in love when there is equal concern — I Corinthians 12:25.
3. Build up in love when we serve one another — Galatians 5:13
4. Build up in love when we bear with one another — Ephesians 4:2
5. Build up in love when we carry each others burdens — Galatians 6:2
6. Build up in love when we submit to each other — Ephesians 5:21
7. Build up in love when we forgive one another — Ephesians 4:32
8. Build up in love when we encourage one another — I Thessalonians 5:11.
9. Build up in love when we are honest with others — Colossians 3:9.
10. Build up in love when we offer hospitality — I Peter 4:9
11. Build up in love when we counsel with wisdom — Colossians 3:16
12. Build up in love when we confess our sins and pray — James 5:16

It is not the talented people who serve the Lord best, but the consecrated ones.

Nothing is so important in your life that it cannot wait while you attend church.

Church attendance is determined more by desire than by distance.

Having his name on a church roll doesn't make a man a Christian any more than owning a piano makes him a musician.

Attend a church? Of course we do,
  Like others in our set,
Except on days that seem too cold
  Or hot or wet.
And then, of course in summer,
  Just to keep them up to par
We take the kids on Sundays
  For a joy ride in the car.
And sometimes, too, in spring and fall
  I take a Sunday off,
And hike me to the country club
  To have a game of golf.
But all the other Sundays
  You will find us in our pew,
For we always go to church
  (When we've nothing else to do.)

Elders and Deacons

Two elders wives sat mending their husbands' pants. One of them said to the other, "My poor John, he is so discouraged in his church work. He said just the other day that he was considering resigning. It seems that nothing goes right for him." The other replied, "Why, my husband was saying just the opposite. He is so enthused, it seems like the Lord is closer to him than ever before."

A hushed silence fell as they continued to mend the trousers, ONE PATCHING THE KNEES AND THE OTHER THE SEAT.

The elder's job is not to crack the whip over the preacher and the congregation but to put their own necks in the yoke.

P.H. WELSHIMER'S SUGGESTIONS FOR ELDERS AND DEACONS

1. Know and understand the New Testament qualifications for these offices (Titus 1:6-11; I Tim. 3:1-7; I Tim. 3:8-12).
2. It is best not to select a man to serve who does not faithfully attend every service of the Lord's church.
3. It is best not to select a man to serve who does not tithe his income to the Lord's church. A man unwilling to give to the local church has no right to vote for expenditures of which he is not willing to pay his rightful share or to vote against expenditures for which other men are willing to pay.
4. It is best not to select a man to serve as elder or deacon who is known to publicly criticize the church, its minister, or its program. This action injures the testimony of the church in the city.
5. It is best not to select a man to serve as elder or deacon whose means of livelihood is questionable, and hence could bring discredit on the Lord's church.
6. It is best not to select a man to serve as an elder or deacon who is not fully committed to the worldwide program of evangelism (missions).
7. It is best not to select a man to serve because he is popular . . . the eldership are not "offices" or "places of honor" . . . they are responsibilities, and you are responsible to God, Mr. Elder or Deacon.
8. It is best not to select a man to serve who is not fully committed to the program of New Testament Christianity.
9. It is best not to select a man to serve who does not fully use his talents for the Lord's church in preference to any other organization or activity.

We talk much about fellowship, but we need to talk about followship. A church can not have good fellowship if she does not follow those chosen to be her leaders.

—Don Earl Boatman

WHAT WOULD YOU DO IF YOU RECEIVED A LETTER LIKE THIS?

Dear _____:

The elders are very concerned about you and they need your help in reaching a decision about you. Your negligence toward things spiritual alarms and distresses us. We have prayed about this grave matter and are deliberating on what should be done. Despite preaching, admonitions in the church bulletin, and personal visits, you are still absent from most of the services. You have promised to "do better," but as yet you haven't kept that promise.

Now, what would you advise us to do? Shall we continue to count you as a member or shall we drop your name from the roll? Do you wish us to come and prayerfully and kindly, but firmly, discuss your problem? Would you advise us to withdraw fellowship from you, because you are a bad influence to other Christians and a hindrance, not a help, to the work? Please use your telephone or write us a letter advising us what you think we should do.

In Christian love,

(signed by the Elders)

—George Tipps

EVIDENCE

The new preacher looked at Deacon Canfield coldly and said, "I'm told that you went to the ball game instead of to church last Sunday."

"That's a lie," cried the deacon hotly, "and I've got the fish to prove it."

A man can not be a leader for God unless he is willing to be led of God.

IF I WERE AN ELDER

E nthusiastically take up my "labor of love" in the shepherding of the fold.
L ovingly tend the sheep along with my fellow elders.
D efend them against the enemy.
E xercise the Christian Spirit at all times.
R ejoice in the opportunity to serve Christ along with my minister.

IF I WERE A DEACON

D edicate myself to my office.
E ncourage my minister
A dvance with "my" church.
C ooperate with my leaders.
O bey my Lord's command to "come" and "go."
N urture every opportunity to serve the Lord, especially as a soul winner.

QUALIFICATIONS

The Word of God states the qualifications for elders and deacons. If they do not matter then the Book takes up wasted space.

If we do not take them seriously, then we do not take God's Word and work seriously.

If we elect 12 men to the offices of elders and deacons and each of them lacks two qualifications, then the church has 24 weak links in the chain.

God's Word established strong qualifications, so that the church will have strength in the times of trial and tribulation.

When we set aside qualifications we are setting aside the authority of God. When God's powerful authority is set aside, the church is set up for trouble ahead.

—Don Earl Boatman

THE CHURCH

GOD'S TEN MOST WANTED MEN

1. The man who puts God's business above any other.
2. The man who brings his children to Bible School rather than sends them.
3. The man who is willing to be the right example to everyone he meets.
4. The man who thinks more of his church service than he does Sunday indulgences.
5. The man who measures his giving by what he has left, rather than the amount he gives.
6. The man who goes to church for Christ's sake.
7. The man who has a passion to help.
8. The man who has a willing mind.
9. The man who sees his own faults before he sees the faults in others.
10. The man who is concerned about winning souls for Christ.

A STAND

If elders and deacons do not first stand on the qualifications for their work, they will not take a stand on other matters when Satan goes to work in the church to teach false doctrine and to scatter the flock.

—Don Earl Boatman

ELECT OF GOD

A man who comes up for election to be an elder or deacon must first prove by his life that he is one of God's elect.

—Don Earl Boatman

THE BEST ELDERS

Generally the best elders were the best workers in the church before they were officially chosen by the congregation.

We must treat leaders like leaders. See the potential in them, expect it of them, and see the results.

Any church leader who fails to support the church with his time, talent and money has forfeited his right to leadership.

Children play follow the leader. Christians must work at it.

The best proof that a man will serve as an elder or deacon is this: Is he already serving?

Preachers

TELL ME WHY?

If a lawyer finds a flaw in the title of property, and does not warn about it, he has not done his duty.

If a sanitary engineer discovers conditions dangerous to health, and fails to report them, he has failed his job.

If a doctor learns of a dangerous condition of our body, and does not properly diagnose, we think he is a quack.

If a bank examiner knows of discrepancies in the accounts of the bank and does not report them, he loses his position.

BUT — if a preacher sees a flaw in our title to a home in heaven, and he warns about it; if he discovers a condition dangerous to spiritual welfare, and reports it, if he finds a diseased condition in our spiritual body, and tells of his diagnosis; if he finds discrepancies in our heavenly account and reports on it, many think he is just meddling and trying to find fault.

FIVE WAYS TO GET RID OF THE PREACHER

1. Sit up front, smile, and say "Amen" every time he says something good. He will preach himself to death.
2. Pat him on the back and tell him what good work he is doing in the church and community. He will work himself to death.
3. Increase your offering to the church. He will suffer from shock.
4. Tell him you've decided to join the visitation group and help win souls for the Lord. He will probably suffer a heart attack.
5. Get the whole church to band together and pray for him. He will get so efficient that some other church will hear about him and give him a call. That will take him off your hands.

A PRAYER FOR MY PASTOR

Let me support him without striving to possess him.

Let me lift his hands without placing shackles around them.

Let me give him help that he may devote more time to working for the salvation of others and less time in gratifying my vanity.

Let me work for him as the pastor of all members and not compel him to spend precious time in bragging on me.

Let me be unselfish in what I do for him and not selfish in demanding that he do more for me.

Let me strive to serve him and the church much and be happy as he serves me less and the church more.

—Robert S. Kerr
Late U.S. Senator

A preacher in Missouri while holding a revival was called the "Rock and Roll" preacher. When he heard about it he said, "They are right, Praise the Lord, I am on the Rock and my name is on the Roll."

The best compliment you can pay our preacher's sermon is to bring along a friend to hear his next one.

THE MISSING PREACHER

Once upon a time there lived a faithful minister, beloved by his people, who year after year went about doing good. But there were empty places in his church. And the parson would invite his people to come to worship and the people would promise and resolve to do so. But there were places to go and things to do, and they did not come. They brought their young people for marriage, and their old for burial; and they knew the church was there and the parson was there, and they depended upon him.

Then the special day arrived, the day the good parson had appointed. And they said, "Something's up! We'll go!" So they brought their friends and filled the church building. The organist played and the people read their bulletins, but the minister did not come. Then all the city was alarmed. Some great tragedy had occurred? But all the week he could not be found. He was not there to marry their sons and bury their dead and give to their poor.

On Saturday he appeared among them and he said, "I will speak to you on Sunday; I will tell you all on Sunday." And on the morrow the people filled the building and the vestibules and the sidewalks around the building. And they waited and read their bulletins and sat and became anxious and minister did not come.

Then they went out to find him. They searched the city. He was seated under a tree in the park reading a book. And the Elders brought him before them, but he said, "I will speak to my people." So the people came and they accused him of breaking the faith with them, of looking lightly upon a great responsibility. And he stood up and spoke: "Why then have you broken faith with me and not kept your appointment with God? I had thought a church service was a minor thing and of little importance in your lives. Will you deny to me the privileges which you demand for yourselves?"

But they accused him saying, "We pay you to be here! There's a difference!" And the preacher said to them kindly: "You pay me, but I do not work for pay. Listen my people, and learn. The CHURCH is not the minister. YOU are the CHURCH and the CHURCH is what you are. In my action I have taught you something. Go now and think about it!"

Then the people began to consider the whole problem of personal individual responsibility.

HOW TO KILL A PREACHER

Many people think preachers are killed by over-work. Honest and happy work makes for health and strength. If you really want to know how to kill a preacher, here are ten good hints:

1. Keep your name on the church roll and never show up for any of the services.
2. Accept an office in the church and then do nothing about it.
3. Sit through the sermon and look like you are bored to death every step of the way.
4. Be active in church work for a while then, all of a sudden drop out of the picture without excuse.
5. Expect your pastor to know of illness in your family by mental telepathy and then criticize him because he doesn't call.
6. Never express appreciation for anything he does, but be loud in your criticism of what he does not do.
7. Start a first class row in the church and expect the preacher to pour oil on the troubled waters.
8. Criticize the program of the church, but refuse to do anything to improve it.
9. Withdraw your financial support and help starve him to death.
10. Use a revolver, a shotgun or a sharp tongue (which ever is handiest).

The preacher should preach a dynamite gospel and not spoil it with a firecracker life.

A PREACHER'S QUALIFICATIONS

A preacher had some fun by sending the following letter to a pulpit committee seeking for a new minister.

"I have many qualifications. I have been a preacher with much success and also as a writer. Some say I'm a good organizer. I've been a leader most places I've been. I am over 50 years of age. I have never preached in one place more than three years. In some places I have left town after my work has caused riots and disturbances. I must admit I have been in jail there or four times, but not because of any wrong doing. My health is not too good, though I still get a great deal done.

The churches I have preached in have been small though located in several large cities. I've not got along too well with religious leaders in towns where I have preached. In fact, some threatened me and even attacked me physically.

I am not good at keeping records. I have even been known to forget whom I have baptized. However, if you can use me, I shall do my best or you."

After reading the letter, the committee member looked at his fellow members and said, "Well, what do you think? Shall we hire him?"

The others were aghast. Hire an unhealthy trouble making, absent minded, ex-jailbird? Was the man who read the letter crazy? Who was the applicant? Who would have such colossal nerve? "Oh," said the letter reader, "It is just signed 'The Apostle Paul'."

Paul's advice to preachers is found in I Timothy 4:1-6; 12-16. A Canadian preacher states that there are two things that will happen to the preacher if he does not heed. They will be whining or reclining. If they heed them, they will be shining for the Lord.

Massillan, famed and gifted French author has said, "I don't want people leaving the church saying what a wonderful sermon or what a wonderful preacher. I want them to go out saying, 'I will do something.' "

THE CHURCH

A PREACHER'S CHOICE

A small town preacher rushed to the railroad station every day to watch the evening train go whistling through town. Members of the church thought it childish and asked him to quit it. "No gentlemen," he said firmly. "I preach your sermons, I teach your classes and have to beg people to attend; I bury your dead, I marry your young, I promote your drives, take the lead in arranging get-togethers for the young people; visit the members, encourage the non-members, listen to your complaints. No, I won't give up watching the train go through. I love it . . . it's the only thing that I don't have to push!"

BURY IS HIS JOB

A young Methodist Minister was asked to conduct the funeral of a prominent Baptist family who did not like their own preacher (pastor). Not knowing if this was ethical, he asked his Bishop for instruction. The Bishop replied, "Bury all the Baptists you can."

THE REQUISITES OF A SUCCESSFUL PREACHER

The successful preacher must have the memory of an elephant, the gentleness of a kitten, the drive of a busy beaver, the patience of a turtle, the determination of a mule, the wisdom of an owl, the persistence of a horsefly, the voice of a bullfrog and the organizational ability of an ant colony.

FOOD FOR THOUGHT

A man came to the minister one day and told him of all the trouble he had had during the past year. He wound up with, "I tell you right now, preacher, it's enough to make a man LOSE his religion." "Seems to me, Jim" the minister told him quietly, "It's enough to make a man USE his religion!"

JUST NEXT TO ME

*The preacher sure did pour it on,
But he just let me be,
He took the starch right out of those,
That sat just next to me.
You should have heard the things he said,
It was true as it could be;
It burned the seat from under those
That sat just next to me.
He hit the nail square on the head;
With him I did agree;
He trimmed the dead limbs off of those
That sat just next to me.
And then I got to thinking, and felt as
Sneakin' as could be.
And when I turned and looked at him,
He had his guns turned on Me!*

VOCABULARY OF SOUR CHRISTIANS

Some church members have a vocabulary that requires translation when they are talking about their preacher.

"He brings politics into the church" . . . means . . . "I do not agree with him."

"He is sowing dissension" . . . meaning . . . "some people are waking up."

"He upsets my faith" . . . meaning . . . "my prejudices are taking a beating."

"He lacks judgment" . . . may mean . . . "He takes the Bible to seriously."

"He neglects the substantial members" . . . means . . . "He is getting the whole church to be active."

"He is playing up to the new members" . . . means . . . "He is by-passing the road blocks set up."

"The whole church is upset" . . . means . . . "I am causing all the trouble I can."

THE IDEAL PREACHER

(Available to churches who prefer to build their own preacher, although at the present time, it seems to be difficult to obtain necessary parts.)

RADAR MIND	Detects every possible illness, problem, disturbance, etc.
AUTOMATIC MIND	Can produce 3 or 4 lively and original messages each week without much study.
EAR	To hear all gossip, grumbling and complaining.
EYES	To see only good in all.
NO BODY	Can't take time to be tired, ill, weak.
ARM	Spring wound, shakes hands, lends help everywhere.
GARMENT	Prosperous appearance on a very minimum salary.
FEET	Able to go everywhere, at all times for all manner of calling.
CHECK VALVE	To insure against mistakes and forgetting.
HAIR	One side cut for youthfulness. One side grey for experience.
FILE CABINET MIND	Remembers all names, guests, retains all popular know-how. Has thousands of programs and new ideas available in seconds. Full record of all Bible knowledge.

NOSE	Big enough to detect every wrong, small enough to stay out of people's business.
MOUTH	To speak only good, smile always, panic people at all social gatherings.
NO HEART	To be hurt, offended, or affected by grumblings, complaints, etc. Instead, an instrument to turn on the passion of great preaching.
SPLIT PERSONALITY	Half is business-like, other half is artistic, idealistic, and dramatic.

THE IDEAL PREACHER'S WIFE

(Available only with Ideal Preacher. We do not break a set! Note: Any resemblance to any particular preacher's wife is not intentional.)

EAR	With built-in automatic sifter to sort out information: (a) that which can be repeated, (b) that which is to be kept confidential.
RADAR MIND	To know exactly where to reach husband at all times.
AUTOMATIC MIND	Can produce Sunday School lessons, youth lessons, assorted devotions for ladies groups. Spontaneous, clever ideas for parties, socials, and ways to build husband's enthusiasm.
EYES	One in front for forward attention during services; one in back to see what the children are doing.
FIGURE	Not too glamorous, and not too "matronly."

THE CHURCH

BODY	Tireless.
FEET	Substantial, able to hold up for hours as she works and works and works.
ESCAPE VALVE	To relieve tensions.
HAIR	Half in the very latest style and half in "motherly" style.
FILE CABINET MIND	Remembers all information that husband is apt not to. Has recipes for 999 ways to prepare hamburger. Retains latest knowledge on marriage problems, psychology of raising children, etc.
MOUTH	Always smiling and saying good things.
FOUR ARMS	To keep a neat, clean house at all times; keep family neat, clean and well dressed; raise children to be intelligent and obedient; keep active in all areas of church-work.
CLOTHING	Not too new, not too old, not too fancy, not too plain, but always neat.

You cannot make Christ the King of your life until you abdicate.

A SUCCESSFUL PREACHER

Every Sunday with few exceptions, for 30 years, Charles Spurgeon preached morning and evening to more than 5,000 people at the Metropolitan Tabernacle in London. Spurgeon was asked many times, "How did you get your congregation?" He replied "I never got it at all. I did not think it my duty to do so. I only had to preach the Gospel. My congregation got my congregation."

THE PREACHER'S COFFEE

Here is a pointed story which has been told in rhyme
  About a certain preacher who lived once upon a time.
At one of his appointments, some members — not a few
  Became sorely troubled about the word "INTO."
The Good Book says quite plainly (Acts 8) "They came into"
  And went down INTO water, as Bible people do.
This parson preached a sermon with zeal and power and might.
  And, to his satisfaction, he set the passage right.
"INTO there doesn't mean INTO, but AT or NEAR or BY,
  They went down TO the water, and got a small supply."
Now, near this place of worship, there lived a Sister Brown,
  Who, by her splendid cooking, had gotten much renown.
And her delicious coffee, on all the circuit round
  The preacher oft said boldly, "It's like could not be found."
When he would preach a sermon of extra power and length
  He liked at her good table to recuperate his strength.
She was a simple Christian — no better in the land,
  And oft reproved the daring for changing God's command.
She heard Jones' "INTO" sermon, and thought the matter o'er,
  Then asked him home to dinner, as she had done before.
She ground her well-known coffee — the kettle steaming hot
  And put it AT, not INTO the famous coffee pot.
She poured for him a cupful — I think she did not sin;
  "Why, Sister, you've forgotten to put the coffee in."
"No, no, dear sir, that's coffee, I ground a good supply
  And then down by the vessel I put it AT, near BY.
By logic of your sermon (I thought it very thin)
  If AT or NEAR mean INTO, I put the coffee IN.
But if you now will promise no more such stuff to teach,
  I'll go and put the coffee IN and place it in your reach."

A preacher shouldn't apologize for repeating old truths any more than a cow should be embarrassed to give milk today because it was milk she gave yesterday.

THE CHURCH

THE PREACHER'S MISTAKE

The Parish Priest of Austerity
Climbed up in a church steeple
To be near God
So that he might hand
His Word down to his people.

When the sun was high
When the sun was low
The good man sat unheeding
Sublunary things
From transcendency
Was he forever reading.

And now and again
When he heard the creak
Of the weather vane a turning,
He closed his eyes
And said of a truth
From God I now am learning.

And in sermon script
He daily wrote
What he thought was sent from heaven
And he dropped this down
On his people's heads
Two times one day in seven.

In his age God said
"Come down and die."
And he cried from the steeple
"Where art Thou, Lord?"
And the Lord replied,
"Down here among my people."

A PRAYER A PREACHER MIGHT LIKE TO PRAY ON MANY A SUNDAY MORNING!

Dear God: Forgive me if I complain; forgive me if I wish ill on anyone; but, just for this day, I'd like to see all the fishermen come home empty handed. I'd like to have all the golfers be "Duffers" just for today. I'd like to have all the parents who let their children think today was only "a day for children" at Sunday School see their children twenty or thirty years from now. I'd like to have those who stayed at home to work on the house or yard, as I could have done, find that the mower won't mow, the sewer won't sew, the cleaner won't clean, and the wife a little mean.

Having wished all this, dear Father above, and knowing full well it shows lack of love, I ask for Thy help in speaking Thy Word. For somehow, someway, Thy voice will be heard by those who at home stay. Use me dear Lord, in what way Thou will, for it is Thy will and not mine, that will be done. Amen!

THE EMPTY SEAT

The preacher does better when You are there,
'Tis hard to preach to an empty chair.
But your seat is not empty when you're away,
For Satan's imps are there that day.
They're making faces at the preacher's text.
They're nudging the folks who are sitting next.
They're showing how the church is down,
And it's all because you are not around.

A preacher who had trouble getting his congregation to occupy front seats was surprised one Sunday when a man came down and took his place on the front seat. After the service he asked why the man did so. The reply came, "Well, I'm a bus driver and I came to find out how you get folks to move to the rear."

HOW DID YOU GET SUCCESSFUL?

A famous preacher states that his early success in the ministry was because his people said to non-church people, "You ought to hear this young man."

A prominent citizen of a certain community met a minister one day and asked, "Preacher, do you think I'll be able to recognize my loved ones in Heaven?"

"Not at the distance from which you'll be looking," was the quick reply.

The disadvantage of practicing what you preach is that you have to put in so much overtime.

Teachers

    The Lord is my teacher, I shall not lose the way.
    He leadeth me in the lowly paths of learning.
    He prepareth a lesson for me every day;
    He bringeth me to the clear fountains of instruction.
    Little by little he showeth me the beauty of truth.
    The world is a great book which He hath written.
    He turneth the leaves for me slowly.
    They are all inscribed with images and letters.
    He poureth light on the pictures and the words.
    He taketh me by the hand to the hilltop of vision.
    And my soul is glad when I perceive His meaning.
    In the valley also He walketh beside me,
    In the darkness He whispereth to my heart.
    Even though my lesson be hard it is not hopeless,
    For the Lord is patient with His slow scholar;
    He will wait awhile for my weakness,
    And help me to read the truth through tears.

THE TEACHER AND THE ABSENTEE

"Someone is absent," the Shepherd said,
As over my classbook He bent His head;
"For several Sundays absent, too;
So tell me TEACHER, what did you do?"

"I didn't visit as perhaps I should;
I wrote some cards, but they did no good:
I've never heard and she never came,
So I decided to drop her name."

He answered gravely, "A flock was mine,
A hundred — no, there were ninety and nine,
For one was lost in the dark and cold —
So I sought that sheep which had left the fold.

The path was stony and edged with thorns,
My feet were wounded, and bruised and torn;
But I kept on seeking, nor counted the cost,
And, oh, the joy when I found the lost."

Thus spoke the Shepherd in tender tone,
I looked, and lo . . . I was all alone;
But God a vision had sent to me
To show His will toward the absentee.

I saw tomorrow marching by on little children's feet; within their forms and faces I read her prophecy complete. I saw tomorrow look at me, from little children's eyes, and thought how carefully we'd build and teach if we were truly wise.

Mothers and teachers of children fill places so great that there isn't an angel in heaven that wouldn't be glad to give a bushel of diamonds to come down here and take their place.

Some think teachers are born. They can improve their skill if they are born again.

A TEACHER'S PRAYER

A teacher prayed this prayer at the close of Bible School:
"Thank you, Lord for using me to be a teaching tool.
Thank you for enduring strength, I've needed it each day,
When faith seemed to falter, I had only but to pray.
Forgive me, Lord, for days when my patience seemed to fail,
When my flesh grew weak, I longed to rant and rail.
We've loved these children, Lord, enjoyed each girl and boy,
Forgive us when we failed, bless us for each joy,
Just one question, Lord, and it's with love I dare
To wonder at my teaching, do they really care?
Did they listen, Lord, to lessons that I taught?
Will their lives be touched by Scriptures I have brought?
Forgive me, Lord, for doubting, my words sounds so unfair,
But, let me see just one thing, Lord, to show they really care . . ."
This teacher's prayer is echoed in pure lives everywhere,
Do the children listen? Do they really care?
As the program ended, an older woman came,
Touched her on the arm, called her by her name.
"I came to talk to you because I felt God led,
Wonder no more, teacher," with this she simply said,
"God still answers prayers, as the years unfurl,
I prayed a prayer like yours, when you were just a girl."
—Jane Hale

> Whatever you write on the heart of a child —
>   A story of gladness, or care
> That heaven has blessed, or that earth had defiled,
>   Will linger unchangeably there.
> Who writes it has sealed it forever and aye;
>   He must answer to God on the great judgment day.

THE TEACHER

Write no poem men's hearts to thrill, no song I sing to lift men's souls; no battle front, no soldiers lead; in halls of state I boast no skill; I just teach school.

I just teach school. But poet's thrill, and singer's joy, and soldier's fire, and stateman's power — all, all are mine; I have all this whene'er I will, as I teach school.

The poets, soldiers, statesmen — all; I see them in the speaking eye, in face aglow with purpose strong, in straightened bodies, tense and tall, when I teach school.

And they, uplifted, gaze intent on cherished heights they soon shall reach. And mine the hands that led them on! If I inspired them, I'm content, and still teach school.

And when I see the world of men and know my touch has guided some, I ne'er regret a moment's toil; and if I'd have my choice again, I'd still teach school.

A Bible School teacher is a person whose job is to welcome a lot of live wires and see that they are all well grounded.

JESUS, THE EXAMPLE

Measured by the best standards of pedagogy, Jesus was the greatest teacher in the world:
He knew His subject.
He knew His people.
He knew how to live what He taught.
He knew how to illustrate His truths.

THE IMPORTANCE

The best of teachers sees the potential good future as she sees her students eyes. For that reason she does not major on content but how to be moral and wise.

A PIECE OF CLAY

*I took a piece of plastic clay
And idly fashioned it one day.
And as my fingers pressed it still,
It moved and yielded to my will.
I came again, when days were passed;
The bit of clay was hard at last.
The form I gave it, still it bore,
But I could change that form no more.*

*I took a piece of living clay,
And deftly formed it one day.
And molded, with my power and art
A young child's soft yielding heart.
I came again, when years were gone;
It was a man I looked upon.
He still that early impress bore,
But I could change it never more.*

WHEN I COME TO THE LORD'S TABLE

I come not because I am worthy, nor for any righteousness of mine, for I have sinned and fallen short of what, by God's help, I might have been.

I come not that there is any magic in partaking of the symbols of Christ's body and blood, but I come because Christ bids me come. It is His table. He invited me.

I come because it is a memorial to Him as oft as it is done in remembrance of Him, and when I remember Him — His life, His suffering, and death, I find myself humbled in His presence and bowing before Him in worship.

I come because here is portrayed Christian self-denial and I am taught forcibly the virtue of sacrifice on behalf of another, which has salvation in it.

Only the teachable people make good teachers.

Look upon the child as a garden where good and bad seeds will grow and be challenged to sow only seeds of goodness.

Be sure that what you teach, the students will never forget.

You cannot teach what you do not know, nor can you lead where you will not go.

The student learns something but the teachers learns much more.

No one is saved by works of merit, but no one can be saved without works of obedience to Jesus, our Lord!

Missions

Once a missionary who was earning about $1200 a year was approached by the representative of a business concern who offered him $5000 to work for his company. When the missionary refused, he raised the offer to $7000 and then to $10,000. When asked why he refused, the missionary replied, "I prefer the job I have." When asked if the salary offered was enough he answered, "Oh, yes, but the JOB is not big enough."

We will never win the world to Christ with spare cash.

THE CHURCH

WE WILL TELL YOUR GOD ON YOU

Night is falling on the Congo,
O'er the jungles far and near—
Every heathen village knows it,
Soon the blackness stark and stere,
Will be brooding, brooding, brooding;
He who walks will walk in fear!

Yet no black man seeks his hut,
All are waiting on the shore,
Gazing, peering, thru the twilight;
Gazing, peering, — something more!
Longing, ah, with what wild longing,
Longing never known before!

For the drums have beat the word:
"Comes again the river spirit,
A great ship — white man aboard!"
And the black men do not fear it!
For the word has passed along:
"White man's message, hear it, hear it!"

List, there is the sounded horn!
Into view the great boat presses!
"Hasten, heathen, gather close
In canoes, address it! Stresses
On the strokes you black men there!
Tell the white men our distresses!"

Slowly the great boat draws near
Heeds the signal from the land;
Then a voice from white to black men:
"What is it, my brother, friend?"
And the aged chief doth answer,
Mighty chieftain of the band:

"Come and tell the story, white man,
Tell the story that you know,
That you've told the other black men
In the villages below,
Of a Christ who came to save us,
Of a Christ who'll ease our woe!"

Troubled then the tired white man
Who is going home to rest
To America his homeland,
To America the blest;
As he speaks his heart is breaking,
Sighs and groans upheave his breast;
Wrenched is his soul within him;
Faint is he and sore distressed.

"Black chief, giant of the village,
I am coming back again!
Now I hasten to my homeland!
Time permits me not my friend!
For the path is long that leads me,
And I seek the journey's end!
But a year from now you'll see me!
I will tell the story then!"

But the black chief turned away—
Bent his head and sunk his chest,
Limp and swaying all his frame,
Then resolve did fill his breast:
"I will tell your God on you,
White man, who so loveth rest!"

"I will tell your God on you!
White man, make my heart to burn
With the story that you tell:
White man, tell me! Let me learn!
See, my race is almost done!
I shall die with set of sun!"

But the white man dropped his head,
Slowly, sadly, turned and fled!
Down the river the ship sped!
Ne'er before was heard or read
By White man or his crew:
"I will tell your God on you!"

In the heathen village there
Darkness deepened to despair,
Fallen stark and dead the chief!
Stricken every soul with grief!
And the horror of the night
Stalked and brooded till the light.
But the black men took a vow.
Will you hear it, white men, now!
"We will tell your God on you!
Surely as your God is true!"

"We will tell your God on you!"
White men do you hear the cry?
"We will tell your God on you!"
May it prod you till you die!
May it, oh, become the cry
That will quicken every breast
That hath known our God in heaven!
May it never be suppressed!
May it prod and prick you thru
Till you rise and duty do!
"We will tell your God on you!
We will tell your God on you!"

—Amy Carson Phillips

The cost of the first atom bomb was $2,000,000,000. This amount would have put 10,000 missionaries in the field for a period of 100 years at $2,000 a year.

COMPULSION

So long as hungry faces
Ask and are denied
So long as barefoot bodies
Shiver far and wide;
So long as there are hearts
That never heard of Christ;
So long as there is sorrow
And youth is sacrificed . . .
I have to give.

So long as there is heartache
Or suffering anywhere;
So long as men are homeless
With burdens I can share;
So long as life abundant
Is lived by, oh so few;
So long as the Kingdom calls
Some thing I have to do . . .
I have to give.

—Mayme Garner Miller

EVERY CHRISTIAN A MISSIONARY

Admiral Foote invited the royalty of Sion to a dinner on his vessel. As soon as the guests were seated, the admiral as was his custom prayed a blessing upon the food. The king in surprise said, "I thought only missionaries asked blessing." "True," the admiral said, "but every Christian is a missionary."

Paul Rader, "A world man — that is, a man with a whole world on his heart — is a rare man and a man close to God, for God alone loves the world."

It is possible that we may forget the divine commission of the church is to save the world, not gain it.

Some churches have a missions committee but most of the people belong to the omission committee.

The best remedy for a sick church is to put it on a missionary diet.

THE BIBLE A MISSIONARY BOOK

Every book in the New Testament was written by a foreign missionary.

Every epistle in the New Testament that was written to a church was written to a foreign missionary church.

Every New Testament letter written to an individual was written to the convert of a foreign missionary.

The one book of prophecy in the New Testament was written to seven foreign missionary churches in Asia.

The language of the books of the New Testament is a missionary's language.

The map of the early Christian world is the tracings of the missionary journeys of the apostles.

Of the twelve apostles chosen by the Lord, every apostle except one became a missionary.

The one man among the twelve apostles who did not become a missionary became a traitor.

—The Kings Business

Those who call themselves Christians and yet do not wish all others to be Christians are confessing the insecurity of their own faith. A church that is not dreaming in terms of presenting the Gospel to all men is tacitly admitting that it has no message for any man.

—Kenneth Scott Latourette

IS IT NOTHING TO YOU?

Is it nothing to you
   That lost ones are crying?
Is there nothing you'll do
   To keep them from dying?

They're dying without Jesus
   For lack of a preacher,
They're crying, come see us
   Or send us a teacher.

Is it nothing to you?
   My Jesus is pleading.
A world I died to resuce
   From Satan's leading.

You're safe in my fold
   And one of my children,
But others must be told
   And a world must be won.

So please, my saved one,
   Arise to meet this need;
There's a job to be done
   That this world might be freed.
             —David Savage

TO A MISSIONARY

For me 'twas not the truth you taught,
To you so clear, to me so dim,
But when you came you brought a sense to Him.
And through your eyes He beckoned me,
And through your heart His love was shed,
Till I lost sight of you and saw the Christ instead.

Missionary giving depends not so much on the condition of the people's purses as on the state of the soul.

MISSIONS is not a minor charity; it is the Church's chief business. The Christian has the best news in the world to tell, namely, that God has come into the world in Jesus Christ to save the world from itself to Himself. It is every Christian's responsibility to give out the Gospel, in every way possible as often as possible, to everyone possible. He cannot reach everyone, but he can reach someone, and it is for those whom he can reach that he will have to give an answer.
—Johnson

Charles Haddon Spurgeon, British pastor: "If called to be a missionary, don't stoop to be a king."

BELIEVE IN MISSIONS

People who don't believe in missions should turn to the pages of history and read of the life lived by their ancestors before the missionaries reached them.

We are saved because of past missionary efforts. That should make us concerned about the coming generations.

If a church will not reach out, then it faces the danger of passing out.
—Jesse Bade

Christ accepted makes you a Christian. Christ obeyed makes you a missionary.

Jim Elliot, "He is no fool who gives what he cannot keep to gain what he cannot lose."

THE HOME

Home, Marriage

THE IDEAL HOME

*An ideal home cannot be built
With compass, rule or square.
An ideal home cannot exist
Without our Jesus there.*

*An ideal home, where Jesus reigns
And all on Him depend,
Alone can save our nation, doomed,
From her untimely end.*

*An ideal home is filled with faith,
And work will coincide.
Where trust will ever rest in Thee,
Our all, the Crucified.*

*The place you find just filled with love
No matter where you roam,
Where Jesus Christ does reign supreme,
There — is the ideal home.*   —Selected

Many American homes are now on a three shift basis. Father is on the night shift, Mother on the day shift and the children shift for themselves.

The most ideal home temperature is maintained by warm hearts instead of hot heads.

THE HOME

A COOKIE OR A KISS

A house should have a cookie jar, for when it's half past three
  And children hurry home from school as hungry as can be,
There's nothing quite so splendid for filling children up
  As spicy, fluffy ginger cakes and sweet milk from a cup.

A house should have a mother waiting with a hug,
  No matter what a boy brings home — a puppy or a bug;
For children only loiter when the bell rings to dismiss
  If no one's home to greet them with a cookie or a kiss.
—Helen Welshimer

One reason why many children are found on the streets these days is that they are afraid to stay home alone.

The greatest educational institution in the world is the home. There are 8,760 hours in a year. The average child will spend 8 hours a day sleeping, or 2,920 hours per year. If he attended Bible School every Sunday, and IF the teacher taught for a whole hour, he would only receive 52 hours of instruction during the year. If he attended other services of the church he would perhaps receive an additional 100 hours or so of religious instruction. This still leaves 5,688 hours in the year to be accounted for. If this child attends the public school 6 hours per day, 5 days a week, for 9 month, he has spent 1,080 hours in public school. There are still 4,608 hours left in the year. Most of these hours will be spent in the environment of the home. This will amount to approximately 4,000 hours of instruction in the home every year.

Be it ever so humble there is no place like home, when you return from a camping trip.

There are more home permanents, than permanent homes.

THANKS FOR DIRTY DISHES

Thank God for dirty dishes
They have a tale to tell.
While others may go hungry
We are eating well.

With home, health and happiness
I shouldn't want to fuss,
By the stack of evidence
God's been very good to us.

Blessed are the husband and wife who are as polite and courteous to one another as they are to their friends.

A true home is not built by hands but by hearts.

A small house can hold as much happiness as a large one.

If a man is unhappy at home, he should find out if his wife has married a grouch.

To bring up a child in the home in the way he should go, parents must be going that way.

Children at play may tear up a house but they never break up a home.

Home is the best place where our stomachs get 3 meals a day and our hearts a thousand.

THE HOME

YOUR HOME IS BUGGED

Yes, your house is bugged. In every home there are two microphones per child — one in each ear. These highly sensitive instruments pick up table prayers, ordinary conversations, incidental remarks, various types of words, radio, TV commercials and many things not intended for them.

These all-absorbing microphones transmit all they hear to highly impressionable minds. These sounds become the child's vocabulary and the basis for this thinking and action. What they think they may grow up to be.

Home is the first school. Be careful what is caught. It may be more powerful than what is taught.

Many very fine houses ought to be remodeled into Christian homes.

DOWNFALL OF A NATION AND HOMES

1. When the state does the educating and has to admit that it has done a poor job.
2. Parental neglect of the children, when parents are more interested in government care than personal care.
3. When parents lack self-discipline and let the children grow up the same way.
4. Doting parents who can see no wrong in their children and who defend them before the school teacher and the police when they are caught.

Rough hands build houses, but gentle hearts build homes.

Every human being should have three homes, a domestic home, a church home, and an eternal home.

MORE SPACE IN THE HOUSE

"You have two small children who need more growing space," observed a neighbor when she visited the couple in their much too small apartment. "Why don't you move out of your apartment and get a home?" The mother replied, "We've got the home we just don't have a house to put it in."

A realtor described a beautiful property for sale. It had everything that people dream about but can't afford. The price was greatly reduced. A prospective buyer asked why. He replied, "The couple is getting a divorce." A beautiful house is not the same as a beautiful home.

HOME

We may plan a new world charter
And its pros and cons debate.
How to build a higher order,
And a better world create.
But they build in vain who trust in
Starry places and domes,
For no nation is worse or better
Than the fiber of its homes.

A Puritan once said, "If you are a child of God and marry a child of the devil, you can expect to have trouble with your father-in-law."

Home should be something more than a filling station.

Some men who can't run a home can go down to the park, sit on a bench, spit tobacco and run the country.

THE HOME

THREE BOOKS FOR A HAPPY MARRIAGE

Marriage is at its best when the wife uses a good cookbook, the couple asks the Lord to help them keep a well balanced checkbook and the family feeds regularly on the Good Book.
—Don Earl Boatman

A house is no home unless it contains food for the soul as well as the body.

Leave your home with loving words. Life has many dangers — you may never return.

Have you ever wondered why the sound of the words "chocolate pudding" carry farther through the air than the words "pick up your toys"?
—Shari Rodifer

Marriage is an investment that pays you great dividends if you keep up the interest.

KINDNESS IN MARRIAGE

>They were single and went walking
> Her heart did skip a beat
>As she stumbled on the sidewalk
> He said "Oh, be careful sweet."
>
>Now the wedding bells have sounded
> And they walk that very street
>When she stumbles on the sidewalk
> He yells, "Awkward, pick up your feet."

BEATITUDES FOR CHRISTIAN MARRIED COUPLES

Blessed are the husband and wife who continue to be affectionate, considerate, and loving after the wedding bells have ceased ringing.

Blessed are the husband and wife who are as polite and courteous to one another as when they were just friends.

Blessed are they who have a sense of humor, or this attribute will be a handy shock absorber.

Blessed are the married couples who abstain from the use of alcoholic beverages.

Blessed are they who love their mates more than any other person in the world and who joyfully fulfill their marriage vow of a lifetime of fidelity and mutual helpfulness to one another.

Blessed are they who attain parenthood, for children are a heritage of the Lord.

Blessed are they who remember to thank God for their food before they partake of it and who set apart some time each day for the reading of the Bible and for prayer.

Blessed are the husband and wife who faithfully attend the worship services of the church and who work together in the church for the advancement of Christ's Kingdom.

Blessed are the husband and wife who can work out the problems of adjustments without interference from relatives.

Blessed is the couple who has a complete understanding about financial matters and who has worked out a perfect partnership with all money under the control of both.

Blessed are the husband and wife who humbly dedicate their lives and their home to Christ and who practice the teachings of Christ in the home being unselfish, loyal and loving.

Girls don't marry a man to reform him. The rites will not right him and the altar will not alter him.

Marriages, some think, are made in heaven but all of us know they have to be maintained on earth.

THE HOME

A man teaching young couples advocated a two child family. The best advice is to have a two parent family. God did!

Marriages would be happier if couples seeking the last word, would make the last word a time of prayer.

LOVE IS MANY THINGS

Love is a state of the heart;
Love is a state of the mind.
Love is a feeling of rapture;
Love is being kind.
Love is a pair of ruby lips;
Love is eyes of sparkling blue.
Love is being happy;
Love is crying too.
Love is most times giving;
Love is sometimes taking.
Love is steady strength;
Love is hearts a-quaking.
Love is baby's laughter;
Love is Mother's tears,
Love is Father's pride;
Love is teen-age fears.
Love is heights of ecstasies.
Love is depths of sorrow,
Love is yesterday's memories;
Love is plans for tomorrow.
—Esther Decker

The happiest marriage is where both paries get better mates than they deserve.

Many teen-agers today just go ahead and marry, expecting their folks to be good supports about it.

A happy marriage is when two people are as deeply in love as they are in debt.

Success in marriage is more than finding the right person; it is a matter also of being the right person.

Trouble often starts in marriage when a man is so busy earning his salt that he forgets his sugar at home.

Adam and Eve had special advantages. He did not have to hear about all the men who she might have married and she didn't have to hear about how good his mother cooked.

If young people would use "horse" sense before marriage they would avoid some "nightmare" later on.

Sometimes when you are depressed, think back over the person you might have married.

Marriage probably has the poorest public relations of any institution in the world, but its business is only slightly short of spectacular.
—Douglas Meador

Some people in winter are prone to freeze
While others sweat and smother.
By some tricky quirk of fate
They get married to each other!

—Georgie Starbuck Galbraith

Many modern houses have everything in them except a happy family.

Home is the place where a child must be helped to learn from his mistakes, not be forced to suffer from them.

The most influential of all educational factors is the conversation in a child's home.

Father, Man

While MEN look for better organizations through which to do God's work, GOD looks for better men to work through His organization — the church.

When a man finds no peace within himself it is useless to seek it elsewhere.

The man who really wants to do something finds a way; the other finds an excuse.

A man can be strong without being brutal, can be firm without being mean, can exercise authority without being arrogant, and can instruct, teach, and guide without being unkind.

We have learned to fly through the air like birds and to swim through the seas like fish. When will we learn to walk the earth like men?

Strange, but it seems to be true: charm is a woman's strength, while strength is a man's charm.

Every man is worth just as much as the things are worth about which he busies himself.

WHAT IS HE WORTH?

Not infrequently one hears the query, "Wonder what he is worth?" by which the questioner is asking how much money does he have, how much property, what is the size of his holdings. If a man has a large bank account, lives in a beautiful home in a restricted residential district, drives an expensive car, takes long and costly trips to the far reaches of the world, and in many similar ways evidences wealth, we think of him as being worth a lot. Actually he may be next to worthless. If he lacks character, integrity, and is devoid of spiritual life he isn't worth much to himself or to anyone else. If what he has he gained by dishonest practices and outright chicanery, what he has is ill-gotten, and he has sold himself for a mess of pottage. Many a man who does not own the house in which he lives, seldom takes a trip, owns very little of anything, lives in a not-too-prosperous neighborhood, is worth everything because he has a sterling character, lives with God, is a man of integrity. The worth of a man is not determined by the amount of worldly possessions he has or has not, whether he travels or stays at home. His worth depends entirely on what he IS, his relationship to other men, and to God, what he does with his time, his abilities, and his opportunities. What he IS determines WHAT HE IS WORTH!

When God measures a man He puts the tape around the heart instead of the head.

Foolish men say something but wise men have something to say.

THE LITTLE CHAP WHO FOLLOWS ME

A careful man I want to be
A little fellow follows me
I do not want to go astray
For fear he'll go the self-same way.

Not once can I escape his eyes
Whatever he sees me do, he tries.
Like me he says he is going to be,
That little chap who follows me.

He thinks that I am good and fine,
Believes in every word of mine.
The base in me he must not see,
That little chap who follows me.

I must remember as I go
Thru summer sun and winter snow,
I am building for the year to be
That little chap who follows me.

Many a farmer wants only thorough-bred animals on his farm but he lives like a mongrel that shows he has no breeding.

WATCHFUL EYE

While driving a car, I watched the traffic before me and behind me through the rear view mirrors. Naturally I was concerned about speed limits and a police car that appeared in view.

I became far more conscious of my driving, obedience to the law when my little boy Roger looked over my shoulder for the first time and said, "Daddy, you are going 60 miles an hour." A good example is much better than good advice on any subject.

—Don Earl Boatman

A foolish man might never be known to be foolish if he would keep his mouth shut.

THE KEY TO WORLD CONSTRUCTION

A young man prepared to spend the evening reading a long magazine article dealing with post war world. He was frequently interrupted by a noisy young son. Tearing off the back cover of the magazine on which was a map of the world, the father cut it into bits and made a jigsaw puzzle. "Here is a puzzle for you," he said. "Put the map of the world together." The man returned to his reading, but in a short time he heard the boy say, "Here it is, Dad; I've finished." "How did you finish it so quickly?" asked the father. The boy answered, "On the other side was a picture of a man. I put the man together and found the world in perfect order."

For 20 years a mother asks her son where he is going. It is wonderful to have a faithful wife who inquires, "Where are you going?" It is a shame when at the end of life the mourners ask the same question.

Any weakling can abuse a little child. It takes a strong man to treat them tenderly.

Sincere men who love their children see things differently when they look through the eyes of their little ones.

TEACHERS OF MEN

New words are bing coined daily in our society. We have more than 7,000 English words. Our children will learn many of them, but a Father should teach his family that the greatest word is God.

A dog is known as man's best friend. It is a reproach upon our society that an animal would be better than our fellow man.

Man and rivers grow crooked by following the path of least resistance.

If the sheep go wrong, it will not be long till the lambs be wrong as they.

A wise man thinks all he says; a fool simply says all he thinks.

A man should be like tea: his real strength appearing when he gets in hot water.

THE WORLD NEEDS MEN

. . . who cannot be bought.
. . . whose word is their bond.
. . . who put character above wealth.
. . . who possess opinions and a will.
. . . who are larger than their vocation.
. . . who do not hesitate to take chances.
. . . who will not lose their individuality in a crowd.
. . . who will be as honest in small things as in great things.
. . . who will make no compromise with wrong.
. . . whose ambitions are not conformed to their own selfish desires.
. . . who gives thirty-six inches to the yard and thirty-two quarts to the bushel.
. . . who will not say they do it "because everybody else does it."
. . . who will not have one brand of honesty for business purposes and another for private life.
. . . who are not ashamed or afraid to stand for the truth when it is unpopular; who can say "no" with emphasis, although the rest of the world says "yes."

The good man even though overwhelmed by misfortune, loses never his inborn greatness of soul. Camphorwood burnt in the fire becomes all the more fragrant.

—Satake

ILL-USTRIOUS BEHAVIOR

Men are so impervious
 To illness and to pain;
Sickness may surround them
 Yet they will not complain.
They're calm, resigned, and stalwart
 And will not sigh or moan
Unless, of course, that ache or pain
 Turns out to be their own.

If you find a person who feels God has let him down, look closely and you will see it is probably the other way.

The best gift a father can give to his children is to love their mother.

Mother, Woman

A vacationer reported seeing a sign in a restaurant as follows: "Pies like mother used to make before she took up bridge and cigarettes."

"Stick to your washing, ironing, scrubbing and cooking" the husband said, "No wife of mine is going out to work."

Mothers are selfless, with tender devotion, asking no thanks for the love which they give.
Mothers are brave, their bright courage enduring agony, pain that their children might live.
Mothers are artists, and mothers are poets, etching and writing, the life of a child.
Gardner, they, who are tending their seedling, weeding with care lest a flower be defiled.
Mothers forgive our too frequent omission, cherish our virtues, which others ignore,
Lift us by faith to our highest attainment. We honor, this day, those we ever adore.

MOTHER'S DAY

Let every day be Mother's Day.
Make roses grow along the way.
And beauty everywhere.
Oh, never let her eyes be wet
With tears of sorrow and regret,
And never cease to care.
Come, grown-up children, and rejoice
That you can hear your mother's voice.
A day for her? For you she gave
Long years of love and service brave
For you her youth was spent.
There was no weight or hurt or care
Too heavy for her strength to bear.
She followed where you went;
Her courage and her love sublime
You can depend on all the time.

—*Guest*

Wife, homemaker, teacher, maid, cook, referee, rescue squad, tutor, chauffeur, psychiatrist, and example. All put together they spell Mother.

A young daughter paid her mother the highest compliment when she introduced her at a Mother-Daughter Banquet, by saying, "She's my mother, I had nothing to say about that. But I can choose my friends, and she's first on the list."

THE SHINING MOMENT

One Sunday I was entertained in a farm home of a member of a rural church. I was impressed by the intelligence and unusually good behavior of the only child in the home, a little four-year-old boy.

Then I discovered one reason for the child's charm. The mother was at the kitchen sink, washing the intricate parts of the cream separator when the little fellow came to her with a magazine. "Mother," he asked, "what is this man in the picture doing?" To my surprise she dried her hands, sat down on a chair and taking the boy in her lap she spent ten minutes answering his questions.

After the child had left I commented on her having interrupted her chores to answer the boy's questions, saying, "Most mothers wouldn't have bothered."

"I expect to be washing cream separators for the rest of my life," she told me, "But never again will my son ask me that question!"

THE ARITHMETIC OF LOVE

When George was a baby upon my knee
I wondered if I could love another as much as he.
Maydene was added, and then there were two.
Love wasn't divided; love just grew.
Then when wee Charles came along,
My love for him was just as strong.
When Jerry and Merry joined our group,
My mother-love took a loop-de-loop.
Love didn't subtract; love didn't divide-
God's gift of love just multiplied!
—Beulah Aydelotte Curtiss

MOTHER'S OPPORTUNITY

Teach the child obedience in the play pen to save him from the state pen.
Teach the offspring in the high chair to save them from the electric chair.
Let the children break up each others toys and they will break your heart when they are boys.

MOTHER AND AN ANGEL'S WORK

I have done an angel's work today, yes such an honor came my way;
Real angel's work, and lest you doubt it, I'm going to tell you all about it;
Well, first I cooked. It was so nice to plan the pies, stewed fruit and rice.
God sent His angel once to make cakes for a poor wayfarer's sake.
But just today he honored me and sent the task my way, you see!
Back of my mind this thought would lurk, that I was still at angel's work—
Putting away the coats and dresses and moving all unsightliness—
For oh, 'tis such a lovesome thing, just straightening out and refreshening.
And after that I washed a few small, wooly garments, old and new,
And as I hung them on the line I thought, "What God-like work is mine
To cleanse, ah me, to wash out stains "til not a single spot remains."
So, later in the day "twas sweet to sit and rest my tired feet,
Mending the clothes and planning, too, how to make old things into new.
For surely 'tis and angel's way to put things right from day to day,
To find thin places and repair the old things for the sturdy wear,
Since wear and tear must surely be on this side of Eternity.
I'm feeling very proud to say, "I've done an angel's work today!"

The bravest battle that ever was fought
I'll tell you where and when
On the maps of the world you will find it not
It was fought by the mothers of men.

MOTHER — AND OTHERS

Others weary of the noise,
Mothers play with girls and boys.
Others scold because we fell,
Mothers "kiss and make it well."
Others work with patient will,
Mothers labor later still.
Others love is more or less,
Mothers love with steadiness.
Others keep the ancient score,
Mothers never shut the door.
Others grow incredulous,
Mothers still believe in us.
Others throw their faith away,
Mothers pray, and pray, and pray.
—Amos R. Wells

MOTHER

God made a wonderful mother,
A mother who never grows old,
He made her smile of the sunshine,
And He molded her heart of pure gold;
In her eyes He placed bright shining stars,
In her cheeks fair roses you see;
God made a wonderful mother,
And He gave that dear mother to me.

WATCHFUL MOTHERS

She always leaned to watch for us,
　Anxious if we were late,
In winter by the window
In summer by the gate.

And though we mocked her tenderly,
　Who had such foolish care,
The long way home would be more safe,
　Because she waited there.

Her thoughts were all so full of us,
　She never could forget!
And so I think that where she is
　She must be waiting yet.

Waiting until we come home to her
　Anxious if we are late.
Watching from Heaven's window
　Leaning on Heaven's gate.

　　　　　—Margaret Widdemer

CHRISTIAN MOTHERS

A mother's arms are the child's best cradle, her heart is the child's classroom and her knees are his altar. She has balm for baby's bruises, cheer for childish woes, comfort for daily catastrophies, counsel for her children's concerns and hopeful visions for the eventual blessing and success in life for all of her children. Above all she is concerned about their salvation and their spiritual welfare.

The child that does not hear about Christ at his mother's knee may listen to some evil ideas at some other joint.

A MOTHER'S SECRET

Someone asked a mother whose children had turned out very well, the secret by which she prepared them for usefulness and for the Christian life.

Without hesitation she said: "When in the morning I washed my children, I prayed that they might be cleansed by the Savior's precious blood.

When I put on their garments, I prayed that they might be arrayed in the garments of salvation and in the robe of God's righteousness.

When I gave them food, I prayed that they might be fed with the Bread of Life.

When I started them on the road to school, I prayed that their faith might be as the shining light, brighter and brighter to the perfect day.

When I put them to sleep, I prayed that they might be enfolded in the Savior's everlasting arms."

No wonder her children were early led to a saving knowledge of the Lord Jesus Christ; and became adornments to the doctrine of God our Savior in the things!

A MOTHER'S PRAYER

Lord Jesus, you who bade the children come and took them in your
  gentle arms and smiled,
Grant me unfailing patience through the days to understand and help
  my child;
I would not only give his body care and guide his young dependent steps
  along the wholesome ways,
But I would know his heart, attuning mine to childhood's grief and song;
Oh, give me vision to discern the child behind whatever he may do or
  say,
The wise humility to learn from him the while I strive to teach him day
  by day.

—Adelaide Love

THE HOME

A man reported that he had the meanest mother in the neighborhood. When other kids ate candy for breakfast his mother made him eat cereal, eggs, toast and drink milk.

GOD'S WORTHY WOMEN

The world loves a wonderful woman:
One who is worthy in her way,
For her price is far above rubies;
God is her anchor and stay.

She works from sunrise to sunset,
Cheerfully setting her pace,
Being thrifty, true, and trusting,
With honor, love and grace.

Her hands are eager, helping others,
Working willfully, wanting to erase
The poverty, needs, and dark clouds
With a gentle smiling face.

She never neglects her homely duties;
Always a thought for kith or kin,
Her work she faithfully masters,
Her husband's approval to win.

She is a guiding star to her husband,
The leader and lover at home,
And she is versatile in her talents;
Her home is a stepping stone.

She is tactful through trials always;
Her ambition ever soars high;
Her spiritual strength a well of water,
Her treasures in heaven lie.

—Elizabeth Harris

CONDITIONING

A machine will air condition a house but a mother is in the process of heir conditioning.

An old-fashioned woman is the gal who tries to make one husband last a lifetime.

ARE ALL THE CHILDREN IN?

*I think oftimes as the night draws nigh
  Of an old house on the hill,
Of a yard all wide and blossom starred
  Where the children played at will.
And when the night at last came down,
  Hushing the merry din,
Mother would look around and ask,
  "Are all the children in?"*

*Tis many and many a year since then,
  And the old house on the hill
No longer echoes to childish feet,
  And the yard is still, so still.
But I see it all, as the shadows creep
  And though many the years have been
Since then, I can hear my mother ask
  "Are all the children in?"*

*I wonder if when the shadows fall
  On the last short earthly day,
When we say good-bye to world outside,
  All tired with our childish play.
When we step out into that Other Land
  Where mother so long has been,
Will we hear her ask, just as of old,
  "Are all the children in?"*

GOOD MOTHERS AND A NATION

Rulers of men speak of priorities in government. If a nation does not have good mothers, our nation will be busy governing the ungovernable.

FROM THE HEART OF ONE WOMAN

What is a woman? She is a complex entity: she can be a wife, a mother, a grandmother, a career woman, a teacher, a student — all these and more — wrapped up into one being which is above all, a dedicated servant of God.

Human life and human character are so many-sided, the Bible approaches every side from several different angles. As the final analysis, "by their fruits ye shall know them." Since we are essentially spiritual and eternal, we strive to bring forth those fruits of the spirit; love, joy, peace, patience, kindness, goodness, faithfulness, gentleness, self-control. The state of your soul is always expressed in your outer condition and the intangible influence which you radiate at large. The soul that abides with God cannot be hidden, and actually does its best work unconsciously, by the radiation of peace and joy. "Do you not know that you are God's temple and that God's spirit dwells in you? Make love your aim and earnestly desire the spiritual gifts." The only way of earning these gifts is by practicing the presence of God. Our entire beings are absorbed by love, and our every thought and every act are motivated by purest love. Let us serve God better by loving those around us with a deeper and more compassionate devotion.

When a woman lives such a life, it may be said of her, "She is far more precious than jewels; her children (and grandchildren) rise up and call her blessed; her husband also, and he praises her." If her influence extends beyond her home, as a teacher or student or leader of women in the church family, only the distant shores of eternity will show how far have spread the ripples of righteousness which were caused by the paddles of her little craft on the ocean of life.

JUST LIKE MOTHER

He criticized her pudding, he didn't like her cake;
He wished she'd make the biscuits like his mother used to make
She didn't wash the dishes and she didn't make a stew;
And she didn't darn his socks like his mother used to do.
And then one day he went the same old ritual through;
She turned and boxed his ears — just like mother used to do!

God thought to give the sweetest thing
In His almighty power, and deeply pondering
What it should be — one hour in fondest joy and love of heart
Outweighting every other.
He moved the gates of heaven apart
And gave to earth — A Mother!

GAINED?

Woman has gained footing in nearly every profession, but along with woman's elevation to respectable position in the business world has come the temptation to neglect a top job. It is the God-given, honorable, powerful, influential and wonderful many faceted task of being a mother.

Mothers who scold little boys for carrying crazy things in their pockets should look in their own handbags.

It has been said of children — "Unless we reach their hearts today, they will break our hearts tomorrow." It is the word of GOD — taught, believed, and practiced — that will keep our children from sin."

Just about the time a woman thinks her work is all done, she becomes a grandmother.

THE HOME

PRAYER TIME

The while she darns the children's socks,
She prays for little stumbling feet;
Each folded pair within its box
Fit faith's bright sandals, sure and fleet.

While washing out, with mother pains
Small dusty suits and frocks and slips,
She prays that God may cleanse the stains,
From little hands, and hearts and lips.

And when she breaks the fragrant bread,
Or pours a portion in each cup,
For grace to keep their spirits fed,
Her mother-heart is lifted up.

O busy ones, whose souls grow faint,
Whose tasks seem longer than the day,
It doesn't take a cloistered saint
To find a little time to pray.

❦

Parents, Grandparents

NO SECOND SHOWING

Now is the best time to be the best parents. It is the only time. In film of childhood there are no re-runs. There are no re-plays. What is done is done. What we have taught is final — our example can not be recalled. The mistakes we make can not be undone. While the child is in the high chair we should start to teach him to be high-minded. More attention to the high chair lesson will put cobwebs on the electric chair.

Parent's discipline should be based on four "F's." They are firmness, fondness, frankness and fairness. Parents who can not say "NO" to a child often rear offspring who have contempt for authority.

TRAINING IN CHRISTIAN TEACHING

Some parents who are indifferent to Christianity say they do not want to influence the children in matters of religion. They should realize that many influences are at work and it may be antagonistic to moral values.

Tobacco ads, if believed, will injure health. While teens they may get get into nicotine.

Beer ads may influence them to be addicts, drunks, murderous drivers.

Pornography may cause them to produce children while they are in grade school.

Movies, T.V., magazines influence their behavior.

Ungodly companionship may turn them away from the parents and into a life of debauchery.

The schools may convince them that they are animals.

Peer pressure may be their downfall.

Parents who will not take a stand may help their kids to be victimized by wrong influences.

The church is the most powerful influence for good in the society. Parents need the church for re-inforcement.

DO WHAT YOU CAN

Parents can't change the color of their children's eyes, but they can give them enlightenment. They can't alter the child's features but they can shape what the child will do with his talent.

The child that has love, kindness, sympathy and a desire for good has something better than a beauty contest trophy.

GOOD PARENTS — GOOD CHILDREN

Good parents seldom have delinquent children. It is because the parents decisions are controlled, not by the child's wants but by the child's needs.

OH, GOD MAKE ME A BETTER PARENT

Help me to understand my children, to listen patiently to what they have to say and to answer all their questions kindly. Keep me from interrupting them, talking back to them and contradicting them. Make me as courteous to them as I would have them be to me. Give me the courage to confess my sins against my children and to ask of them forgiveness, when I know that I have done them wrong.

May I not vainly hurt the feelings of my children. Forbid that I should laugh at their mistakes or resort to shame and ridicule as punishment. Let me not tempt a child to lie and steal. So guide me hour by hour that I may demonstrate by all I say and do that honesty produces happiness.

Reduce, I pray, the meanness in me. May I cease to nag; and when I am out of sorts, help me, Oh Lord, to hold my tongue.

Blind me to the little errors of my children and help me to see the good things that they do. Give me a ready word for honest praise.

Help me to treat my children as those of their own age, but let me not exact of them the judgments and conventions of adults. Allow me not to rob them of the opportunity to wait upon themselves, to think, to choose, and to make decisions.

Forbid that I should ever punish them for my selfish satisfaction. May I grant them all of their wishes that are reasonable and have the courage always to withhold a privilege which I know will do them harm.

Make me so fair and just, so considerate and companionable to my children that they will have a genuine esteem for me. Fit me to be loved and imitated by my children.

With all thy gifts, Oh God, do give me calm and poise and self-control.

NEGLECT

It is almost criminal to neglect the spiritual life of a child. Yet many parents feel that when they have given their children clothing, food, shelter, medicine and public education, they have given them everything. In school they are taught evolution, thus without spiritual foundation, the children act like animals. Thus society becomes zoo keepers and the animals multiply.

Parents give their children heredity and that they can not help, thus it behooves them to be greatly concerned about their environment. That they can help.

When parents cannot control children in the home, it is difficult for the government to control them on the streets.

WHY I GO TO CHURCH

Because my youth is watching me,
To note whatever he can see
That tells him what his father thinks,
And with his eager soul he drinks
The things I do in daily walk,
The things I say in daily talk;
If I with him the church will share,
My youth will make his friendship there.

Because my youth needs to go—
His faith in right is rather low;
He needs the church to hold him fast
To those great truths that always last;
And when he sees me on my way,
It draws him to the church to pray;
And both our hearts are lifted up
To heavely places where we sup.

A PARABLE FROM NATURE

Once upon a time there was a Papa Rooster and a Mama Hen and they had a cute little baby chick. They were the proudest papa and mama you ever did see! "This little chick is never going to scratch out his living like I did," declared Papa Rooster. "I shall see that he has everything he needs to grow up and be a fine chicken."

And they did. They worked their beaks off trying to provide things for their little chick. He wore the finest, shiniest feathers in the whole chicken yard. They taught him the finest manners and allowed him to associate with only the very best chickens. "I want" is all the baby needed to say and his want was provided. The other chicks were so envious that he had parents who took such pride in the meeting of his every wish!

In chicken school he was always the leader. He led in reading, writing, and arithmetic; played both chicken football and basketball and held down first chair in the school crowing choir. He was valedictorian of his chicken class and was voted the chicken most likely to make tracks.

He went to Barnfowl U. and continued his education. Once there he performed brilliantly and Papa Rooster and Mama Hen bought a slick convertible. He graduated with honors and finally earned a Master's degree in coopology. He met a cute little chick co-ed and was wed in an elaborate barnyard affair that had the henhouse talking for weeks afterwards. His career seemed assured and the future bright but one morning tragedy struck. He disappeared and was never again seen. The last anybody ever saw of him he was tucked under the arm of a very hungry looking hobo who was headed for a campfire down by the railroad tracks.

Alas for the little chick! His parents did everything for him except one thing that was absolutely needful: THEY NEVER taught him how to SAVE HIS OWN LIFE!

Of course the moral of all this is that unless your child is in the church program and learns all he can about how to save his own soul, he doesn't have a chance. THE WORLD IS A HUNGRY HOBO.

The ability to say no is perhaps the greatest gift a parent has.

TOO YOUNG TO LEARN

A parent who says that their child is too young to go to Bible School is in need of learning something. The child recognizes Santa Claus, toys, "Twinkle, Twinkle Little Star." The child knows how to wrap such mothers around her/his little finger. Mothers need to realize that children learn very young and sometimes conclude that parents are not very smart.

The time will come when the child with a soul white as snow, will not want to go to church because his parents wouldn't go.

If you want to keep your child in the fold stay near the good shepherd.

—Charles Willbanks

CHURCH ORPHANS

I was an orphan when it came time for church. I had to get myself ready to go alone. The others had their parents, but I was by myself. I sat with the other kids but they had their parents sitting back there. How I wished for a mother and father to sit between. I would have been so proud! I would have sat just as straight and still. I wouldn't have wiggled an inch. I'd have listened to every word, and when church was over I wouldn't have run out with the others, but would have walked quietly beside mom and dad. I would have been so good, if I had a mother and father in church.

Every day at mealtime I had a mother to get dinner. She washed my clothes and mended the tears. I had a mother to teach me how to hold my fork and say "please" and "thank you." She was there to bandage a cut or care for me when I was sick, but I was an orphan when it came time for church.

I had a father who worked hard to buy the food and clothes I needed. He wrestled with me and was a real pal. But I was an orphan when it came time for church.

PARENTS ARE TEACHERS

1. You are the child's first teacher.
2. By age three the child you have has shaped a personality.
3. Before he goes to school you have determined his traits of character.
4. In your house he has learned about moral, ethical values that may last a lifetime.

HOW DO PARENTS TEACH?

1. By what they say, good or bad.
2. By what they are. The child draws conclusions about parents. They see consistency or hypocrisy.
3. By the experiences that parents plan for them — games, social life, church, surprises, celebrations etc.
4. By our attitude toward other people; races, cultures, friends, enemies, etc.
5. By our concern for material things. They may see our desire for "greeds" rather than "needs."
6. By our reactions — violence, kindness, hatred or love. He sees and hears and tends to act out what he observes.
7. By our attitude toward God, Church, and stewardship.
8. By our interaction with our children. They are learning all the time, even though parents have few times when they are actually planning on teaching.

WHAT WILL CHILDREN SAY 25 YEARS LATER

My mother did two things about discipline. Some times she gave us a spanking without a moments hesitation. Other times she would say, "I have a mind to spank you." We soon learned that if we were very quiet she would not spank. Kids sometimes know how to control their parents.

—Don Earl Boatman

SATURDAY WITH A TEENAGE DAUGHTER

"Are you going to sleep all day? . . . Who said you could use my hairspray? . . . Clean the dishes off the table . . . Turn down the radio . . . Have you made your bed? . . . That skirt is much too short . . . Your closet is a mess . . . Stand up straight . . . Somebody has to go to the store . . . Quit chewing your gum like that . . . Your hair is too bushy . . . I don't care if everybody else does have one . . . Turn down that radio . . . have you done your homework? . . . Don't slouch . . . You didn't make your bed . . . Quit banging on the piano . . . Why don't you iron it yourself? . . . Your fingernails are too long . . . Look it up in the dictionary . . . Sit up straight . . . Get off the phone now . . .Why did you ever buy that record? . . . Take the dog out . . . You forgot to dust that table . . . You've been in the bathroom long enough . . .Turn off the radio and get to sleep, NOW!"

Another day gone, and not once did I say, "I love you."

Dear Lord, forgive me.

A wise parent realizes that he is not "all wise" like God, thus he seeks to get new ideas from the best sources. The Church, the Bible and successful friends furnish a deep well of fresh methods.

What the American house needs today is a complete family devoted to God.

Recently a woman told her preacher that though they desired to teach their children the danger of drinking alcohol, yet she and her husband had to attend parties, where for business reasons, they found it necessary to take a drink or two of liquor so as not to offend the hostess. Then she asked, "What shall we do?"

Her preacher said, "Why ask me? By your own admission you consider the feelings of your hostess more important than the setting of a proper example for your children. Never forget this, you cannot fool your children with pious phrases if they see inconsistencies in your life."

Parents, when you walk away from Bible School, worship services and church activities, remember, you are teaching your child WHERE to walk! Chances are he will follow your example.

GRANDMA ON RELIGION

My Grandma once said, "Dear, religion
Is not just a Sunday affair;
It isn't enough that you go to church
Or recite a Sunday vesper prayer . . .
Religion is something you carry
Around in your heart every day;
It's reflected in all your actions,
Plus everything that you say.

Why religion is what you make it
From day to day, so be sure
And remember that God is Love, if
You would have His blessings endure."
And so religion to me is my way of life,
My conduct from day to day;
It permeates thought and action
And reflects in each word that I say.

Religion to me is a blending
Of the spiritual with the mundane;
It holds twin places, first in my heart,
Yet there's room for it too in my brain.
For my brain tells me time without number
That my heart would be like a cold cell,
If the Spirit of God the Father
Would cease in it ever to dwell.
—Loretta Power Wilson

Once God was pronounced dead, but God has been around for a long time and He intends to stay. Only the pronouncer is dead.

TWO SPECIAL PEOPLE

My grandma is made with
A soft double chin
And gentle, kind eyes
That twinkle, "Come in!
And have a fresh cookie
Or possibly two—
I baked them this morning
For someone like you!"

My grandpa is made with
A whiskery chin
And sparkly fun eyes
That twinkle, "Come in!
I'll tell you a story
Or possibly two—
I saved them for telling
To someone like you!"

A genius usually remains a crackpot until he hits the jackpot with his invention.

Some men try to use God, but the best way, is to be used of God.

LIFE

Do not look at life as an arena in which we play and fight to get fun and to accumulate money. It is a time for us to fight for the privilege to honor Christ and to be a blessing to our fellow man.

A good archer is not known by his arrows but by his good aim.

THE HOME

Children, Teenagers

GROWING UP

We think our babies are beautiful angels, soon we find out that the angelic wings grow shorter as fast as their legs grow longer.

Little girls seem in a hurry to grow up and wear the spike heel shoes that are killing their mothers.

We are so anxious to teach our children to talk, but we soon learn that the next step may be to "shut up."

Children are a comfort to parents, but as they grow up they help parents to grow old faster.

A CHILD TO REAR

I have a child to rear. I would be strong,
That something of my strength may flow to him;
I would be glad, that something of my song
May lift within his heart and mind to brim
Into some clearer cadence all his own,
A lovelier song than I have ever known.

I have a child to rear. I would be wise
To say to him, nay, if that command be best;
I would be honest that his earnest eyes
May find no hidden shame within my breast.
I would be kind and just that he may know
There is but one straight open road to go.

I have a child to rear. Lord God, I ask
Thy help in doing my great blessed task.
—Grace Noll Crowell

MARY HAD A LITTLE BOY

Mary had a little boy, his soul was white as snow;
He never went to Sunday School, 'cause Mary wouldn't go
He never heard the tales of Christ that thrilled the childish mind;
While other children went to class, this child was left behind.
And as he grew from babe to youth, she saw to her dismay
A soul that once was snowy white became a dingy gray.
Realizing he was lost she tried to win him back
But now the soul that once was white had turned an ugly black.
She even started back to church and Bible study too.
She begged the preacher, "Isn't there a thing that you can do?"
The preacher tried — failed and said, "We're just too far behind.
I tried to tell you years ago, but you would pay no mind."
And so, another soul is lost, that once was white as snow.
Sunday School could have helped, but Mary wouldn't go.

BIRDS OF A FEATHER

A farmer loaded up his shotgun and slipped out along the fence, to make it warm for the crows that were pulling up his corn. The farmer had a very sociable parrot who, discovering the crows, flew over and joined them. The farmer saw the crows, but not the parrot. He fired among them and then climbed over the fence to see the execution done. There lay three dead crows, and his pet parrot with ruffled feathers and a broken leg. When the bird was taken home, the children asked, "What did it, Papa? Who hurt our pretty Polly?" "Bad company! Bad company!" answered the parrot in solemn voice. "Aye, that it was," said the father. "Polly was with those crows when I fired and received a shot intended for them. Remember the parrot's fate, children. Beware of bad company."

Tip to a youthful male driver: forget the girl and hug the road.

THE HOME

POWERFUL CHANGES

A baby, so sweet, cooing happily in the crib can grow up to be a hairy dirty militant, "high" on drugs, stooping to pick up a rock or hurling a Molotov cocktail at a police car.

Take another look at the baby daughter, fresh from her morning bath, powdered with fragrance. Visualize her 16 years from now, shouting obscenities in the street, following a rock band, having sex, not knowing which one of many made her pregnant.

What has gone wrong when a society has turned to defiance and drugs as common as chewing gum.

These realities in the streets of the world cause us to realize that children are potentially dangerous and capable of breaking parents hearts and causing a nation to fall.

BAD OPINIONS

Some teenagers seem to think that the family circle includes a couple of squares.

Some think they are being clever when they light up a smoke, down their liquor and take advantage of a girl — what fools!

Some think that once they pass their driving test that they should pass everyone on the road.

FOR WHAT IT'S WORTH DEPARTMENT

Two live cows in a Chicago department store attracted much attention. A radio station placed the two cows in the show window of a store. Both cows wore earphones. One cow listened to the "contented" music of the station while the other cow heard Rock 'N Roll all day. What do you suppose happened? The cow with the musical diet of Rock 'N Roll became restless, upset, agitated, and the experiment was called off. The other cow listening to the soothing strain of good music did famously, even giving a hundred pounds more milk than the upset cow. What lesson might we learn from this experiment? Well if you're upset, you might be listening to the wrong kind of programs.

TEEN CODE OF CONDUCT URGED BY BILLY GRAHAM

1. Avoid the wrong company.
2. Watch your eyes; you cannot help the first look, but you can help the second look.
3. Watch your lips. Refrain from telling dirty or off-color stories.
4. Watch your heart. Don't let evil thoughts stay in your mind long.
5. **Watch your dress.**
6. Watch your recreation and amusements. Be careful about the films and TV shows you watch.
7. Be careful what you read. The newstands are filled with pornographic literature. Avoid it like a plague.
8. Watch your idleness. Too much leisure and idleness for **young people is harmful in many ways.**
9. Have Christ in your heart and life.
10. Take a delight in the Word of God. The Bible says, "Thy word have I hid in my heart, that I might not sin against Thee."

TEEN COMMANDMENTS

1. Don't let your parents down; they brought you up.
2. Choose your companions with care; you become what they are.
3. Be master of your habits or they will master you.
4. Treasure your time; don't spend it; invest it.
5. Stand for something or you'll fall for anything.
6. Select only a date who would make a good mate.
7. See what you can do for others; not what they can do for you.
8. Guard your thoughts; what you think, you are.
9. Don't fill up on this world's crumbs; feed your soul on the **Living Bread.**
10. Give your all to Christ; He gave His all for you.

THE HOME

TEENAGER SPEAKS

I guess I am what is commonly called a teenager. I suppose in some instances I have been called a juvenile delinquent. Therefore, I feel justified in discussing juvenile delinquency.

As adults you are our leaders, our example, and our inspiration — for good or bad. As children, we should have standards to guide and rule our lives. But by what and whom do we receive these standards? You give us no belief or faith in anything. We set our standards by your standards of divorce, crime, greed, prejudice and lust. And yet, these are the very things you condemn in us and why you now have good reason to look and weep over us.

You talk big — "juvenile delinquency must be wiped out. We'll build parks; we'll have teenage canteens." Yes, you talk big, but your actions talk louder and bigger. You make movies that contaminate immature minds and show them to us. You serve drinks when you want to because money is first with you. You write books on immorality and proclaim them best sellers. You sell us magazines which are filled with vulgarity and lust, magazines which no adult should read, let alone a juvenile. You laugh and agree with a designer whose moronic mind has thought of a new way of immodesty and vice.

You put on stage plays that are filled with smut. You tell jokes on the radio, the stage, the TV, in the movies, and wherever you can that ridicule women, marriage, motherhood, and all decent things kids once believe in. And we hear you laugh at these things. We hear you and we will follow you and you'll lament over us and go on talking big — but acting bigger.

HOW MUCH IS A TEENAGER WORTH?

When a business man was asked how much he thought a teenager was worth, he was quick to give this answer. "Teenagers are worth about nine billion dollars annually for movies, food, cars, books and other items. That is to say nothing of three billion dollars for clothes alone. The teenagers gave one Rock 'N Roll singer a four million dollar profit in a single year. A teenager is worth billions to the business world."

A statesman answered, "The future of America, yes, the very destiny of the free world rests in the hands of our youth. Hitler gained control of Germany, and almost conquered the whole of Europe by winning the hearts of the German youth. The Communists conquered China, they are conquering India and you can be sure that their eyes are on the youth of America. I am convinced that the destiny of America and the hope of the free world rests with the teenager. They're worth everything to us."

What is a teenager worth? Ask again this question to yourself and then consider that if the powers of the world are striving so diligently to win the hearts of our youth and to cultivate their ways of thinking, can we sit idly by? WE CAN NOT!

WHAT CAN WE DO?

"Always we hear the plaintive cry of the teenagers: 'What can we do? Where can we go?'

The answer is, 'Go home! Hang the storm windows! Paint the woodwork! Rake the leaves! Mow the lawn! Shovel the walk! Wash the car! Learn to cook! Scrub the floors! Repair the sink! Build a boat! Get a job! Help the minister, priest or rabbi, the Red Cross, the Salvation Army! Visit the sick! Assist the poor! Study your lessons! And then, when you are through — and not tired, read a book!

Your parents do not owe you entertainment. Your village does not owe you recreation facilities. The world does not owe you a living. You owe the world something. You owe it your time and energy and your talents so that no one will be at war or in poverty, or sick, or lonely again.'

In simple words: 'Grow up! Quit being a cry-baby! Get out of your dream world! Start acting like a man or a lady'!"

—L.D. Harris,
Chief of Police, Manasses Park, West Virginia

THE HOME

FLING

A foolish generation of adults that adopted the foolish philosophy that kids need to have their fling are now fearing what the kids are flinging.

DOING WORSE

Young people have pointed out that they didn't cause all the world's trouble. That is great, but they should not be so determined to make so many on their own.

Aged

I LIKE IT BETTER THIS WAY

My face in the mirror
Isn't wrinkled or drawn.
My house isn't dusty,
The cobwebs are gone,
The garden looks lovely,
And so does the lawn,
I think I might never
Put my glasses back on.

OLD AGE IDEAS

To avoid old age, keep over-eating, drinking, smoking being a crank and hating your existence.
The best thing for gray hair is a sensible head.
Middle age is where the memory gets shorter, experiences longer, stamina lower, forehead higher and hair thinner.

BE YOUNG IN HEART

1. Do something useful every day even though you had to retire from your job.
2. Make a habit of happiness. Gloom spreads doom and drives away pleasant ideas and pleasant people.
3. Think well of others. Don't think "how people are treating me," but "how am I treating others."
4. Try to broaden your interests, for this will make life newer for you.
5. Don't count hurts imaginary slights but blessings!
6. Don't dread about something awful that might happen but rejoice in the good things of today.
7. Read your Bible. Anticipate the blessings promised to the faithful.

GET RID OF IT

A group of senior citizens attending a lecture heard the speaker condemning our enemies. He said, "The time has come when we need to get rid of socialism, Communism, Anarchism and" at this point a little lady trying to stand up shouted "while we are at it let's get rid of rheumatism, too"!

Middle age is that period when a narrow waist and a broad mind may change places.

Old age is like everything else. To make a success of it you must start young.

All people are young only once. Some stay immature indefinitely.

Middle age is when a person starts planning his resignation from the Jet Set and joining the Sit Set.

One good thing about living in the past is that it is so much cheaper.

THE HOME

BEATITUDES FOR FRIENDS OF THE AGED

Blessed are they who understand.
My faltering step and palsied hand.
Blessed are they who know my ears today
Must strain to catch the things they say.
Blessed are they who seem to know
That my eyes are dim and my wits are slow
Blessed are they who looked away
When coffee spilled at the table today.
Blessed are they with a cheery smile
Who stop to chat a little while.
Blessed are they who never say,
"You've told that story twice today."
Blessed are they who know the ways
To bring back memories of yesterdays.
Blessed are they who make it known
That I'm loved, respected and not alone.
Blessed are they who know I'm to find
The strength to carry this cross of mine.
Blessed are they who ease the days
On my journey Home in loving ways.
  —Esther May Walker

Nobody grows old merely by living a number of years. People grow old only by deserting their ideals. Years wrinkle the skin, but to give up enthusiasm wrinkles the soul. Worry, doubt, self-distrust, fear and despair . . . these are the long, long years that bow the head and turn the growing spirit back to dust. Whether seventy or seventeen there is in every being's heart the love of wonder, the sweet amazement of the stars, and the star-like things and thoughts, the undaunted challenge of events, the unfailing child-like appetite for what is next and the game of life. You are as young as your faith, as old as your doubts; as young as your self-confidence, as old as your fears; as young as your hope, as old as your despair.

—Author Unknown

A PRAYER FOR THE MIDDLE-AGED

Lord, thou knowest better than I know myself that I am growing older and will some day be old. Keep me from the fatal habit of thinking I must say something on every occasion. Release me from trying to straighten out everybody's affairs.

Make me thoughtful, but not moody; helpful, but not bossy. With my vast store of wisdom, it seems a pity not to use it all — but Thou knowest that I want a few friends at the end.

Keep my mind free from the recital of endless details — give me wings to get to the point. Seal my lips on my aches and pains. They are increasing and love of rehearsing them is becoming sweeter as the years go by. I dare not ask for grace enough to enjoy the tales of others pains, but help me to endure them with patience.

I dare not ask for improved memory but for a growing humility and lessening of cock-sureness when my memory seems to clash with memories of others. Teach me the glorious lesson that occasionally I may be mistaken.

Keep me reasonably sweet. I do not want to be a saint — some of them are so hard to live with; but, a sour old person is one of the crowning works of the devil. Give me the ability to see good things in unexpected places and talent in unexpected people. Give me the grace to tell them so.

Amen.

Be like the marathon runner. He is happy to be over the hill.

Once a man, twice a child? No, the Christian "thrice a child" for he is born again.

It's not miserable to be old; it's miserable not to be capable of living your age.

If you dread growing old think of the millions who have not had the privilege.

YOU NEED NOT LET AGE HINDER YOUR SERVICE TO CHRIST!

John Wesley preached every day at 88.
Tennyson published "Crossing the Bar" at 88
Michelangelo painted the ceiling of the Sistine Chapel in his late 80's.
Benjamin Franklin went to France to serve his country at 78 years of age, and wrote his autobiography when past 80.
Thomas Jefferson was active in public life until his death at the age of 83.
Paderewski at 79 played the piano superbly before large audiences.
Stradivarius made his finest violins between ages 60 and 70 and continued making them until his 93rd year.
Grandma Moses, who began painting at 70, is regarded as the most outstanding primitive artist of our time.
Henry Lytton, president of Chicago's HUB, retired at 83. At 87 he came back into the business and was still there at age 100.
Anna was used of God though she was close to 100 years old (Luke 2:36-38).
Moses gave Deuteronomy to the world at the time of his death.
Some of Paul's finest letters were written as an "aged" man (Philemon).

—Author Unknown

It is wonderful to grow old — if you remember to keep young while doing it.

One blessing about becoming older is that you and your children eventually are on the same side of the generation gap.

Happy old people are doubling their length of life, for as they look back on their experiences with pleasure, they are living twice.

Old codgers who always complain that the world is changing and it isn't what it used to be should remember that neither are they.

If I can grow old like a garden,
I never shall mind growing old;
The summer will die, and the autumn
Leaves color scarlet and gold,
But beauty will burnish my garden
With glorious yellows and blues,
And the sunrise will touch it with silver,
The sunset with lavender hues;
When winter winds blow on my garden,
The roses will all be asleep
And a blanket of snowflakes above them
The souls of the roses will keep;
If I can grow old like a garden,
My soul will awake in the spring,
For death will be only a winter
To prepare for new blossoming.
—Anne Campbell

OLD AGE AND MONEY

Some Christians are very careful stewards while alive but forget the church enterprises in their will. This is not wise.

It is not Christian to leave ones estate to non-Christians, even though they are relatives.

Children who do not honor parents while they are alive will not love their parents after inheriting an estate.

Millions of dollars are left each year to children who do not need it and who will waste it in riotous living.
—Don Earl Boatman

No matter what may be our lot in life, build something on it.

Senior citizens are graduates from the college of hard knocks.

THE CHRISTIAN LIFE

Accomplishment

SUCCESS is not confined to any one part of your personality but is related to the development of all the parts: body, mind, heart and spirit. It is making the most of your total self.

SUCCESS is discovering your best talents, skills and abilities and applying them where they will make the most effective contribution to your fellow men.

SUCCESS is focusing the full power of all you are on what you have a burning desire to achieve.

SUCCESS is ninety-nine percent mental attitude. It calls for love, joy, optimism, confidence, serenity, poise, faith, courage, cheerfulness, imagination, initiative, tolerance, honesty, humility, patience and enthusiasm.

SUCCESS is not arriving at the summit of a mountain as a final destination. It is a continuing upward spiral of progress. It is perpetual growth.

SUCCESS is having the courage to meet failure without being defeated. It is refusing to let present loss interfere with your long-range goal.

SUCCESS is accepting the challenge of the difficult. In the inspiring words of Phillips Brooks: "Do not pray for tasks equal to your powers. Pray for powers equal to your tasks. Then the doing of your work shall be no miracle."

—Wilferd A. Peterson

Help us, oh Lord, to forget our accomplishments in the view of the tremendous work that yet needs to be done!

"There is no limit to what can be accomplished if it doesn't matter who gets the credit."

—Emerson

After all is said and done, more is said than done.

The only things we can be sure of accomplishing are the things we do today.

JUST FOR TODAY

Just for today I will try to live through this day only, and not tackle my whole life problem at once. I can do something for twelve hours that would appall me if I felt that I had to keep it up for a lifetime.

Just for today I will be happy, enjoying the blessings that are mine.

Just for today I will adjust myself to what is, and not try to adjust everything to my own desires.

Just for today I will try to strengthen my mind. I will study. I will learn something useful. I will not be a mental loafer. I will read something that requires effort, thought and concentration.

Just for today I will exercise my soul by doing somebody a good turn.

Just for today I will have a program. I may not follow it exactly, but I will have it. I will save myself from two pests: hurry and indecision.

Just for today I will be agreeable. I will look as well as I can, dress becomingly, talk low, act courteously, criticize not one bit.

Just for today I will be unafraid. Especially I will not be afraid to enjoy what is beautiful, and to believe that as I give to the world, so the world will give to me.

Just for today I will have a quiet half hour all by myself, and relax. During this half hour I will try to get a better perspective of my life.

"Lord, grant that I may always desire more than I accomplish."
—Michelangelo

That you may find success, let me tell you how to proceed. Tonight begin your great plan of life. You have but one life to live, and it is most important that you should not make a mistake. Tonight begin carefully. Fix your eye on the fortieth year of your age, and then say to yourself: "At the age of forty, I will be an industrious man, benevolent man, a well-read man, a religious man, and a useful man. I resolve, and will stand to it!"

SUCCESS

The father of Success is named Work. The mother of Success is named Ambition. The oldest son is called Common Sense and some of the boys are called Stability, Perseverance, Honesty, Thoroughness, Foresight, Enthusiasm and Co-operation.

The oldest daughter is Character. Some of the other sisters are Cheerfulness, Loyalty, Care, Courtesy, Economy, Sincerity and Harmony. The baby is Opportunity.

Get acquainted with the "old man" and you will be able to get along with the rest of the family.

—Royal Neighbor

Reprinted from *This Week* magazine. Copyright 1962 by Wilferd A. Peterson.

"Out of the will of God there is no such thing as success; in the will of God there is no such thing as failure."

—David Amstutz

"The talent of success is nothing more than doing what you can do well without a thought of fame."

Longfellow

People who wake up famous, have not been asleep all the time.

THE CHRISTIAN LIFE

TAKE TIME

Take time to live. That is what time is for. Killing time is suicide.
Take time to work. It is the price of success.
Take time to think. It is the source of power.
Take time to play. It is the mountain of wisdom.
Take time to be friendly. It is the road to happiness.
Take time to dream. It is hitching your wagon to a star.
Take time to look around. It is too short a day to be selfish.
Take time to laugh. It is the music of the soul.
Take time to play with children. It is the joy of joys.
Take time to be courteous. It is the mark of a gentleman.
—Santa Fe Magazine

JUST A MINUTE

I have only just a minute,
Only sixty seconds in it,
Forced upon me, can't refuse it.
But it's up to me to use it,
I must suffer if I lose it.
Just a tiny little minute,
But eternity is in it.

"Acrophobia is the fear of heights; it may also be the fear of high ideals, high thoughts, and high ambition. There are people who avoid high ideals because they are content with low ones. The tragedy of this age is that people with minds to think and souls that are hungry are so afraid to reach up and seek the things that are high. So do not ever underestimate what you can do. You have the courage to cast off acrophobia and to dream big, and to aim high, if you do it with God's help."
—Peter Marshall

One does not hit the weathervane on the steeple by aiming at the barn door.

You will never stub your toe standing still. The faster you go the more chance there is of stubbing your toe, but the more chance you have of getting somewhere!
—Charles Kettering

It is better to resolve and fail than to resolve not to resolve and be a failure.

Goals

OBJECTIVE

One ship drives east and another drives west
With the self-same wind that blows.
'Tis the set of the sail and not the gale
That tells us which way it goes.
Like the winds of the sea are the ways of fate,
As we journey along through life;
'Tis the set of the soul that determines the goal
And neither the calm nor the strife.

Strive to be like a well-regulated watch of pure gold, with an open face, busy hands and full of good works!

DON'T BE SATISFIED

Sad is the day for every man when he becomes absolutely satisfied with the life he is leading, with the thoughts he is thinking, with the deeds he is doing — when there is not forever beating at the doors of his soul some great desire.

THE CHRISTIAN LIFE

EXPECTANCY

There are many who wait for their ships to come in,
  For their ships to come in from the sea.
This question they ask as they watch and wait:
  "Will a ship come home for me?"
The answer comes swift from a voyager old,
  A voyager weathered and gray:
"Have you sent forth a craft with a cargo, friend?
  A craft that might come in today?"
There are many who long for their ships to come in,
  That they from their cares may be free;
But how could a ship come home to them
  When they've sent no craft to sea?

"Unhappiness is not knowing what we want and killing ourselves to get it. Therefore it was no casual question when Jesus asked His followers, 'What seek ye?' In that day He needed disciples who knew what they were after in life. He still needs disciples with a clear objective. Only they can reach the goal. As David Starr Jordan wrote; 'The world stands aside to let anyone pass who knows where he is going.' Do we know where we want to go in the Christian life?"

—Christian Herald

Reaching high keeps a man on his toes.

No matter what others are doing, my friend,
Or what they are leaving undone,
God is counting on you to keep on with the job,
Until the very last battle is won!
He is counting on you to be faithful,
He is counting on you to be true
Yes, others may work, or others may shirk, but remember,
God is counting on you!

REACH HIGH

Reach high! Do not be satisfied
With goals in easy reach—
A thing too easy to come by
Has little power to teach
The heart and mind to prize those things
More difficultly done.
Effort expended adds a lot
Of value to goals won.
—Helen Howland Prommel

This is the day to press forward
To strive for a higher aim,
A day for mastering problems
That make up life's little game.

This is the day to be busy
Sowing the seeds of good cheer,
Spreading a few words of kindness
On pathways otherwise drear.
—Georgia Adams

The great use of life is to spend it for something that will outlast it.

I'd rather be a Will-be
Than a Would-be-if-I-tried,
For a Would-be is a Won't-be,
'Til he stretches out his stride.

I'd rather be a Can-be,
Than a Could-be-if-I'd-cram
For a Could-be is a drone bee,
While a Can-be is an Am.

Yesterday is gone; tomorrow is uncertain; today is here. Use it.

Yesterday is a cancelled check. Tomorrow is a promissory note. Today is Cash on hand.

It takes a certain amount of push to accomplish anything even with a wheelbarrow.

The laborer with plenty of "push" in him doesn't depend upon a "pull" to elevate him to the station of success.

Let us endeavor so to live that, when we come to die even the undertaker will be sorry.

The man of the hour is generally one who has made every minute count.

Don't wait for your ship to come in — row out and meet it.

Determination

GIANTS AND GRASSHOPPERS

In any worthy endeavor there are difficulties to be faced, hazards to be overcome, and obstacles to surmount — and the fainthearted will fall by the wayside (Numbers 13:33).

DISCOURAGED?

When you feel like tossing in the sponge and quitting, take a minute to consider this man's record: Failed in business 1831; defeated for legislature 1832; failed again in 1833; elected to legislature 1834; sweetheart died in 1835; nervous breakdown 1833; defeated for speaker 1838; defeated for congress 1843; elected to congress 1846; defeated for re-election 1848; defeated for Senate 1858; elected for President of the United States in 1860.

Who was he? A man with very few advantages in life; only fierce determination. Although he was uneducated he refused to stay that way and learned by himself. Though beset by failure he refused to say life and people were against him. He believed in simple virtue, honesty, hard work, love for all humanity and faith. He was Abraham Lincoln.

KEEP ON GOING

One step won't take you very far;
  You've got to keep on walking.
One word won't tell folks who you are;
  You've got to keep on talking.
One inch won't make you very tall;
  You've got to keep on growing.
One little deed won't do it all;
  You've got to keep on going.

—*Author Unknown*

THE ART OF SUCCESS

There are no secrets of success. Success is doing the things you know you should do. Success is not doing the things you know you should not do.

SUCCESS is not limited to any one area of your life. It encompasses all of the facets of your relationships: as parent, as wife or husband, as citizen, neighbor, worker and all of the others.

THE CHRISTIAN LIFE

I WILL

I will start anew this morning,
  With a higher, fairer creed;
I will cease to stand complaining,
  Of my ruthless neighbor's greed;
I will cease to sit repining,
  While my duty's call is clear;
I will waste no moment whining,
  And my heart shall know no fear.
I will look sometimes about me,
  For the things that merit praise;
I will search for hidden beauties,
  That elude the grumbler's gaze;
I will try to find contentment,
  In the paths that I must tread;
I will cease to have resentment,
  When another moves ahead.
I will not be swayed by envy,
  When my rival's strength is shown;
I will not deny his merit.
  But shall strive to prove my own;
I will strive to see the beauty,
  Spread before me rain or shine;
I will cease to preach your duty,
  And be more concerned with mine.

—Anonymous

There's no skill in easy sailing
When the skies are clear and blue . . .
There's no joy in merely doing . . .
Things that anyone can do.
But there's great satisfaction
That is mighty sweet to take
When you reach a destination . . .
That they said you couldn't make.

—Author Unknown

A determined soul will do more with a rusty monkey-wrench than a loafer will accomplish with all the tools in a machine shop.
—Rupert Hughes

YOU MUSTN'T QUIT

When things go wrong, as they sometimes will,
When the road you're trudging seems all uphill,
When the funds are low, and the debts are high,
And you want to smile, but you have to sigh,
When care is pressing you down a bit,
Rest, if you must, but don't you quit.

Life is queer with its twists and turns,
As everyone of us sometimes learns,
And many a failure turns about
When he might have won, had he held out.
So don't give up, though the pace seems slow,
For you may succeed with another blow.

Often the goal is nearer than
It seems to a faint and faltering man.
Often the struggler has given up,
When he might have captured the victor's cup,
And he learned too late, when the night slipped down,
How close he was to the golden crown.

Success is failure turned inside out,
The silver tint of the clouds of doubt.
And you never can tell how close you are
It may be near, when it seems afar.
So stick to the fight, when you're hardest hit—
It's when things seem worst that you mustn't quit.

The man in earnest finds a way; and if he cannot find it he makes it.

THE CHRISTIAN LIFE

Resolution is omnipotent. Determine to be something in the world, and you will be something. Aim at excellence and excellence will be attained. This is the great secret of effort and eminence. "I cannot do it," never accomplished anything. "I will try," has wrought wonders.
—J. Hawes

I am not bound to win, but I am bound to be true. I am not bound to succeed, but I am bound to live by the light that I have. I must stand with anybody that stands right, stand with him while he is right, and part with him when he goes wrong.
—Abraham Lincoln

"I won't" is a tramp.
"I can't" is a quitter.
"I don't know" is lazy.
"I might" is waking up.
"I will try" is on his feet.
"I can" is on his way.
"I will" is at work.
"I did" is now the boss!

"When you are through improving yourself — you are through."
—Ruth Smeltzer

'Tain't what we have,
But what we give,
'Tain't what we are,
But how we live;
'Tain't what we do,
But how we do it—
That makes this life
Worth goin' through it.

It does a man no good to "sit up and take notice," if he keeps on sitting.

❦

Stewardship

What if God gave to you the way you give to Him?

THE CHRISTIAN AND MONEY

In the administration of his money the Christian finds for the character of his profession both a test of sincerity and means of culture. Here is an unmistakable revelation of the sentiment of his soul. "Money talks." Its use speaks a message, the meaning of which verbiage can not conceal. Hereby he tells truly what he would hesitate to express with his tongue. *This reveals the range of his vision, and the goal of his desire.* It proclaims the character of his emotions, his attitude to society, and the object of his devotion. It testifies to the world concerning the virility of his faith and the vitality of his hope.
—E. Lynwood Crystal in *The Christian and His Money*. (Italics mine).

Making money is a process by which we exchange our life's energy, our skill, our brains, our heart, our reserve force for what should be their equivalent. We are "coining our life" when we work. That is what makes the matter of spending money so important. We are spending our life. If we waste our money, we are wasting our life. If we fritter it away, we are frittering away our life. If we invest it wisely, we are making a wise investment of life. "Ye are not your own," so you have no right to squander your life. Spending money is one of the highest tests of character.
—Chas. A. Brooks

A church in San Antonio, Texas was planning the year's budget. One woman told them: "My husband lost his job, and we are on unemployment compensation for $28 a week and so we are going to revise our contribution. We will give $2.80 a week."

A check of the church people revealed that if the entire membership had been on unemployment compensation and had given 10%, or the tithe, the total offerings would have doubled!

Some years ago a London paper offered a prize for the best definition of money. This was the winning answer: "Money is an instrument that can buy you everything but happiness, and pay your fare to every place but heaven."

—Rays of Sunshine

People are funny. They spend money they don't have, to buy things they don't need, to impress folks they don't like.

WHY SHOULD I GIVE?

Giving is the Law of Life.
There is no harvest without seed, no gain without investment, no success without sacrifice. The richest life is the life of service.
Giving is the Law of Love.
The motive of love is sharing. The greatest joy is the joy of helping those we truly love. We give because we love. Giving increases love, makes it more real.
Giving is the Law of Growth
An unused muscle becomes weakened; an unexpressed thought soon dies; an unexercised talent declines. In the natural, social, or spiritual realm we gain in strength by use.

THE MORE YOU GIVE
THE MORE YOU WILL HAVE TO GIVE
—The Centralian

A great portion of our time, energies and attention is given over to money matters. Christian motives certainly can not dominate our lives without entering into our economic affairs.

A Christian's real character — the state of his love for God and his love for man — is shown in (1) the way he gets money, (2) the way he feels about what he has and what others have, and (3) the way he uses money.

—Seth Wilson

We believe in a Christ-like world.
We know nothing better;
We can be content with nothing less.
We cannot live without Christ,
And we cannot bear to think of men
Living without Him.
Christ is our motive,
And Christ is our end.
We must give nothing less
And we can give nothing more.

Jesus was not crucified because He said, "Consider the lilies of the field — how they grow," but because He said, "Consider the thieves in the temple, how they steal."

GIFT BEYOND VALUE

Give to the Lord, as He has blessed thee,
Even when he seems far away,
Know that His love has e'er possessed thee,
Shelters and feeds thee every day.
Heaven and earth are God's alone
Wilt thou hold back from His own?

—James Boeringer

I NEVER PLEDGE

"I never sign a pledge of any kind," said a man whom I was soliciting.

"Are you sure?" I asked.

"Yes," he replied.

"Do you own your home?" I questioned.

"Yes, but it is mortgaged for half its value."

"Did you promise to pay interest on your mortgate?"

"Yes."

"When your telephone was installed, did you agree to pay monthly charges?"

"Yes. What are you driving at?"

"As a matter of fact," I answered, "have you not committed the larger portion of your income to everything your home needs except the church?"

"I surrender," he said.

—Robert Cashman

The story is told of a good farmer who loved the Lord and believed in stewardship. He was generous indeed, and was asked by his friends why he gave so much and yet remained so prosperous. "We cannot understand you," his friends said, "why you seem to give more than the rest of us, and yet always seem to have greater prosperity."

"Oh," said the farmer, "that is easy to explain. You see, I keep shoveling into God's bins, and God keeps shoveling more and more into mine, and God has a bigger shovel."

MONEY

Workers earn it, spendthrifts burn it, bankers lend it, women spend it, forgers fake it, taxes take it, dying leave it, heirs receive it, thrifty save it, misers crave it, robbers receive it, rich increase it, gamblers lose it . . . *we could use it!*

—Max Hickerson

A STEWARDSHIP CREDO

Stewardship is more than the giving of money; although it is that. It is more than giving of my talents, although it involves that, too. It is the offering of my total self to Him.

This means that in all the relationships of life, I shall seek to give a good account of my stewardship. In the home, I shall, along with the other members of my family, worship Him. I shall share in the closeness of the family council my concerns, my hopes, my wisdom, my experiences, so that together we may fulfill the purpose God has for us. I shall so organize my life that the way I earn my money and the way I use my money shall contribute to the advancement of God's will and the Kingdom among men.

It means that in my church I shall seek to be faithful to the responsibilities that I carry as a member of the body of Christ. I shall attend church regularly. I shall consecrate my talents to God's service at the place where I can make the fullest possible contribution to His Kingdom. I shall give of my money directly; proportionately, as God has prospered me.

All this I shall do, not out of any compulsion, save the compulsion of my gratitude to God for what He has done for me.

Life for some folks is the practice of sowing wild oats six days a week, and on the seventh going to church and praying for a crop failure.

If the power to do hard work is not talent, it is the best possible substitute for it.

Take responsibility on your shoulders, and it will leave no room for chips.

An offertory prayer: Dear Lord, in spite of all we say and do, this is what we really think of you.

THE CHRISTIAN LIFE

THE MASTER CAME

*The master came today,
I think it saddened Him to call.
He noted not how fine the chairs
How deep the rugs, my lovely home,
He paid no heed at all.
He didn't see my antique clock,
My dishes and my silver, Oh,
I hoped he'd stay for lunch and see
How richly we would dine.
In voice so filled with love and pain,
He spoke of things apart,
The unloved and the homeless, and
The peoples of all races, I
Must take unto my heart.
He is gone. And suddenly,
A flash of knowing brings
Awareness, and I realize
How much of life is wasted
In accumulating things.*

*We are not here to play, to dream, to drift,
We have hard work to do, and loads to lift;
Shun not the struggle, face it, 'tis God's gift.*
—Maltbie B. Babcock

Stewardship is the ordering of one's life so that time, ability, possessions, and all of one's personality are administered as belonging to God.

When it comes to giving, some people stop at nothing!
—Reader's Digest

MONEY TALKS

A big silver dollar and a little brown cent,
  Rolling along together they went;
Rolling along the smooth sidewalk,
  When the dollar remarked — for the dollar can talk:

"You poor little cent, you cheap little mite,
  I'm bigger than you, and twice as bright.
I'm worth more than you a hundred-fold,
  And written on me, in letters bold,
Is the motto drawn from the pious creed,
'In God We Trust,' which all can read."

"Yes, I know," said the cent; "I'm a cheap little mite,
  And I know I'm not big, nor good, nor bright;
And yet," said the cent, with a meek little sigh,
"You don't go to church as often as I."

ONE QUARTER

He dropped a quarter in the plate,
  Then meekly raised his eyes;
Glad that his weekly rent was paid
  To mansions in the skies.

HOW MUCH OUGHT I TO GIVE?

Give as you would if an angel
  Awaited your gift at the door.
Give as you would if tomorrow
  Found you where giving was o'er.
Give as you would to the Master,
  If you met His loving look.
Give as you would of your substance,
  If His hand the offering took.

THE CHRISTIAN LIFE

THE VOICE OF MONEY

Dug from the mountain side,
  Washed in the glen,
Servant am I or the MASTER OF MEN!
  Steal me, I curse you,
Earn me, I bless you;
  Grasp me and hoard me and a
Friend shall possess you.
  Lie for me, die for me,
Covet me, take me,
  Angel or devil, I am just what
You make me.

But what you cannot buy you can receive as a gift. "For the wages of sin is death; but the gift of God is eternal life through Jesus Christ our Lord."

WHAT I LIVE FOR

What dost thou live for, brother mine?
I live to give.
To give myself, my life, my all
To Him who notes the sparrow's fall,
And keeps me ev'ry day
Upon His holy way—
For this I live.

What dost thou live for, brother mine?
I live to give.
To give a word of hope and cheer,
To dry, perchance, some falling tear,
To forward on life's road
Some pilgrim with his load—
For this I live.

CHRISTIANS CAN BE LED ASTRAY!

Use your money while you're living;
  Do not hoard it to be proud;
You can never take it with you,
  There's no pocket in a shroud.
Gold can help you on no farther
  Than the graveyard where you lie,
And tho' you are rich while living
  You're a pauper when you die.
Use it then some lives to brighten
  As through life they weary plod;
Place your bank account in heaven,
  And grow rich towards your God.

Gold in the hand is all right; in the heart it is all wrong!

MONEY WILL BUY

A bed but not sleep,
Books but not brains,
Food but not appetite,
Finery but not beauty,
A house but not home,
Medicine but not health,
Luxuries but not culture,
Amusements but not happiness,
A crucifix but not a Saviour,
A church but not a heaven.

"Stewardship is the acceptance from God of personal responsibility for all of life and life's affairs."

—R.C. Long

THE CHRISTIAN LIFE

THE BALLAD OF DESERT PETE

In a desert store in Southern California is a letter written on a sheet of brown wrapping paper. It was found in a baking powder can wired to the handle of an old pump, the only hope of drinking water on a very long and seldom used trail across the Amarogosa desert. The letter reads:

"This pump is all right as of June, 1932. I put a new sucker washer into it and it ought to last five years. But the washer dries out and the pump has got to be primed. Under the white rock I buried a bottle of water, out of the sun and the cork end up. There's enough water in it to prime the pump, but not if you drink some first. Pour about one-fourth and let her soak to wet the leather. Then pour in the rest medium fast and pump like thunder. You'll git water. The well never has run dry. Have faith. When you get watered up, fill the bottle and put it back like you found it for the next feller.

signed, Desert Pete

P.S. Don't go drinkin up the water first. Prime the pump with it and you'll git all you can hold."

That would be quite a choice for a really thirsty man wouldn't it? A bottle of water with which you could satisfy your thirst for the moment or the big risk of pouring the water into a dry pump with the hope and trust that Desert Pete really knew what he was talking about, that the pump really would bring up fresh water.

I think you have heard this basic choice of life stated before. Shall I use this little bottle of water, my life, to satisfy my greed, my pleasures and my vanity right now, knowing that when it is gone there will be no more? Or shall I take the risk of faith and pour out my life for Christ in the trust that the return will be a crystal flow of water springing up unto eternal life? Or to put it another way — "Whoever would save his life will lose it, and whoever loses his life for my sake will find it."

That's the choice. And that's what Christian stewardship is all about. You'd better prime the pump.

Possessions weigh me down in life — I never feel quite free — I wonder if I own my things or if my things own me.

> *Do your givin' while you're livin'*
> *Then you're knowin' where it's goin'.*

Money cannot go to heaven, but it can do something heavenly here on earth.

... sacrificial giving is a grace — the lack of which is a disgrace ...

We make a living by what we get; we make a life by what we give.

Prayer

What you say on your knees won't have much effect unless you practice it on your feet.

THE REASON

We mutter and sputter;
We fume and we spurt.
We mumble and grumble;
Our feelings get hurt.
We can't understand things;
Our vision grows dim,
When all that we need
Is a moment with Him.

THE CHRISTIAN LIFE

TAKE TIME TO PRAY

I got up early one morning
And rushed right into the day;
I had so much to accomplish
That I didn't have time to pray!
Problems came tumbling about me
And heavier came each task;
"Why doesn't God help me?" I wondered.
He answered, "You didn't ask!"
I wanted to see joy and beauty,
But the day toiled on gray and bleak;
I wondered why God didn't show me.
He said, "But you didn't seek!"
I tried to come into God's presence
And used all my keys at the lock;
God gently and lovingly chided,
"My child, you didn't knock!"
I woke up early this morning
And paused before entering the day;
I had so much to accomplish that
I had to take time to pray!

Not so in haste, my heart,
Have faith in God and wait;
Although He seems to linger long,
He never comes too late;
Until He cometh, rest;
Nor grudge the hours that roll;
The feet that wait for God,
'Tis they are soonest at the goal—
Are soonest at the goal
That is not gained by speed;
Then hold thee still, O restless heart,
For I shall wait his lead.

Strength in prayer is better than length in prayer.

God answers prayer . . . when our hands reach out to clasp His hand . . . and our hearts respond to His command!

"Give me Thy strength for the day, Lord, that whereso'er I go
There shall no danger daunt me and I shall fear no foe;
So shall no task o'ercome me, so shall no trial fret,
So shall I walk unwearied the path where my feet are set;
So shall I find no burden greater than I can bear,
So shall I have a courage equal to all my care;
So shall no grief o'erwhelm me, so shall no wave o'erflow;
Give me Thy strength for my day, Lord, cover my weakness so."
—Annie Johnson Flint

THE SECRET

I met God in the morning
When my day was at its best,
And His presence came like sunrise,
Like a glory in my breast;
All day long the Presence lingered,
All day long He stayed with me,
And we sailed in perfect calmness
O'er a very troubled sea;
Other ships were blown and battered,
Other ships were sore distressed,
But the winds that seemed to drive them
Brought to us a peace and rest;
Then I thought of other mornings,
With a keen remorse of mind,
When I, too, had loosed the moorings
With the Presence left behind;
So I think I know the secret,
Learned from many a troubled way—
You must seek Him in the morning
If you want Him through the day.
—Ralph Cushman

PRAYER OF THE EVANGELIST

Lord, give me a passion for the lost,
For souls so deep in sin,
That I may lead them to the Cross—
That one You died to win!

Give me a burden for that heart
Bowed down in deep despair.
Then come, dear Lord, and heal the wound
That sin has planted there.

Lord, lay someone upon my heart—
Give me the grace to go
And tell them of Thy saving power,
And how You loved them so!

A PRAYER

Give me courage, Lord, I stumble
Faltering feet are mine today,
Hold me fast lest ideals crumble
Into dust along the way.
Give me faith, O, Lord I need it,
Seeming rudderless I ride.
Take the helm and guide my spirit
Through this overpowering tide,
Give me patience, Lord, I, blinded,
Stagger through the misty night,
Keep my vision fixed, clearminded
On the stable truths and right,
Give me strength, I would not sever
One thin cord of Thy control.
I would keep Thee, Lord, forever
As the force which rules my soul.

—Laura Caroline Fierz

LOOK UP AND PRAY

If you are troubled in your heart
If you are sad today
And if the world is cold and bleak
Look up to God and pray.
Tell Him your problems pour them out
Before His mighty throne
You will not be the first to plead
You will not be alone.
However futile it may seem
How much you may despair
There always is the comfort and
The peace that comes with prayer.
If you are not to blame at all
He knows that you are true
And if you are a sheep that's strayed
He searches now for you.
He is as willing to forgive
The wrongs that you have done
As He is ready to bestow
The glory you have won.

A HAPPY DAY

Today will be a happy day
If first you find some time to pray
If all alone you go apart
From worldly things, and in your heart,
You make resolve to do your best.
And then to God you leave the rest.

Among the nettles and the thorns that grow along the rutted way,
We build a little wayside altar everytime we pause to pray.
—Patience Strong

THE CHRISTIAN LIFE

PRAY THAT YOU MAY BE:

> *Able to suffer without complaining,*
> *To be understood without explaining,*
> *Able to endure without a breaking,*
> *To be forsaken without forsaking;*
> *Able to give without receiving.*
> *To be ignored without grieving;*
> *Able to ask without commanding,*
> *To love despite misunderstanding;*
> *Able to turn to the Lord for guarding,*
> *Able to wait for His own rewarding!*

Bowing the head for a few minutes at the beginning of the day will help one to walk more erect during the hours that follow.

Prayer is a small word for a big thing.

> *You prayed for me . . . You did not know my need,*
> *Or that my heart was very sore indeed,*
> *Or that I had a fear I could not quell;*
> *You sensed that all with me was not quite well,*
> *And so — you prayed for me. . . .*
>
> *You prayed for me . . . God did Himself attend—*
> *Honored the intercession of my friend;*
> *And as your prayer, like incense sweet, did soar,*
> *He did, in love, on me a blessing pour,*
> *The day you prayed for me. . . .*

> *We often say our prayers,*
> *But do we ever pray?*
> *Does the sentiment of our hearts*
> *Go with the words we say?*

A DAILY PRAYER

If I can do some good today,
If I can smooth the rugged way,
If I can something helpful say,
Lord, show me how.

If I can right a human wrong,
If I can help to make one strong,
If I can cheer with smile or song,
Lord, show me how.

If I can aid one in distress,
If I can make a burden less,
If I can spread more happiness,
Lord, show me how.

If I can do a kindly deed,
If I can help someone in need,
If I can sow a fruitful seed,
Lord, show me how.

If I can feed a hungry heart,
If I can give a better start,
If I can fill a nobler part,
Lord, show me how.
—Grenville Kleiser

Thank you Lord for prompt reply to my request,
For I had no other way of knowing what was best.
The answer wasn't the one I sought,
But Your will I'll question not.
For my faith is strengthened,
And my grief is lessened
By the knowledge that You are still there,
Even though You answered "no" to my prayer.
—Cathy McTeer

PRAY OR PREY?

We love to sing about the Beautiful Garden of Prayer. Was Gethsemane a beautiful place of prayer? For Jesus it was. For Simon Peter, who slept instead of praying, it was where he fell prey to Satan. Jesus reminded the disciples to pray lest they fall prey to temptation. Pray or you will pay when you fall prey.

Prayer was natural for Jesus. For the disciples, it was different. Why? Because Jesus lived in complete fellowship with God and He longed to talk with His Father.

Have you prayed today? If not, you are not like Jesus. If you feel the nearness of God, talking with Him is as natural as breathing.

If you do not pray you have already fallen prey to the Evil One. He has made you concerned with the affairs of this life and unconcerned about the Kingdom.

—Don Earl Boatman

KNEE DRILL

A British soldier one night was caught creeping stealthily back to his quarters. He was taken before his commanding officer and charged with having communicated with the enemy. The man pleaded that he had gone into the woods only to pray by himself. That was his only defense.

"Have you been in the habit of spending hours in private prayer?" the officer growled.

"Yes Sir!"

"Then get down on your knees and pray now!" he roared, "You never needed it so much!"

Expecting immediate death, the soldier knelt and poured out his soul in prayer . . . that for eloquence could have been inspired only by the power of the Holy Spirit.

"You may go," said the officer simply, when he had finished. "I believe your story. If you hadn't been often at drill . . . you couldn't have done so well at review."

How would it have been with you?

—Cherryvale Christian

THE PROOF

Some tell us that prayer is all in the mind,
That the only result is the solace we find;
That God does not answer, nor hear when we call;
We commune with our own hearts in prayer: That is all!
But we who have knelt with our burden and care,
And have made all our problems a matter of prayer,
Have seen God reach down from His heaven above,
Move mountains, touch hearts, in His infinite love;
We know that God works in a wonderful way
On behalf of His children who trust Him and pray.
—Barbara Corney Ryberg

He who does not pray when the sun shines, knows not how to pray when the clouds arise.

If you won't talk to God on a clear day, there isn't much use to yell at Him in a storm.

THE LORD'S PRAYER

Thou canst not say the Lord's Prayer
And make one selfish plea;
Thou canst not pray the Lord's Prayer
And even once say "me."

For it's "our, our, our,"
And it's "us, us, us;"
And the fourth time it is "our,"
And fourth time it is "us."

God has one Son who lived without sin, but he has no Son who lived without prayer.

THE CHRISTIAN LIFE

*We all have a secret weapon
Which can cure our deepest woes
It can tear down walls of hatred
And confound our godless foes.*

*Doesn't cost a billion dollars,
Yet can guarantee world peace . . .
Not the A-bomb or the H-bomb,
Yet it makes the war drums cease.*

*It's not guarded from the millions,
Each of us can do our share . . .
It grows stronger as you use it.
For it's better known as prayer!*

MY PRAYER

*I'm just a little child, dear Lord,
But, oh I long to be
Gentle, kind, and loving,
And ever true to Thee!
Take my hand in Thine, dear Lord;
Direct my steps aright;
Keep me close beside Thee
Morning, noon, and night.*

Prayer of a soldier; "Oh, Lord, don't let nothin' get hold of me that you and me can't handle!"

Even when words seem to fail us and our spirits are dull, we should not omit our prayers. At such times we may well use some of the great classic prayers of the past or refresh ourselves with a hymn or find prayer thoughts in a chapter of Scripture. But we should not let the day pass without praying. Someone has said, "When you cannot pray as you would, pray as you can."

*Beat wear and tear
With care and prayer.*

❦

Salvation

DO YOU KNOW?

LONGFELLOW could take a worthless sheet of paper, write a poem on it, and make it worth $6000 — that is genius.

ROCKEFELLER could sign his name to a piece of paper, and make it worth millions — that is capital.

UNCLE SAM can take gold, stamp an eagle on it, and make it worth $20.00 — that is skill.

AN ARTIST can take a fifty-cent piece of canvas, paint a picture on it, and make it worth $1,000,000 — that is art.

GOD can take a worthless, sinful life, wash it in the blood of Christ, put His Spirit into it, and make it a blessing to humanity — that is Salvation

Beware of men who insist on teachings that are not found in the Word of God. A religious dictator is as dangerous as a political one. Some of the cruelest deeds in history were done by religious fanatics. There is a difference in religion and Christianity. Religion is man seeking a god in his own ungodly image. Christianity is God revealing Himself to man. Christianity makes men free, religion places man in bondage.

—Don Earl Boatman

The Christian can only find satisfaction where he found salvation.

ANYONE

*Anyone can come to God
With a trustful heart,
Anyone can say a prayer,
His desires impart,
Anyone can ask in faith
And, believing, find
God will listen, God will hear.
God is just and kind.*

*Anyone can enter in
To the secret place
Of His inner chamber, there
At the throne of grace
He can shut out every thought
Of discord and grief,
Know the presence of the Lord,
Find a true relief.*

*Anyone, whoever will
None are barred or banned,
Sinful, wretched though he be
God will understand.
God, whose name is Love, will lift,
Cleanse, forgive, renew
Anyone who asks in faith
Proves and finds it true.*
　　　　　　　　—Della Adams Leitner

Hearing the Gospel destroys interest in sin.
Believing the Gospel destroys pleasure in sin.
Repentance destroys the practice of sin.
Confession destroys the allegiance to sin.
Baptism destroys the guilt of sin.

THINK IT THROUGH

IF one can be saved without faith, why did Paul say it was impossible to please God without it (Heb. 11:6)?

IF God promised to give faith when we ask for it, why are we told that faith comes by hearing, and hearing by the Word of God (Romans 10:17)?

IF "Faith Alone" is a wholesome doctrine and very full of comfort, why did James say that faith without works is dead (James 2:17)?

IF God has promised to save men regardless of the kind of faith they have, why did Paul make it so plain that "there is one faith" (Eph. 4:4-6)?

IF the Lord will save us without baptism, why did He command it (Matt. 28:19 and Acts 10:48)?

IF the Lord has promised us salvation without baptism why did Peter say it saves (I Pet. 3:21)? Why did Peter say baptism is for the remission of sins (Acts 2:38)?

IF sprinkling and pouring are scriptural baptism, why did Paul say there is one baptism (Eph. 4:4-6) and that it is a burial (Rom. 6:4 and Col. 2:11-12)?

IF we can be born again of the Spirit only, why did Christ say to be born of water and Spirit (John 3:3-5)?

WHY CHRIST DIED

"Well, I cannot understand why a man who has tried to lead a good moral life should not stand a better chance of heaven than a wicked one," said a lady recently, in a conversation with others about the matter of salvation.

"Simply for this cause," answered one. "Suppose you and I wanted to go to a place of amusement where the admission was a dollar. You have half a dollar, and I have nothing. Which would stand the better chance of admission?"

REMEMBER: The plan of Salvation was not provided to suit you, but to save you.

THE CHRISTIAN LIFE

If Christ a thousand times in Bethlehem be born,
Until He's born in me, my soul is all forlorn!

The Bible is so plain in its teaching on salvation that it takes "help" to misunderstand it.

There is not one thing wrong with having your own way — provided you have already accepted God's way as your way.

Forgiveness

FORGIVE, AS WE FORGIVE

Lord, may I live to help the man
  Who tries to keep me down.
May I greet him with a smile
  Who greets me with a frown;
And may I never hold a grudge
  Nor hunt up scattered strife,
May I never seek to judge the
  Faults found in another's life,
And always be too big to see the
  Things that others do to me.
Lord may I ever use good sense
  And always take a stand.
To me nothing is offense, as
  There is no perfect man,
And may I always be too big to
  See the things that others do to me.

—Anonymous

TEN RULES OF FORGIVENESS

1. Determine that you are going to forgive.
2. Remember the harm resentment can do, not to the other person, but to you.
3. Remember that you will never be spiritually blessed until you forgive.
4. Thinking about forgiving is not enough. you must come to a specific moment when you say, "With God's help, I now forgive."
5. Repeat the Lord's Prayer, inserting your offender's name: "Forgive me my trespasses as I forgive_____."
6. Practice praying for the person, asking specific blessings for him.
7. Speak to others in a kindly manner about the person against whom you harbor antagonism.
8. Write a brief letter of good will. Do not be offended if it is not answered. You have cleansed your own heart, and that is what really matters.
9. Study the causes of this unhappy situation to correct the "mistake pattern" in yourself.
10. Ask God now to effect a permanent spiritual change in your nature to forestall future rifts. Secretly want this, pray for it, believe it is given you, and you will surely have it.

A Christian will find it cheaper to pardon than to resent. Forgiveness saves the expense of anger, the cost of hatred, the waste of spirits.
—Meggido Message

It is just that he who asks forgiveness for his offenses should give it in turn.

Two persons will not be friends long if they will not forgive each others little failings.

When we stop to think that God forgives us of our sins not once but many times, that He loves us despite our unworthiness, how is it possible that we can keep unkindness, hatred and resentment in our hearts?

He who does not forgive others burns before him the bridge of God's forgiveness.

It is manlike to punish but Godlike to forgive.

Evangelism

IT MEANT HEAVEN TO HIM

One day I rang a doorbell,
   In a casual sort of way,
'Twas not a formal visit
   And there wasn't much to say.
I don't remember what I said—
   It matters not, I guess—
I found a heart in hunger;
   A soul in deep distress.
He said I came from Heaven,
   And I often wondered why,
He said I came to see him
   When no other help was nigh.
It meant so little to me
   To knock at a stranger's door
But it meant Heaven to him
   And God's presence forevermore.

"Why didn't you tell us sooner,"
  The words came sad and low;
"Oh ye who knew the gospel truth
  Why didn't you let us know?
The Savior died for those who sin,
  He died to save from woe;
But we never heard the story,
  Why didn't you let us know?"

"You say you are Christ's disciple;
  That you try His work to do;
And yet His very last command
  Is disobeyed by you!
'Tis indeed a wonderful story
  He loved the whole world so,
That He came and died to save us,
  Why didn't you let us know?"

One night in a howling hurricane the lookout observed a distress signal from a ship that had gone aground on the dangerous Diamond Shoals, ten miles at sea.

The lifeboats could be easily launched, the lookout thought, but getting them back in again. . . .

Captain Etheridge ordered the boats rolled out.

One of the lifeguards protested, "Captain Pat, we can get out there, but we can never get back."

"Boys," came the reply that has gone down in history, "We don't have to come back — but we have to go"!

Yes, Jesus has given us our marching orders. He has commanded us to preach His gospel in all the world. He has never promised them that they would get back safely from every venture, but He does command us, "GO."

Every loyal Christian; every true Christian, will go without counting the cost.

Do not expect God to use you as a lighthouse somewhere else, if He cannot use you as a candle where you now are.

THE CHRISTIAN LIFE

A CRY FOR LIGHT

There comes a wail of anguish
  Across the ocean wave—
It pleads for help, O Christians,
  Poor dying souls to save.
These far-off heathen natives,
  Who sit in darkest night,
Now stretch their hands imploring
  And cry to us for light.

We have the blessed gospel;
  We know its priceless worth;
We read the grand old story
  Of Christ our Saviour's birth.
O haste ye, faithful workers,
  To them the tidings bear—
Glad tidings of salvation
  That they our light may share.

God has more trouble getting Christians to GO than Sinners to COME.

What spring is to the earth, what the sun is to the flowers, what a physician is to the sick, what a boat is to a drowning man, true evangelism is to a lost soul and a sinful world.

What shall it profit a man if through engineering skills he is able to build massive bridges over which millions may safely pass and neglect the learning, the work and the witnessing that will build the bridge of faith from time into eternity, and lose his own soul and the souls he might have won?

Every Christian is a soul-winner . . . get to work!

YEW AWT TWO REED THIS HEAR ARTIKUL!

An illiterate salesman had been sent on a selling assignment. His letters to the boss are worth reading.

"Dear Boss: I seen this outfit which they ain't never bought a dime's worth of nothing from us — I sole them a couplul hundred thousand dollars worth of guds. I'm now in Chkawgo." Two days later a second letter arrived at the home office. It read "I cum hear and sole them half milyon."

Both letters were posted on the bulletin board with a note added by the company president. Catching the spirit of the situation, the president wrote in this fashion: "We bin spendin to much time hear trying to spel instead of tryin to sel. Let's watch these sails. I want everybody shud reed these letters from Gooch who is on the rode doin a grate job for us, and you shud go out and do like he done."

As a minister, let me say this: "Peoplul are movin into this hear community and we ain't getting 'em invited and vistud. Least wise not fast enuf. Peopul live rite near us and we ain't invitin 'em to church and Bibul Skul and they don't not go nowhere. Les us do like Gooch done and jes do our level bess with what we have and wurk for Christ and Christ's church."

IT PAYS TO ADVERTISE

The codfish lays ten thousand eggs,
The homely hen lays one.
But the codfish never cackles
To tell you what she's done.
And so we scorn the codfish,
While the humble hen we prize,
Which simply goes to show you,
That it pays to adverise.

Nothing else is as successful in bringing people to church as a personal call. Second best is a telephone call.

BECAUSE CHRIST CAME ... WE MUST GO

Some Suggestions About Visiting

I. Preparation
   1. Set regular time
   2. Plan your visit
   3. Prepare your heart
   4. Pray before your visit

II. Personality of Visitor Characterized by:
   1. Cheerfulness
   2. Enthusiasm
   3. A well-groomed appearance
   4. Tactful in conversation
   5. Cordiality

III. The visit
   1. Go out two by two
   2. Make the greeting:
      a. Warm and friendly
      b. To the point
      c. Effective
   3. Let the conversation be:
      a. Tactful, but positive
      b. Specific
      c. Friendly
      d. Constructive
   4. Use your Bible
   5. Know when to leave
   6. Leave cheerfully and optimistically

IV. The follow-up
   1. Engage in prayer privately and in the group or class
   2. Enlist aid of the Pastor where deep spiritual needs are discovered.
   3. Visit again, and again, and again.

The curse of many people is that they have been innoculated with a small dose of Christianity which has prevented them from catching the Real Thing!

If there is one thing that Satan is sensitive about, it is the danger of a Christian harming the cause he loves by speaking of Christ to a needy soul.

Those who call themselves Christian and yet do not wish all others to be Christians are confessing the insecurity of their own faith. A Church that is not dreaming in terms of presenting the gospel to all men is tacitly admitting that it has no message for any man.
—Kenneth Scott Latourette

The old adage: "A stitch in time can save nine." Then certainly: "A prayer in time could save at least one and perhaps many!"

TELL SOMEONE ABOUT JESUS THIS WEEK.

A BILLBOARD in a small village, in front of a church building has this message . . . "Pray for a good harvest, but *keep on hoeing.*"

Lord's Supper

Christians should go to the Lord's house on the Lord's day to worship around the Lord's table, to examine themselves in the light of the Lord's perfect life and to fellowship with the Lord's people.

IN MEMORY — THE LORD'S SUPPER

Nineteen hundred and sixty-four years ago, our Heavenly Father brought forth on this planet a new Kingdom, conceived in love and dedicated to the proposition that all men are in need of a Savior.

We are now engaged in a great spiritual struggle, testing whether this kingdom or any kingdom so conceived and so dedicated can long endure. We are met at the Memorial Table of that conflict. We have come to dedicate this cup and this loaf on this first day of the week in remembrance of HIM who died that we might live.

This we must do in all obedience to the Scriptures. But in a larger sense, we cannot dedicate, we cannot consecrate, we cannot hallow this memorial. The Son of God, having died, and risen again, who struggled and bled for it, has hallowed it far beyond our poor power to add or detract.

The world will little note nor long remember what we say here, but it can never forget what He did there.

It is rather for us, who live through HIM, that we here be dedicated to the great task remaining before us, that from our honored Savior we take increased devotion to that cause for which HE gave HIS last full measure of devotion.

That we here highly resolve that the Lord shall not have died in vain and that this world under God shall have a new birth, of the water and of the Spirit and that this Kingdom from the Father, through the Son, for the people, shall be preached in all the earth.

Each Lord's Day following the services there are at least three cups which tell of one's devotion to the Lord: The *Used* cup, the *Mis-used* cup, and the *Unused* cup. Which cup represents you?

Service

... There never was a person who did anything worth doing, who did not receive more than he gave.

GO FORWARD

The Master says: "Go forward"
  Our part is to obey.
So let us take His message
  To those we meet each day.

Boys, girls, grown men and women,
  Yes, little children, too
The great command, "Go forward,"
  Is meant for me and you.

"Go forward"! Every Christian
  Should hear that great command
And take salvation's story
  To those in every land.

If we will all go forward,
  The Lord will give us strength
And we will surely conquer
  In His blest name at length.

Our leader gave His promise,
  We know His word is true,
And if we serve Him gladly
  We may win others, too.

So let us all go forward
  And work each day for Him,
Alert to hear His orders —
  Our light must not grow dim.
                —Pearl Neilson

Be big enough to speak the truth — and live it . . .
Hold your ideals though the heavens fall . . .
Expect no quarter, yet be big enough to give it . . .
Be big enough to meet the humblest call.

IF

If you were busy being kind,
Before you knew it, you would find
You'd soon forget to think 'twas true
That someone was unkind to you.

If you were busy being glad,
And cheering people who are sad,
Although your heart might ache a bit
You'd soon forget to notice it.

If you were busy being good,
And doing just the best you could,
You'd not have time to blame some man
Who's doing just the best he can.

If you were busy being true
To what you know you ought to do,
You'd be so busy you'd forget
The blunders of the folks you've met.

If you were busy being right,
You'd find yourself too busy quite
To criticize your neighbor long,
Because he's busy being wrong.

Wouldn't it be nice if everyone tempted to point a finger would instead hold out a hand?

I am glad to think
I am not bound to make the world go right,
But only to discover and do,
With cheerful heart, the work that God appoints.

—Jean Ingelow

SITTING BY THE FIRE

An old man sat by the open fire,
  And dreamed the years away;
While outside in the battle of life
  Many perished in the toils of day.
He never did any good, nor did he
  Ever do any wrong—
He just sat by the open fire,
  And dreamed, the whole day long.
Now he's left a vacant chair,
  And they say he's gone up higher,
But if he still does what he used to do . . .
  He's still sitting by the fire.

Too many of us conduct our lives on the cafeteria plan — SELF SERVICE ONLY.

ARE YOU BUSY ENOUGH FOR GOD TO USE?

God never goes to the lazy or the idle when He needs men for His service. When He has work to be done He goes to those who are already at work. When God wants a good servant, He calls a busy man.

MOSES was a busy man with his flock at Horeb.
SAUL was busy searching for this father's lost sheep.
AMOS was busy following the flock.
JAMES and JOHN were busy mending their nets.
PAUL was busy persecuting the friends of Jesus.

The busy man always has time for Christ because his schedule is a full one and he knows he *must* put Christ first on his list. By putting God's work first we find the rest of our schedule seems to run more smoothly. Begin the day with the Lord; begin the week with the Lord, and enjoy the many blessings of the full Christian life that God intended for you.

THE CHRISTIAN LIFE

There are too many of us praying for mountains to be moved . . . when what we really need is the courage to climb them!

Even a mosquito doesn't get a pat on the back until he starts working! If we, as Christians, expect the approval of God, we must work for Him!

>   Oh! God will pardon your blunder, my friend,
>   And regard with pity your fall;
>   But the one big sell that surely means hell
>   Is to simply do — nothing at all.

THE SIZE OF YOUR HEART

It isn't the size of your house so much
*   That matters so much at all,*
It's the gentle hand, its loving touch,
*   That maketh it great or small.*
The friends who come, in the hour they go,
*   Who out of your house depart,*
Will judge it not by the style you show
*   It's all in the size of your heart.*
It isn't the size of your head so much,
*   It isn't the wealth you found,*
That will make you happy — it's how you touch
*   The lives that are all around*
For making money is not so hard —
*   To live life well is an art;*
How men love you, how men regard,
*   Is all in the size of your heart.*

The Spirit is evident in any church where all the Lord's people are working together on the Lord's business under the Lord's direction.

COST OF FOLLOWING GOD:

It cost Abraham the willingness to yield his only son.
It cost Esther the risk of her life.
It cost Daniel being cast into the den of lions.
It cost Shadrach, Meshack and Abednego being put in a fiery furnace.
It cost Stephen death by stoning.
It cost Peter a martyr's death.
It cost Jesus His life.
DOES IT COST YOU ANYTHING?

TROUBLE IN THE TOOL CHEST

The carpenter's tools formed themselves into a church, which seemed the logical action for Servants of the Carpenter.

Trouble developed almost immediately, with accusation, criticism, and counter-charges being hurled at one another. *Mr. Plane*, the preacher, was charged with superficiality and having no depth to his work. *Mr. Screwdriver* was accused of twisting everything he touched. *Deacon Sandpaper* was condemned for roughness and rubbing people the wrong way. And though it was admitted that *Teacher Hammer* could drive his point home, he was disliked for his noisiness and bluntness, while *Sister Ruler* was criticized for her unyielding and uncompromising standards, *Mr. Saw* for his cutting remarks.

In the midst of the trouble the Carpenter came to form his work. In his skilled hands, he took the *Hammer, Plane, Sandpaper, Screwdriver, Ruler, Saw*, and all the rest, put their peculiar characteristics to proper use and made a pulpit from which he could proclaim the gospel to those who needed to hear it. As these tools began to work together for his business and under his direction, accusations, criticism, and counter-charges, died away. In their place came a love and mutual respect they had never dreamed possible. Furthermore, something constructive was accomplished for the Glory of God.

THE CHRISTIAN LIFE

BUT ONCE I PASS THIS WAY

And then — and then, the silent door
Swings on its hinges - Opens -
Closes - and no more I pass this way,
So while I may with all my might,
I will essay sweet comfort and delight
To all I meet upon the Pilgrim way,
For no man travels twice the Great Highway
That climbs through darkness up to light
Through night to day.

"Father, where shall I work today?"
   And my love flowed warm and free.
Then He pointed me out a tiny spot,
   And said, "Tend that for me."
I answered quickly, "Oh, no, not that;
   Why, no one would ever see,
No matter how well my work was done;
   Not that little place for me."
And the word He spoke — it was not stern;
   He answered me tenderly:
"Ah, little one, search that heart of thine,
   Art thou working for them or me?
Nazareth was a little place,
   And so was Galilee."

If you have a minute to waste do not spend it with some one who doesn't have the time.

If more Saints would heed the admonition to "Go," more sinners would heed the admonition to "COME."

God always uses the man nearest Him.

There is no time like the present, but people need to be careful not to waste it like they have so much of the past!

What one does in his spare time is the acid test of his character.

> *If you have not gold and silver*
> *Ever ready to command,*
> *If you cannot toward the needy*
> *Reach an ever-open hand,*
> *You can visit the afflicted,*
> *O'er the erring you can weep;*
> *You can be a true disciple,*
> *Sitting at the Savior's feet.*
>
> *Do not, then, stand idly waiting*
> *For some greater work to do.*
> *Fortune is a lazy goddess—*
> *She will never come to you.*
> *Go and toil in any vineyard,*
> *Do not fear to do or dare;*
> *If you want a field of labor*
> *You can find it anywhere.*

A mistake is evidence that someone tried to do something.

God will forgive those who start late to serve Him, but He will not forgive those who quit early.

Everything we do in the church building is called service. We have song service, worship service, prayer service etc. We need to do some serving outside of the building.

A good place to find a helping hand is at the end of your arm.

Christian Living

A MORNING WISH

The sun is just rising on the morning of another day. What can I wish that this day may bring to me? Nothing that shall make the world or others poorer, nothing at the expense of other men; but just those few things which in their coming do not stop with me, but touch me rather, as they pass and gather strength.

- A few friends who understand me, and yet remain my friends.
- A work to do which has real value, without which the world would feel the poorer.
- A return for such work, small enough not to tax unduly anyone who pays.
- A mind unafraid to travel, even though the trail be not blazed.
- An understanding heart.
- A sight of the eternal hills and unresting sea, and of something beautiful the hand of man has made.
- A sense of humor and the power to laugh.
- A little leisure, with nothing to do.
- A few moments of quiet, silent meditation. The sense of the presence of God.
- And the patience to wait for the coming of these things, with the wisdom to know them when they come.

—W.R. Hunt

"Men will wrangle for religion; write for it; fight for it; die for it; anything but live for it."

—Charles Cotton

INDISPENSABLE FOLKS!

*"They do not ride forth with banners,
But whenever a roof-top falls,
These little, nameless people —
Are rebuilding their shattered walls."*

One cloudy day in London, I clipped that little verse from a London paper knowing that some day it would come in handy. Now — it does.

"Riding forth with banners" is a way of shouting from the rooftops that a heroic patriotic people are meeting the adversities of life — head on — and facing the future with courage. There are other ways to let the world know what is in our hearts.

On another cloudy day, I was riding through the Great Smoky Mountains, and at a sharp dip in the curving road, I came upon a mountain cabin hanging precariously to the mountainside and supplying shelter to the family that called it "home."

On a clothesline, stretched alongside the cabin, there was a white table cloth, and at the edge of the small porch there were tomato cans from which bright flowers lifted their fragrant faces toward the mountaintops. What do those simple things tell you?

Here lives a poor family — possibly uneducated, and shut in by the circumstances of life, but inside that small house is a woman who has a love for the beautiful and a sense of need for the simple elegance as noted by that white cloth and those bright flowers.

Again, here is a man who belongs to a church. He, like hundreds of others, has never spoken at a meeting. He has never been "Chairman" of anything. In listing the "church leaders" his name is not listed. What of him?

Just this. Without him and his unceasing loyalty, his love for the church, and his presence at all services, we could not be the great church we are; THAT makes him as IMPORTANT as any "chairman," as any more talented person who also serves. He, too does not "ride forth with banners" — but his part in the victory is so vital he comes near being "indispensable man." Think on that — and be grateful.

—Dr. Pierce Harris

THE CHRISTIAN LIFE

JUST AN ORDINARY MEMBER

*Just an ordinary member of the church I heard her say,
But you'd always find her present even on a rainy day.
She had a warm handclasp for the stranger in the aisle,
And a friend who was in trouble found sunshine in her smile.*

*When the sermon helped her, she told the preacher so—
And when she needed help, she let the elders know—
She always gave so freely and tried to do her share;
In all the ordinary tasks for which some have no care.*

*Her talents were not many, but her love for God was true.
Her prayers were not public, but she prayed for me and you.
An "ordinary member" — I think that I would say
She was "extra ordinary," in an humble sort of way.*

DIRECTIONS FOR A HAPPY LIFE

A little more patience to bear with the persons whom I do not like;
A little more humility to fulfill my duty, even though I find it difficult;
A little more good judgment to take people as they are and not as I would like them to be;
A little more prudence so as not to bother with the faults of others and not get excited over them;
A little more courage and strength to bear the trials that disturb the peace of mind;
A little more charity so as not to manifest my hurts;
And, above all, a little more prayer to draw the good Lord into my heart and keep him there.

*Our lives are songs; God writes the words
And we set them to music at pleasure;
And the song grows glad, or sweet or sad,
As we choose to fashion the measure.*

IN CHRIST WE HAVE

A love that can never be fathomed;
A life that can never die;
A righteousness that can never be tarnished;
A peace that can never be understood;
A rest that can never be disturbed;
A joy that can never be diminished;
A hope that can never be disappointed;
A glory that can never be clouded;
A light that can never be darkened;
A purity that can never be defiled;
A beauty that can never be marred.

COUNTING THE COST

You have counted the cost of serving Christ
   And find it too much, you say;
But what of the cost of rejecting Him
   And turning His love away?

It will cost you far more than money can buy,
   It will cost you a lifetime of pain;
And then when your life on earth is done,
   You will have to start paying again.

For the cost of rejecting Christ, my friend,
   Is not paid at the close of life;
You must pay with your soul at the bar of God,
   When your conscience will cut like a knife.

It will cost countless ages away from the Lord,
   And leave hopeless pangs of regret;
O! think once again and turn to Christ
   For judgment forever is set.

When things go wrong, don't go with them.

A BETTER WAY TO LIVE

If we pray a little more,
 And scold a little less,
If we bear a little more
 Though things are in a mess
If we work a little more
 Without a bitter groan,
If we talk a little more
 To Jesus when alone,
If we cling a little more
 To faith instead of doubt,
We'll have more peace within
 And spread more joy without.

A SMILE

A smile is something deeper
 Than an affected grin:
It's not just on the surface,
 But from the heart within.
Synthetic smiles are always
 So easy to detect:
Though pleasant for the moment,
 They soon lose their effect.
But when the smile is prompted
 By love sincere and true:
It proves to be contagious
 And warms the whole heart through.

THANKS

It's a gracious word when you think of it.
It's an encouraging word when you say it.
It's an inspiring word when you hear it.
It's a magic word when you mean it.

Many Christians have enough religion to make them decent, but not enough to make them dynamic.

WHY?

The sound of wild geese flying home
   Awakened me tonight;
What is it guides them when they roam?
   Who taught them form of flight?
What is it tell them when to go
   Their north or southward way?
How is it that they seem to know
   To go without delay?
I watched their silver wings tonight,
   Against the darkened sky
And marveled at their ordered flight
   And stopped to ponder why,
If they can trust their Maker's plan,
   Then why can't we, the sons of man?
—Catherine E. Jackson

IF

If man would concentrate on God
   As he does on business schemes,
And give this church the backing
   That he gives his baseball team;
If he could quote the Scripture
   As he does his favorite jokes,
And practice with his prayer
   The way he does his golfing strokes;
If he argued with temptation
   Like he argues with his wife.
The world would soon be full of saints
   Who live a perfect life.
—Richard Smith

THE CHRISTIAN LIFE

> *Help me, dear Lord, this lesson sweet to learn;*
> *To sit at Thy pierced feet and only yearn*
> *To love Thee better, Lord; and feel that still*
> *Waiting is working, if it be Thy will.*

It is motive that gives value to service.

Most of the New Testament is written to tell Christians how to live.

CHRISTIAN LIVING

PRAY	It is the greatest power on earth.
LOVE	It is a God-given privilege.
READ	It is the fountain of wisdom.
THINK	It is the source of power.
BE FRIENDLY	It is the road to happiness.
GIVE	It is too short a day to be selfish.
PLAY	It is the secret of perpetual youth.
LAUGH	It is the music of the soul.
WORK	It is the price of success.
SAVE	It is the secret to security.

Bad habits, like a comfortable bed, are easy to get into, but hard to get out of. Good habits, are the soul's muscles. The more you use them — the stronger they grow.

Quitters in the church are like motors: they start 'sputtering' before they miss, and start 'missing' before they quit.

To make mistakes is human; to repeat old mistakes is stupid.

VICTORIOUS LIVING

When you are forgotten or neglected, or purposely set at naught, and you smile inwardly, glorying in the insult or the oversight, because you are counted worthy to suffer for Christ; this is victory.

When your good is evil spoken of, when your wishes are crossed, your taste offended, your advice disregarded, your opinions ridiculed, and you take it all in patient, loving silence; that is victory.

When you are content with any food, and raiment, any climate, any society, any solitude, any interruption, by the will of God; that is victory.

When you can lovingly and patiently share with any irregularity, any unpunctuality, and any annoyance; that is victory.

When you never care to refer to yourself in conversation or to praise your own good works, or to itch after commendation, when you can truly love to be unknown; that is victory.

When you stand face to face with waste, folly, extravagance, spiritual insensibility, and ignore it; that is victory.

When, like Paul, you can throw all your suffering on Jesus, thus converting it into a means of a surrendered heart, therefore, do take pleasure in infirmities, in reproaches, in necessities, in persecutions, in distresses, for Christ's sake; that is victory (II Cor. 12:7-11).

The New Testament does not use many words to tell us how to be born again but many words how to live so we can live again.

Four things a man must learn to do if he would make his record true:
To think without confusion clearly;
To love his fellowmen sincerely;
To act from honest motives purely;
To trust in God and Heaven securely.

> God give me work
> Till my life shall end,
> And life
> Till my work is done.

Just because you don't care about your soul, don't take your friend to Hell with you. Give him a chance.

TEST OF OUR CHRISTIAN LIFE

"Blessed is the man that endureth temptation, for when he is tried, he shall receive the crown of life, which the Lord hath promised to them that love Him" (James 1:12). Can you pass these tests?

THE WEATHER TEST: Are you a sailboat Christian making progress in the Lord only when the winds are favorable, or are you a tugboat Christian — plowing ahead even though the gales are against you?

THE WORLDLINESS TEST: Do you think as the world thinks, go where the world goes, act as the world acts, or does your life give evidence of having set your affections on things above, not on things on the earth?

THE WALLET TEST: How much energy is being given to the work of the Lord, and is it a reasonable portion of what you are expending in the day-by-day tasks of making a living?

THE WITNESSING TEST: Are you by life and lip commending Christ so that He is attractive to those who do not know Him as a personal Saviour and Lord, and is the vote of your life for Him or against Him?

THE WAITING TEST: The Thessalonian "turned to God from idols to serve the true and living God and to wait for His Son from heaven whom He raised from the dead" (I Thess. 1:9-10). Have you turned, and are you living with His coming in view?

There is a right way to settle all problems and most of our troubles are the result of trying to avoid that way.

Some people go to a lot of trouble trying to hide their light under a bushel, when a tea cup would do the job just as well.

WHICH

There are two ways of beginning the day — with prayer, or without it. You began today in one of these two ways. Which?

There are two ways of spending the Lord's Day — idly or devotionally. You spend the Lord's Day in one of these two ways. Which?

There are two classes of people in the world — the saved and the unsaved. You belong to one of these two classes. Which?

There are two great masters of men in the universe — God and Satan. You are serving under one of these two great masters. Which?

There are two roads which lead through time to eternity - the broad road and the narrow road. You are walking in one of these two roads. Which?

There are two deaths which people die — some "die in the Lord"; others "die in their sins." You will die one of these two deaths. Which?

There are two places to which people go — heaven and hell. You will go to one of these two places. Which?

I see the sun shine in the sky;
At night I see the moon up high;
I know the sun's reflected light
Makes the moon shine in the night.

I feel the love of God for me,
And this is what my prayer shall be;
That I reflect that love and send
It, like a sunbeam, to each friend.

Beware of temptation — the more you see of it the better you like it.

THE CHRISTIAN LIFE

A DEAD WEIGHT

I've been a dead weight many years
    Around the church's neck;
I've let the other carry me
    And always pay the check.
I've had my name upon the rolls,
    For years and years gone by.
I've criticized and grumbled too,
    Nothing could satisfy.

I've been a dead weight long enough
    Upon the church's back;
Beginning now, I'm going to take
    A wholly different tac.
I'm going to pray, pay, and work
    And carry loads instead;
And not have others carry me—
    As people do — THE DEAD.

YOU HAVE A PART

All have a share in the beauty
    All have a part in the plan.
What does it matter what duty
    Falls to the lot of man?

Someone has blended the plaster,
    And someone has carried the stone;
Neither the man nor the master
    Ever has built alone.

Making the roof from the weather,
    Or building a house for a king,
Only by working together
    Have men accomplished a thing.

AT THE DOOR

He wiped his shoes before his door,
But ere he entered he did more;
'Twas not enough to cleanse his feet
Of dirt they'd gathered in the street;
He stood and dusted off his mind
And left all trace of care behind.
"In here I will not take," said he,
"The stains the day has brought to me."

Beyond this door shall never go
The burdens that are mine to know;
The day is done, and here I leave
The petty things that vex and grieve;
What clings to me of hate and sin
To them I will not carry in;
Only the good shall go with me
For their devoted eye to see.

I will not burden them with cares,
Nor track the home with grim affairs;
I will not at my table sit
With soul unclean, and mind unfit;
Beyond this door I will not take
The outward signs of inward ache;
I will not take a dreary mind
Into this house for them to find.

He wiped his shoes before his door,
But paused to do a little more.
He dusted off the stains of strife,
The mud that's incident to life,
The blemishes of careless thought,
The traces of the fight he'd fought,
The selfish humors and the mean,
And when he entered he was clean.
—Edgar A. Guest

THE CHRISTIAN LIFE

Wouldst thou be chief? Then lowly serve.
Wouldst thou go up? Go down;
But go as low as e're you will,
The Highest has been lower still.

When God measures a man he puts the tape around the heart — not the head. God measured Saul the new king of Israel with a different yard stick. Tall and handsome and impressive to the people he was not impressive to God.

Silence is not always golden, it is yellow cowardly.

The silent Christian is working for Satan.

Repentance

You've been speeding and you get a ticket. You don't like it, but you know you've been wrong. With little or no argument, you pay your fine.

You've been staying home from church on Sundays for one of a dozen reasons. Maybe you like to sleep late. Maybe you don't consider yourself the church-goer type. Whatever your alibi — nobody's going to come after you.

This is a summons you'll have to serve on yourself. For an infraction of God's law is something that can't be ignored. Until you declare yourself guilty, you will be deliberately shutting yourself off from the greatest fellowship in the world. No judge in history has ever pronounced a sterner sentence.

—Ross Sloan

WHEN A PERSON IS WRONG

There are several thing he can do:
1. He can become angry and take it out on the Lord.
2. He can stir up trouble by creating a faction in an effort to justify himself.
3. He can become blind and excuse His own fault.
4. He can play the martyr and explain it as someone else's fault.
5. He can run away from the place of his sin.
6. He can humbly and sincerely repent of his sins and get right with God.

Giving our best today is the receipe for a better tomorrow.

ON THE WRONG TRACK

One morning a train pulled into the Union Station at Washington, D.C. but had to back up and get on the right track. It had been going in on the wrong track when suddenly the engineer discovered it and had to back up about a quarter of a mile and get back on the right track.

Don't you imagine the engineer was embarrassed that he had gone wrong, but think of the lesson we can learn from the engineer's courage and wisdom to correct his mistake.

There are many times when we get on the wrong track. A boy might be sure he is going into forestry and end up being a doctor. He may think he loves Sue and a week later loves Mary. It is good to have sense enough to change a job or a girl (or boy) if you realize you are on the wrong track.

One of the most tragic things is to get on the wrong track morally or spiritually and be unwilling to "back up" and change. We start doing things that are wrong, maybe just little things, but then we are embarrassed to admit it.

Jesus said, "Unless you repent you shall all likewise perish" (Luke 13:3). Repentance means to stop, back up and get on the right track NOW.

Repentance means to quit sinning. Doing penance is paying a penalty for it under a church authority that has usurped God's authority.

SPIRITUAL SUICIDE

IF YOU PASS THIS POINT YOU LOSE YOUR LAST CHANCE OF ESCAPE. Thus read the warning posted at a dangerous point along the Scottish coast. But the traveler passed on, unheeding.

At great risk a man climbed partly down the cliff to give the warning; "The tides are rising; they have already covered the road you have passed, and they are near the foot of the cliffs before you. By this ascent alone you can escape."

His effort was in vain. The traveler thought he knew better and hurried on. Soon he reached a point where he found it impossible to proceed. Retreat, too, was impossible. He was engulfed by the rising tide — a victim of his foolhardiness.

Pilate missed his chance when he delivered Christ to be crucified (John 19:16).

Judas missed his opportunity when he sold Christ for 30 pieces of silver (Matt. 27:3-5).

Felix missed his chance when he excused himself until a "convenient season" (Acts 24:24-26).

Agrippa missed his chance when he dulled his ears against Paul's appeal (Acts 26:1-28).

The Jewish Council missed their chance when they resisted the address of Stephen and put him to death (Acts 7:1-58).

And you miss your chance when you continue in your sins. Christ declares that those who die in their sins cannot come where He is (John 8:21,24).

Unrepented and unconfessed sin is spiritually a loaded gun pointed right at your head.

The Swiss painter, Willy Fries, has set the story of the passion in his own village of Toggenburg. His first picture shows the triumphal entry of Christ; but behind the crowd a man kneels beneath a tree and while the crowd shouts "Blessed be the King that cometh," his cry is "Lord, have mercy upon me." The lonely figure — truly representative of all mankind — will still be there when the crowd is gone.

To put off repentance another day means one more to repent of, and one less to repent in.

Repent now. Avoid the rush on judgment day.

HOW TO BE PERFECTLY MISERABLE

1. Think about yourself.
2. Talk about yourself.
3. Use "I" as often as possible.
4. Mirror yourself continually in the opinion of others.
5. Listen greedily to what people say about you.
6. Be suspicious.
7. Be jealous and envious.
8. Be sensitive to slights.
9. Never forgive a criticism.
10. Trust nobody but yourself.
11. Insist on consideration and respect.
12. Demand agreement with your own views on everything.
13. Sulk if people are not grateful to you for favors shown them.
14. Never forget a service you may have rendered.
15. Be on the lookout for a good time for yourself.
16. Shirk your duties if you can.
17. Do as little as possible for others.
18. Love yourself supremely.
19. Be selfish.

Art thou weary, tender heart? Be glad of pain;
  In sorrow sweetest things will grow as flowers in rain
God watches, and thou wilt have sun
  When clouds their perfect work have done.

Continual dwelling on the inventory of your short-comings is one of the surest ways of losing all the joy of life.

A man needs a little trouble to give him strength — just as he needs something besides sugar to eat.

Count your blessings, not your bruises.

JUST THINKING

Some day, in years to come, you will be wrestling with the great temptation, or trembling under the great sorrow of your life. But the real struggle is here, now, in these quiet weeks. Now it is being decided whether, in the day of your supreme sorrow or temptation, you shall miserably fair or gloriously conquer. Character cannot be made except by a steady, long continued process.
—Phillip Brooks

"When anxiety arises it must be met. The more we push it from us, denying it, gritting our teeth till the moment passes and then forgetting it, the more it will return to haunt us. It has to be met face to face.
—Cyril C. Richardson

"The caliber of a man is found in his ability to meet disappointment successfully, enriched rather than narrowed by it."
—Thomas R. Kelly

There are no hopeless situations; there are only men who grow hopeless about them.

When God puts a tear in your eye it's because He wants to put a rainbow in your heart.

BRIDGES

When anything in life brings pain,
Or anyone upsets my day,
If I can build a bridge to God
His peace will chase my fears away.

When problems leave me tense, unstrung,
And peace of mind cannot be found,
If I can build a bridge of faith,
He'll lift me up to higher ground.

If I can build a bridge of trust
To span the tensions of my day,
God's grace and understanding love
Will be a light upon my way.

No difficulty large or small,
Can come between my Lord and me
If I can build a bridge of prayer
To feel His presence constantly.

If you could kick the person responsible for most of your troubles, you wouldn't be able to sit down for six months.
—*The Plea*

God has promised forgiveness to your repentance, but He has not promised tomorrow to your procrastination.

THE CHRISTIAN LIFE

> *Oh, do not pray for easy lives,*
> *Pray to be stronger men!*
> *Do not pray for tasks equal to your powers,*
> *But powers equal to your tasks.*
> *Then the doing of the work shall be no miracle.*
> *But you shall be a miracle*
> *And every day you shall wonder at yourself*
> *At the richness of your life that has come*
> *To you by the grace of God.*
> —Phillip Brooks

Horizontal tensions pull an individual apart; vertical tensions pull him together.

When God wants to make a man, He puts him into some kind of storm.

He who occupies a place in the sun must expect some blisters.

Carry your cross patiently, and in the end it will carry you.

The most trouble is produced by those who do not produce anything.

We die by living to ourselves. We live by dying to self.

Trials and Tribulations

There are various ways of looking at the rainstorms of adversity. We can lament our misfortunes until our hearts forget the sunshine. Or we can meet the challenge, believing that out of these rainy days will come new growth and beauty to our lives.

SATAN'S AUCTION

It is said that Satan announced once upon a time that he was thinking of retiring from business, and would offer all of his diabolical inventions for sale to anyone who would pay the price.

On the day of the sale, the tools were all attractively displayed, despite the ugliness of most of then. Malice, hatred, jealousy, sensuality, deceit, and all the other instrumentalities of evil each was marked with its price.

Apart from the rest lay a plain wedge-shaped tool, much worn, and priced much higher than any of the others. Someone asked Satan what it was.

"That's Discouragement," was the reply.

"Why have you priced such a simple tool so high?"

"Because," Satan answered, "it is more useful to me than any of the others. I can pry open and get inside a man's consciousness with that when I could not get near him with any of the others; and once inside I can use him in whatever way suits me best. It is much worn because I have used it on nearly everybody, yet few, very few, know that it belongs to me."

THERE IS A VAST DIFFERENCE

Between — being sorry for sin and being sorry you got caught;
Between — confessing your sins and confessing another fellow's;
Between — seeing our own faults and seeing the other person's;
Between — conversion of the head only and conversion of the heart.

Half of our troubles come from our wanting to have our own way; the other half comes from being allowed to have it.

OUR THOUGHT FOR THE WEEK: "The bright crowns that are worn in heaven have been tried and smelted and polished and glorified through the furnace of tribulation."

THE CHRISTIAN LIFE

If there is no sorrow for sin — there is no joy for salvation.

If none were sick and none were sad,
   What service could we render?
I think if we were always glad
   We scarcely could be tender.

If sorrow never claimed our heart
   And every wish were granted,
Patience would die and hope depart,
   Life would be disenchanted.

A gem cannot be polished without friction, nor a man perfected without trials.

The tree that never had to fight
For sun and sky and air and light,
That stood out in the open plain,
And always got its share of rain,
Never became a forest king,
But lived and died a scrubby thing.

The man who never had to toil,
Who never had to win his share
Of sun and sky and light and air,
Never became a manly man,
But lived and died as he began.

Good timber does not grow in ease;
The stronger wind, the tougher trees;
The farther sky, the greater length;
The more the storm, the more the strength;
By sun and cold, by rain and snows;
In tree or man good timber grows.

                              —R.C. Hanks

MARCHING WITHOUT MUSIC

It is said that Benedict Arnold was a better general than was George Washington. He was a handsomer man and a more interesting conversationalist. But he had one conspicuous weakness — he was unwilling to "march without music." Whenever General Arnold performed a task in a competent manner, he expected praise and acclaim, and if these were not forthcoming he sulked and became morose.

In the hurry and scurry of war there were times when the feats of General Arnold went unnoticed. This hurt his most vital spot, his vanity. So he committed the act unpardonable . . . he quit his job and placed the secrets of his employer in the hands of the competition

HOW BIG ARE WE?

We all have times of stress and strain. How we meet them determines how "BIG" we are spiritually. Anyone can live for the Lord when things go smoothly, but how do we live when the going gets rough?

To be a BIG Christian we must:
1. Be free from getting our feelings hurt.
2. Avail ourselves of every opportunity to pray, boost, and attend ALL the services of the Church regularly.
3. Be able to love those who do not like us and do all within our power to make them like us.
4. Be able to face tragedy (serious illness, death, financial reverses, etc.) with trust in the Lord.
5. Cooperate with the group by helping with whatever we feel is best for the church as a whole.
6. Be critical — NOT of others but our own Christian life.
7. Be willing to sacrifice to the limit for God, and be faithful to the Church in spite of all.

We stumble over pebbles — not mountains.

*'Tis my happiness below not to live without the cross,
But the Savior's power to know, sanctifying every loss;
Trials must and will befall, but with humble faith to see
Love inscribed upon them all — this is happiness to me;
Aliens may escape the rod, sunk in earthly, vain delight,
But the true-born child of God must not, would not, if he might.*

*A heartache crippled my spirit; I've nursed it for several days;
Perhaps I've been too kind to it, and that's the reason it stays!*
—Marilyn Townsend

The shortest way is not always right, nor the smoothest the safest; therefore, be not surprised if the Lord choose the farthest and roughest, but be sure of this — He will choose the best!

HISTORY'S GREAT MEN OVERCAME HARDSHIP

Beethoven composed most of his musical works only after he lost his hearing at the age of 32.

Alexander Graham Bell was laughed at for his invention of the telephone as "a crank who says he can talk through a wire."

Louis Braille, developer of the braille system of reading for the blind, was sightless himself.

Dostoevski survived four years in a Siberian prison camp and the afflictions of epilepsy to become one of the world's greatest novelists.

St. Paul generously endured endless sufferings to bring Christ to all men; "We are afflicted in every way, but not crushed; perplexed, but not driven to despair; persecuted, but not forsaken" (II Cor. 4:8).

CHRIST'S MEASURE

I give Him my burdens,
  He gives me His BLESSINGS.
I give Him my trials,
  He gives me His PATIENCE.
I give Him my sorrow,
  He gives me His STRENGTH.
I give Him my blindness,
  He gives me His LIGHT.
I give Him my cold heart,
  He gives me His LOVE.
I give Christ my all,
  And He gives me HEAVEN.

WE CAN'T ASK GOD

For help if we are not making an effort.
For strength if we have strength we are not using.
For guidance if we are ignoring the guidance we now have.
For prosperity if we have proved we cannot be trusted with it.
For faith when we are afraid to act on what we already know.
For forgiveness if we continue hating someone.
For mercy if we intend to commit the same sin again.
—Roy L. Smith

THY WILL BE DONE

Thy will be done. No greater words than these
Can pass from human lips, than these which rent
Their way through agony and bloody sweat,
And broke the silence of Gethsemane
  To save the world from sin.
—G.A. Studdert-Kennedy

A pessimist is one who makes difficulties of his opportunities. An optimist is one who makes opportunities of his difficulties.

HE KNOWS

Sometimes I'm tempted just to say,
 "I can't go on Lord — not this way."
He says, "Lo, always I'm with thee
 To the end of the world, so shall I be.
One day I, too, walked down that road
 And just like you, I carried that load.
But I carried not only temptation and scorn,
 But the sins of the whole world I have borne.
That you've a hard road to walk I know well,
 But the other road leads to hell"!

GETHSEMANE

All those who journey, soon or late,
Must pass within the garden's gate;
Must kneel alone in darkness there,
And battle with some fierce despair.
God pity those who cannot say:
"Not mine but thine"; who only pray:
"Let this cup pass," and cannot see
The purpose in Gethsemane
—Ella Wheeler Wilcox

Many trials today and those we worry about tomorrow will look to be very small when we look back on them.

Many men owe the grandeur of their lives to their tremendous difficulties.

Little things that fret and worry,
Little sins that grow and gain,
These are "foxes" we must watch for
Lest we suffer loss and pain.

Influence

EXAMPLE

On Sunday I have no difficulty in seeing the people of God's church. Our members have gathered for Worship and I see the worshippers from the pulpit. On Sunday, in worship, we are a majority people. Very few who come to worship are unsaved and unchurched. From Monday to Saturday, in God's world, we are a minority. Most of the people about us have little confidence of relation to Christ with meager, if any, commitment to Christ and His church.

I do then pray for you as I picture you in my mind, out in God's world. You are in areas of life that take on the character of good or evil in business, government, education, community, and home. God's presence in you is the salt of the earth. During the week you are closer to more people who need to commit their lives to Christ and His Church than you are with in Sunday worship. God's presence in you is the light which can lead them to Christian decision.

People take your example far more seriously than they take your advice.

When the invitation's given . . . Sinners beckoned one and all,
The Christians start to fidget and the lost ones miss the call.

THE CHRISTIAN LIFE

CHRISTIAN LIVING

There's a sweet old story translated for men,
  But writ in the long, long ago—
The Gospel according to Mark, Luke, and John,
  Of Christ and His mission below.

Men read and admire the Gospel of Christ
  With it's love so unfailing and true;
But what do they say and what do they think
  Of the Gospel according to you?

'Tis a wonderful story, that gospel of love,
  As it shines in the Christ life divine;
And oh! that its truth might be told again
  In the story of your life and mine!

You are writing each day, a letter to men,
  Take care that the writing is true,
'Tis the only gospel that some men will read,
  This gospel according to you.

If you wish your neighbor to see what God is like, let them see what He can make you like!

HAS SOMEONE SEEN CHRIST IN YOU TODAY?

Christian, look to your life, I pray;
Examine your heart this very day.
There are aching hearts and blighted souls;
Being lost in sin's destructive shoals,
And perhaps of Christ their only view
May be what they see of Him in you.
Will they see enough to bring hope and cheer?
Look to your light! Does it shine out clear?
  —Mrs. P.O. Marvel

There are little eyes upon you,
    And they're watching night and day;
There are little ears that quickly
    Take in every word you say;
There are little hands all eager
    To do everything you do,
And a little boy who's dreaming
    Of the day he'll be like you.

You're the little fellow's idol;
    You're the wisest of the wise;
In his little mind about you
    No suspicions ever rise;
He believes in you devoutly,
    Holds that all you say and do,
He will say and do in your way
    When he's grown up just like you.

There's a wide eyed little fellow
    Who believes you're always right,
And his ears are always open,
    And he watches day and night.
You are setting an example
    Every day in all you do,
For the little boy who's waiting
    To grow up to be like you.

A candle can light others only when it consumes itself. So with any servant of the public good: Spare yourself, and your light goes out!

Have your thoughts been pure,
Your words been kind?
Have you sought to have the Saviour's mind?
The world — with a criticizing view —
Has watched, but did it see Christ in You?

THE CHRISTIAN LIFE

A pint of example is worth a gallon of advice.

I SHALL NOT PASS AGAIN THIS WAY

The bread that giveth strength I want to give:
The water pure that bids the thirsty live;
I want to help the fainting day by day:
I'm sure I shall not pass again this way.

I want to give the oil of joy for tears,
The faith to conquer cruel doubts and fears.
Beauty for ashes may I give alway:
I'm sure I shall not pass again this way.

I want to give good measure running o'er,
And into angry hearts I want to pour
The answer soft that turneth wrath away;
I'm sure I shall not pass again this way.

I want to give to others hope and faith;
I want to do all that the Master saith;
I want to live aright from day to day;
I'm sure I shall not pass again this way.
—Ellen H. Underwood

MY INFLUENCE

My life shall touch a dozen lives,
  Before this day is done,
Leave countless marks, for good or ill,
  'ere sets the evening sun.

This is the wish I always wish,
  The prayer I always pray:
Lord, may my life help other lives,
  It touches by the way.

A CERTAIN SAMARITAN

A man went down from Jerusalem
On an old road long ago,
Blithely he walked that far-off day,
Going to Jericho.
But thieves lay waiting, who stripped him bare,
Wounding him, leaving him lying there.

A priest came, mumbling through his beard
Pious prayers, as the hurt one cried,
Pleading for help, and seeing his plight,
Passed by on the other side.
A Levite, also, after one look,
Departed, conning his holy book.

But "a certain Samaritan," going that way,
Had compassion, and kneeling down,
He bound his wounds, and he slaked his thirst,
And he carried him into the town.
"Which was the neighbor?" —which of these?
The question rings down the centuries.

"A certain Samaritan," name unknown.
Lives still because of a kindness shown.
—Grace Noll Crowell

Always be careful what you do.
For you'll never know who'll be watching you.
It may be someone old and wise.
It could be someone young and small.
It might be someone just your size.
Perhaps it's someone you don't know at all.
But whoever it is — whether stranger or friend—
Be a good example to the end!
—Ruth Annella White

THE CHRISTIAN LIFE

We can't teach everyone by our tongue. Let us live in such a way that good things will be caught by those who see our light.

A man's Sunday self and his weekly self are like two halves of a round-trip ticket; not good if detached.

Let your religion be seen. Lamps do not talk . . . they shine.

I would rather light one candle than to curse the darkness.

FRUITS OF THE SPIRIT

Faith

IF

IF one can be saved without faith, why did Paul say it was impossible to please God without it (Heb. 11:6)?

IF God promised to give faith when we ask for it, why are we told that faith comes by hearing and hearing by the Word of God (Rom. 10:17)?

IF "faith alone" is a wholesome doctrine and very full of comfort, why did James say that faith without works is dead (James 2:26)?

IF God has promised to save men regardless of the kind of faith they have, why did Paul make it so plain that "THERE IS ONE FAITH" (Eph. 4:4-6)?

IF the Lord will save without baptism, why did He command it (Acts 10:48)?

IF the Lord has promised us salvation without baptism, why did Peter say that it saves (I Peter 3:21)?

IF sprinkling and pouring are Scriptural baptism, why did Paul say there is one baptism, (Eph. 4:4-6) and that it is a burial (Rom. 6:4; Col. 2:11-12)?

IF we can receive remission of sins without baptism, why did Peter say baptism is for the remission of sins (Acts 2:28)?

IF we can get into Christ without baptism, why did Paul say we are baptized into His body (I Cor. 12:13)? Remember, the body and the church are the same thing (Col. 1:18).

IF we can be born again of the Spirit only, why did Christ say to be born of water and the Spirit (John 3:3-5)?

IF infant baptism is Scriptural, why did Christ command to baptize those who believe (Mark 16:15-16)? Remember, infants cannot believe.

IF infants are sinners, why did Christ teach that we must become like them to be saved (Matt. 18:3)?

IF God has promised salvation outside of the church, why did

Christ die for it (Acts 20:28, Eph. 5:25-27)?

IF the church has nothing to do about our salvation, why did the Lord add us to the church (Acts 2:47)?

IF men have the right to make laws and put them in the church, why did Christ say He had all authority (Matt. 28:18-20)?

IF man can be saved by obeying the commandments and doctrines of men, why did Christ say it is vain to worship and follow them (Mark 7:7)?

IF the Word of God is complete and can furnish us unto all good works, how can we make it better by adding or taking from it (II Tim. 3:16)?

IF the Word of God is able to save men, what need have we of anything else (John 8:32; 17:17)?

IF there is nothing in a name, why did Peter say that salvation is in the name of Christ (Acts 4:10-12)?

IF Christ taught that it is all right to wear any name, why did He call His family by His name (Eph. 3:14-15)?

IF a man cannot fall from grace, why did Peter say that one can be entangled and overcome, and that the latter end is worse than the first (II Pet. 2:20-22)?

IF it is not necessary to meet on the first day of the week, why did Paul say not to forsake the assembly (Heb. 10-25)?

IF there is no punishment for the wicked after death, why did Christ say they would go into everlasting punishment (Matt. 25:46)?

IF one can be saved without wholehearted obedience to the Lord, why did Paul say to "OBEY FROM THE HEART" (Rom. 6:17-18)? and the author of the Hebrews Book says Christ is "AUTHOR OF SALVATION TO ALL WHO OBEY HIM"(Hebrews 5:9)?

IF there is no hell but the grave, what is meant by "the damnation of Hell"(Matt. 23:33)?

IF one becomes a Christian when he believes, why wasn't King Agrippa a Christian (Acts 26:27-28)?

IF one can be saved and not be faithful, why did the Lord say to be "FAITHFUL UNTO DEATH" (Rev. 2:10)? Why did he also declare in Matthew 10:22 "HE THAT ENDURETH TO THE END SHALL BE SAVED"?

There's nothing so bad that it could not be worse;
There's little that time may not mend,
And troubles, no matter how thickly they come,
Most surely will come to an end.
Don't despond, don't give up, but just be yourself—
The self that is highest and best;
Just live every day in a sensible way,
And then leave to God all the rest.

Faith is deaf to doubt, dumb to discouragements, and blind to impossibilities.
Faith makes the uplook good, the outlook bright, and the future glorious.

FAITH

Do not say your are full of faith unless you are faithful.

God's servants can take criticism andd persecution. They serve under all kinds of pressure and without appreciation until the job is done.

They do things that need to be done — for the sake of Christ, not for the credit and honor.

When the crowd is cheering some will attempt to be heroic but God's man keeps at it, when nobody is around.

God's man is steadfast, unmovable always abounding in the work of the Lord. Men lacking in faith are always shirking.

The name of the game is score in sports, but in God's game of life it is "faithful unto death." Jesus said it.

Faith is the response we make to God.

Faith either removes mountains or tunnels through.

I PLACE MY HAND IN GOD'S

Each morning when I awake I say
I place my hand in God's today,
I know He'll walk close to my side
My every wandering step to guide.

He leads me with the tenderest care
When paths are dark and I despair—
No need for me to understand
If I but hold fast to His hand.

My hand in His, no surer way
To walk in safety through the day.
By His great bounty I am fed
Warmed by His love, and comforted.

When at the day's end I seek my rest
And realize how much I'm blessed.
My thanks pour out to Him, and then
I place my hand in God's again.

FAITH

Repentance is faith willing (Luke 13:6).
Confession is faith speaking (Matt. 10:32).
Baptism is faith acting (Acts 2:38).
Prayer is faith communing (Acts 2:42).
Lord's Supper is faith remembering (Acts 20:7).
Life is faith serving (Rev. 2:10c).
Giving is faith proving (I Cor. 16:2; II Cor. 8:1-5,24).

Faith is the soul's intake; love the soul's outlet.

When faith is lost, and honor dies, the man is dead!

THE BEST OF OUT OF MY TREASURE

HIS WAY IS BEST

I may not always know
 The way, wherein
 God leads my feet;
But this I know,
 That round my path,
 His love and wisdom meet.
And so I rest,
 Content to know,
 He guides my feet
 Where'er I go.
O, precious peace
 Within my heart;
O blessed rest to know
A Father's love
 Keeps constant watch
 Amid life's ebb and flow;
I ask no more than this;
 I rest content
 And know His way is best.

If we could push ajar the gates of life and stand within, and all God's
 working see,
We could interpret all our doubt and strife and for each mystery we'd
 find a key.
But not today! Then be content, dear heart, God's plans, like lilies pure
 and white, unfold;
We must not tear the close-shut leaves apart — Time will reveal the
 calyxes of gold.
And when some day we reach the land where wearied feet, with sandals
 loosed, may rest,
When clearly we shall see and understand, I know that we shall say,
 "God knew the best."

—Mary Riley Smith

FRUITS OF THE SPIRIT

There are some who believe the Bible,
And some who believe in part,
And some who trust with a reservation,
And some with all their heart,
But I know that its every promise
Is firm and true always;
It is tried as the precious silver
And it means just what it says

It is strange we trust each other,
And only doubt our Lord;
We will take the word of mortals,
And yet distrust His Word.
But, O, what light and glory
Would shine o'er our days,
If always we would remember
That He means just what He says.

It takes a lot of courage to put things in God's hands,
To give ourselves completely, our lives, our hopes, or plans;
To follow where He leads us, and make His will our own.
But all it takes is foolishness to go the way alone.

I cannot see the why or how
Of things the Lord doth now allow;
But this I know, my will must bow,
Then shall I know "hereafter."

The man who trusts men will make fewer mistakes than he who distrusts them.

Faith is letting down our nets into the untransparent depths at divine command, not knowing what we shall take!

> *Build a little fence of trust around today;*
> *Fill each space with loving work and therein stay;*
> *Look not through the sheltering bars upon tomorrow,*
> *God will help thee bear what comes, of joy or sorrow.*
> —Mary Frances Butts

Living without trust is like driving in the fog.

Faith is knowing there is an ocean because you have seen a brook.

Faith on a full stomach may be simply contentment — but if you have it when you're hungry, it's genuine.

Faith is built like a strong wall, with one worthy brick resting upon another.

The intuitions of faith are more certain than the conclusions of logic.

When faith is most difficult, it is most necessary.

> *HOLD FAST TO FAITH. Doubts, deeply multiplying*
> *Would draw the clouds of darkness closer down,*
> *And unbelief, like valley mists now lying,*
> *Shut out the glow of heaven's starry crown.*

With Christ no one can ever come to a "dead end." Faith always opens a way to the fulfillment of the divine purposes.
—Christian observer

The beginning of anxiety is the end of faith, and the beginning of true faith is the end of anxiety.
—Geo. Muller

With constant faith, surpassing doubt, I stand and watch the tide run out;
It will come back, I say to you; I do not know, and yet, I do!
At eventide I see the day put night on guard and go away;
Will morning come, the mists to woo? I do not know, and yet, I do!
I see the sear that autumns bring; will verdure come with waking spring?
My faith alone can answer true — I do not know, and yet, I do!
We see our loved ones droop and die; hath Heaven a brighter life on high?
Is death the vale that leads thereto? I do not know, and yet, I do!

Faith sees the invisible, believes the incredible, and receives the impossible.

Faith is the outstretched hand of the soul taking what Christ offers.

Faith sees farther than sight and trusts God the rest of the way.

Faith is a higher faculty than reason.

Hope

An atheist has a reason but no hope in his reason.
A hypocrite has a hope, but no reason for his hope.
A Christian has a reason for his hope and a hope for his reason.

The hopeful man sees success where others see failure, sunshine where others see shadows and storm.

CONSOLATION

We know not why there's sorrow, pain and grief.
We only know that we must have belief
That some time in a fairer, happier land
We'll meet our loved ones and will understand.
So courage, faith, and hope down life's highway
Must be our guardian angels 'till that day.
—Edna B. Zimmers

When hope is alive, the night is less dark; the solitude less deep, fear less acute.

Hope is faith going places.

Love

THE FRUIT OF THE SPIRIT

The fruit of the Spirit in terms of love are:
Joy is love exulting.
Peace is love in repose
Long-suffering is love untiring.
Gentleness is love enduring.
Goodness is love in action.
Faith is love on the battlefield.
Meekness is love under discipline.
Temperance is love in training.

FRUITS OF THE SPIRIT

LOVE

*Love that's pure and holy,
Love that's strong and true,
Love to save the sinner
And make his heart like new,
Love that's everlasting,
Love that will not fail,
Love to keep us happy
Through every stormy gale,
Love that keeps us faithful,
Love that drives out fear—
Such love comes from Jesus,
Our Lord who's ever near!*

—Rosie Krain

LOVE

*Great is the power of might and mind,
But only Love can make us kind . . .
And all we are or hope to be is empty
   pride and vanity . . .
If love is not a part of all,
The greatest man is very small!*

Selfishness with much can do little, but love with little can do much.

WHOM WE LOVE

*We flatter those we scarely know,
We please the fleeting guest,
And deal full many a thoughtless blow
To those we love the best.*

ONLY ONE POWER

Love is the bread that feeds the multitudes;
Love is the healing of the hospitals;
Love is the light that breaks through prison doors;
Love knows not rich, nor poor, nor good, nor bad.
But only the beloved, in every heart
One and the same, the incorruptible
Spirit divine, whose tabernacle is life.
Love, more than hunger, feeds the soul's desire;
Love more the spirit then the body heals;
Love is a star unto the darkened mind;
And they who truly are Love's servants leave,
And follow him, undoubting, to the end,
Past Justice and past Mercy, find at last,
Past Charity, past Pardon, Love enthroned,
Lord of all hearts, incarnate in man's soul.
—George Edward Woodberry

Hide in your heart a bitter thought,
Still it has power to blight;
Think love, although you speak it not,
It gives the world more light.
Ella Wheeler Wilcox

WHAT IS CHARITY?

It's silence when your words would hurt.
It's patience when your neighbor is curt.
It's deafness when the scandal flows.
It's thoughtfulness for another's woes.
It's promptness when stern duty calls.
It's duty when misfortune falls.

What may be bitter to endure, is oft sweet to remember.

*The love of God is greater
Than the measure of man's mind
And the heart of the Eternal
Is most wonderfully kind.*

CHRISTIAN LOVE

Christian love is a kind that cannot be found in any other religion or society. There are three Greek words translated "love" in English, but the one describing Christian love is a new and unique word. Let us look briefly at these three words, since our New Testament was originally written in Greek.

1. "Eros" is physical love, the glamorous "Hollywood" type. It lives on physical charms and is responsible for filling our divorce courts. It is a type of love that is selfish and departs as easily as it comes.

2. "Philos" is the love of a friend, parent, child, and even for God. It is a love that is willing to sacrifice, is for fellowship and communion among family and friends, and in the church. It is good, but not the highest type.

3. "Agape" presents a type of love that is so holy and overwhelming that the word is used when we are told that "God is love." It is used in John 3:16 " . . . God so loved the world. . . ." A self-giving love that knows no limits, and loves whether or not there is any response. The word is found 198 times in the New Testament referring to God's love to us, our love to God, and our love for our brethren.

This kind of love is received from God as we meditate to comprehend His love for lost sinners and for erring Christians. During communion our love may deepen. This "agape" love must underlay our Stewardship, our Service and our Worship. Think on these things.

—Francis M. Arant

Love divine has seen and counted every tear it caused to fall,
And the storm which love appointed was its choicest gift of all.

Give me wide walls to build my house of life—
The North shall be of Love, against the winds of fate;
The South of Tolerance, that I may outreach hate;
The East of Faith, that rises clear and new each day;
The West of Hope, that e'en dies a glorious way;
The threshold 'neath my feet shall be Humility;
The roof — the very sky itself — Infinity.
Give me wide walls to build my house of life.

Those who deserve love least, need it most.

To love abundantly is to live abundantly,
And to love forever is to live forever.
Hence, eternal life is inextricably bound up with love.
—Henry Drummond

CHARITY

There is so much good in the worst of us,
And so much bad in the best of us,
That it ill behooves any of us,
To find fault with the rest of us.

LOVE LISTENS

Love listens	Self's too busy
When someone talks	When someone talks
Love pauses	Self runs
And then walks	And often balks
Love hears	Self is deaf
When someone calls	When someone calls
Love lifts	Self disdains
When someone falls	When someone falls.

—Helyn C. Nelson

Love the one the most, who most needs it at the time.

A MUST FOR LIFE

The babies in the foundling home were dying and the doctors could not determine why. The children had no signs of disease; they simply lost interest in their food and toys, then grew weaker until they died. The team of United Nations doctors happened to be in the South American country, and the local doctors summoned them for help. After studying the children for a few days, the UN doctors gave this prescription: "For ten minutes of every waking hour, each child is to be picked up, hugged and kissed, petted and played with, then hugged and kissed some more." Within a short time, the strange epidemic disappeared, the children brightened, they ate again and played with their toys, and when their ten minutes came they held out their arms as the nurses approached. The UN doctors identified the fatal lethargy as "Marasmus," a mysterious and gradual emaciation of the body which seems to strike the very young and very old when people in between do not take time to show them enough love.

The measure of a Christian is not in the height of his grasp but in the depth of his love.

LOVE IS —

Slow to suspect, quick to trust;
Slow to condemn, quick to justify;
Slow to offend, quick to defend;
Slow to demand, quick to give.

The more one judges, the less one loves.

Joy

THE EXCHANGE

*If all my righteousness should buy
Joy-full thousand times it's worth
'Twould fill my cup with misery
But not one drop if mirth,
And all of Hell's deep searing flame
Of fires great I've built
Would only multiply my shame
But ne'er consume my guilt.*

*But praise the Lord who cleansed my cup,
On which I should have fed,
For now the wrath I need not sup
Christ took it in my stead.
His agony I can not tell,
Nor Calvary's grueling pain
He bore to save my soul from Hell
By cleansing every stain.*

*Lo now to me by grace divine
From Jesus' boundless store,
If I will but myself resign
To gain that open door
Through righteousness of Christ my King
Comes Joy beyond degree
With every breath God let me sing
Of Him who died for me.*
—Don Wort

The man who radiates good cheer, who makes life happier wherever he meets it, is always a man of vision and of faith.

FRUITS OF THE SPIRIT

CARRY SUNSHINE

Many people carry shadows
By the gloomy lives they live;
By their grouchy way of speaking,
And by what they do and give;
But there is a way of living
That is better far than this,
Blessing men with sunny brightness,
Helping them to joy and bliss.

You can carry sunshine, neighbor,
Carry sunshine day by day,
Which is done by righteous living—
Yes, by what you do and say;
And it makes you feel much better,
And your fellows that you meet,
When your face is wearing brightness
And your voice is kind and sweet.

Carry sunshine by your smiling,
By our gentleness and grace,
By the prayers you breathe for others
And the kindness of your face;
Though sometimes 'twill cost you money,
Cost you effort, work, and time;
Yet to be a sunshine toter
Is both noble and sublime.
—Walter E. Isenhour

When'er a noble deed is wrought,
When'er is spoken a nobel thought,
Our hearts in glad surprise
To higher levels rise.
—Longfellow

RADIATE JOY

It is man's essential duty to be joyous at all times. Sadness and joy have a deep influence on those around us; both are contagious emotions. It is therefore of utmost importance that man should radiate joy at all times.

—Szekely

Peace

PEACE AFTER A STORM

When darkness long has veiled my mind,
And smiling day once more appears,
Then, my Redeemer, then I find
The folly of my doubts and fears.

Oh, let me then at length be taught
What I am still so slow to learn:
That God is love, and changes not,
Nor knows the shadow of a turn.

Sweet truth, and easy to repeat!
But when my faith is sharply tried
I find myself a learner yet.
Unskilled, weak, and apt to slide.

But, O my Lord, one look from Thee
Subdues my disobedient will;
Drive doubt and discontent away,
And Thy rebellious one is still.

Thou art as ready to forgive
As I am ready to repine:
Thou therefore, all the praise receive;
Be shame and self-abhorrence mine.

SHUT IN

I know not why He has taken
  The work that I loved from my hand—
The work over which I have labored,
  And for which I had hoped and planned.

Nor why He has led me hither,
  With no one to help or teach;
But I trust in His infinite wisdom—
  He knows what is best for each.

Perhaps even here He has waiting
  Some work I have failed to see;
Some mission of love and compassion
  He has kindly reserved for me.

By keeping both cheerful and hopeful,
  When others are sad and depressed;
By doing each day what He bids me,
  And trusting to Him for the rest.

I know there are ways of serving,
  Which He only can understand;
He has taken the larger work from me,
  But the smaller is still at hand.

And so I will lovingly labor
  Just where He has placed me today,
And trust to His wisdom for guidance
  To walk in His own chosen way.

—Unknown

Those who bring sunshine to the lives of others cannot keep it from themselves.

—Sir James M. Barrie

AFTER THE STORM

Oh, blessed quietness that comes after strife.
Striving to want God's will,
Striving to trust that God is good,
Struggling to believe that God loves even me,
Fighting for certainty that God has a plan for my life,
Beating back great waves of selfish desires that
Surge and beat against the door of high resolve,
And then cease, to fight no more.
But to know, to know that God does love,
That God will guide, and to be not afraid.
—Clara Richardson

WHAT IS PEACE?

It is a calmness when the trials press;
It is a confidence that God knows best;
It is gentleness that's undisturbed;
It is a holy hush that is unpreturbed;
It is a quiet trust as on we plod;
It is a sweet reliance on our God!
—Georgia B. Adams

Goodness

Goodness consists not in the outward things we do, but in the inward things we are.

That which is striking and beautiful is not always good, but that which is good is always beautiful.

One of these days I must go shopping; I am completely out of self-respect. I want to exchange some self-righteousness I picked up the other day for some humility which they say is less expensive and wears longer. I want to look at some tolerance which is being used for wraps this season. Someone showed me some pretty samples of peace. We are a little low on that and one can never have too much of it. And by the way, I must try to match some patience that my neighbor wears. It is very becoming to her and I think it might look well on me. I might try on that little garment of longsuffering they are displaying. I never thought I wanted to wear it, but I feel myself coming to it. Also, I must not forget to have my sense of appreciation mended, and look around for some inexpensive everyday goodness. It is surprising how quickly one's stock of goodness is depleted.

FATHER IN HEAVEN

When I consider Thy goodness to me,
I seem to search in vain
For proper words of praise
To speak my thanks to Thee.

Yet, while fine words of praise
Could tell the way I feel—
Sharing something dear to me
Will make it seem more real.

Kindness

We flatter those we know the least,
And please the fleeting guest,
But many a thoughtless blow we give,
To those we love the best.

LET ME DO THE LITTLE THINGS

Lord, let me do the little things
Which may fall to my lot;
Those little inconspicuous ones
By others oft forgot.
A staff for age to lean upon,
Strong hands to help the weak;
A loving heart with open door
To all who solace seek.
To hold my tongue when hot words rise,
Speak kindly ones instead;
Nor harshly judge my fellowmen
In what they've done or said.
To share another's heavy load
By word or courage given;
And bring him nearer Heaven.
If, like the master, I can give
Myself for those I love,
Rich joy and peace shall come to me,
Sweet rest in Heaven above,
I know not when the day shall close
But when life's curfew rings,
I want my Lord to find me then
Still doing little things.

KINDLINESS

If you can think kindly and act kindly, too,
Wherever you are or whatever you do,
You will find through the day,
Along the way,
That folks will take kindly to you.
—Edna Huntington

If you are not kind, you are the wrong kind.

If any little word of mine
  May make a life the brighter,
If any little song of mine
  May make a heart the lighter,
God help me speak the little word
  And take my bit of singing
And drop it in some lonely vale,
  To set the echoes ringing!

No one is useless in this world who lightens the burden for someone else.

A GENTLE WORD

One gentle word that we may speak
Or one kind, loving deed,
May, though a trifle, poor and weak
Prove like a tiny seed;
And who can tell what good can spring
From such a very little thing?

TEACH US TO SHARE

God, thou hast given us so much—
We have a plenteous store!
Teach us to share, to yearn, to care—
Teach us to love Thee more.
Open our eyes, our ears, our hearts—
To every human need.
Help us to glory in Thy light
Instead of caste or creed.
Let us not rest content and safe
While hungry children call;
Teach us to love as Thou hast loved—
Thou, who art Lord of all.
              —Mary C. Adams

He who has conferred a kindness should be silent; he who has received one should speak of it.

HELP SOMEONE!

*Is there somebody who needs your help—
Someone that you've forgot—
That you might cheer by smile or song,
Perhaps someone you've taught?
There oft came times when everything
Seems to just go wrong;
You might forget your own troubles
And cheer someone along.
So look around! You'll find someone
That needs a kind word from you;
By helping others on the way,
God may be helping you.*

Kindness always pays, but it pays best when not done for pay.

*A careless word may kindle strife;
A cruel word may wreck a life;
A bitter word may hate instill;
A brutal word may smite and kill;
A gracious word may smooth away;
A joyous word may light the day;
A timely word may lessen stress;
A loving word may heal and bless.*

Never put off until tomorrow a kindness you can do today; never do today an unkindness that you can put off forever.

Every moment is the right one to be kind.

FRUITS OF THE SPIRIT

There's an old Chinese proverb
   That, if practiced each day,
Would change the whole world
   In a wonderful way . . .

Its truth is so simple,
   It's so easy to do,
And it works every time,
   And successfully, too . . .

For you can't do a kindness
   Without a reward,
Not in silver nor gold,
   But in joy from the Lord . . .

You can't light a candle
   To show others the way,
Without feeling the warmth
   Of that bright little ray . . .

And you can't pluck a rose,
   All fragrant with dew,
Without part of its fragrance
   Remaining with you.

If you sow kindness, you will reap a crop of friends.

      If you were busy being kind,
      Before you knew it you would find
      You'd soon forget to think 'twas true
      That someone was unkind to you.

      If you were busy being glad
      And cheering people who are sad,
      Although your heart might ache a bit,
      You'd soon forget to notice it.

Kindness is a hard thing to give away: It usually comes back.

CONFESSION

I missed the last auxiliary, Thursday night.
My little Timmy — well I couldn't turn out the light
And leave him sobbing in his little bed
With e'en a kindly sitter, as the ladies said.

And then the mothers' luncheon, Tuesday noon.
I meant to go, but my poor neighbor's wife
Was ill and sad; the time flew all too soon
While I fixed lunch and cheered her troubled life.

The church bazaar, now two weeks past—
I promised I would try to come!
But John came home, so dear and tired;
I could not go, for rarely are we two alone.

The ladies say I'm missing half my life
To stay at home when so much beckons me.
But how, friend, can I find the time?
My humble home claims all there is of me.

My hours are spent in drying little tears,
Loving my neighbors, caring for my own,
Tending the garden, hearing children's prayers.
And my reward? A heaven within my home.

—Lucy Hamilton

WASTE

A lovely deed was on my heart,
 I never set it free;
It died from lack of exercise
 And made its tomb in me.

Watch the little girl playing with her doll and you may discover if her mother is kind to her.

Patience

PATIENCE

To him who waits all things will come,
   But patience is not sitting down
   Upon the curbstones of the town;
Waits when skies are overcast and glum.
Nor is it watching day by day,
   Indifferent to the tasks at hand,
   Content in idleness to stand
Till something better comes our way.

The truly patient man is one
   Who, checked and hindered by the fates,
   Still bravely works the while he waits,
And holding fast unto his dream
   Though halted now, still plays the man
   And does whatever task he can,
However humble it may seem.

Day after day and week after week,
   Against the odds must patience fight,
   Clinging forever to the right.
'Tis not a virtue, pale and meek,
That merely sits beside the road
   And waits for luck to come along,
   But its alive, alert and strong
And bravely bears a heavy load!

—Edgar A. Guest

I have not so great a struggle with my voices, great and numerous as they are, as I have with my impatience.

THE PATIENCE OF A BULLDOG

I once knew a cow named "Patience." And it's no wonder. For as we use it today, the word "patient" means to be somewhat like a very tame old cow, not easily excited.

Patience is an important Christian virtue, often mentioned in the Bible, but very often misunderstood. The King James Bible did not use "patience" just as we use it. The original Greek word meant to be more like a bulldog than that old cow. It was not indifference but endurance; not politeness but persistence.

You have heard of the patience of Job, but probably haven't heard that Job would not have been called patient by most of us. "Patience" makes us think of taking things as they come without complaining, not being ruffled by difficulties. Job complained bitterly and cursed the day he was born, yet he held unwaveringly to his principles and would not give up his faith in God (James 5:7-11).

One who is truly "patient" (as it is used in the ancient English of the King James Bible) might be called stubborn. He certainly would not give in easily to evil, or give up his hope in Christ.

Some people call the same quality "Stick-to-it-iveness."

Steadfastness of faith persistence of hope, and unwavering loyalty in love are all parts of the virtue called "patience." How we need it!

"In your patience possess ye your souls" is not an order to hold your temper. It is a promise that if you are steadfast under persecution you will gain your lives (Luke 21:16-19).

One preacher used to say, "There are three abilities; know-ability, do-ability, and stick-ability, and the greatest of these is stick."

—Seth Wilson

Patience is bitter, but its fruit is sweet!

> *God grant us the serenity*
> *To live just day by day*
> *Not borrowing any troubles*
> *That may later come our way;*
> *To remember Jesus taught us*
> *To ask for daily bread;*
> *We should not ask for flour*
> *To bake for months ahead!*

Flowers leave their fragrance on the hand that bestows them.

Bees do not make honey and sting at the same time.

Patience is the ability to idle your motor when you feel like stripping your gears.

Temper is a funny thing; it spoils children, ruins men, and strengthens steel.

Humility

To seek humility is always dangerous. I discovered long ago that the best antidote to pride is not humility but gratitude. The more we cultivate a spirit of thankfulness for happy events and even unhappy ones . . . the more we shall be at leisure from ourselves and therefore free to think about God and other people. I think this is what moves us more and more toward Christian humility.

The test of a person's strength is the knowledge of his weakness.

If your your ears would save from jeers,
These things keep meekly hid;
Myself and I, and mine and my,
And how I do and did.

SECOND FIDDLE

The famous conductor of a great symphony orchestra was once asked which instrument he considered the most difficult to play. He thought for a moment and then said, "The second fiddle. I can get plenty of first violinists, but to find one who can play second fiddle with enthusiasm, that's a problem. And if we have no second fiddle we have no harmony." In our struggle to achieve success we must have humility to be able to play it expertly while waiting for assignment to the selection of the first violinist. HE THAT HUMBLETH HIMSELF SHALL BE EXALTED.

Humility is that vital ingredient in a man that makes him feel smaller as he becomes greater.

Humility is a strange thing. When you think you have it, you have lost it.

A fault which humbles a man is of more use to him than a virtue which puffs him up.

Mercy

Romans 6 tells us that in baptism we died to sin. The new creature is not to test God's mercy by sinning again.

THINK TWICE

Before you push a brother down, THINK TWICE.
Before at another's sin you frown, THINK TWICE.
For who are you in judgment hall
Your brother to the bar to call
To-morrow you may slip and fall — THINK TWICE.

Before the stinging gibe and quip — THINK TWICE.
Lest you yourself should feel the ship, THINK TWICE.
Withhold the gossip's idle sneer,
The thrust that draws the bitter tear,
For fortune's favoring gale may veer; THINK TWICE.

Is charity a quickened art? THINK TWICE
And does it thrill both hand and heart? THINK TWICE.
The mercy you to others show,
That mercy you should some day know;
With other's faults be kind, be slow —THINK TWICE.
—Boston Traveler

UNFAILING MERCIES

God never changes! Things and people alter;
   And blessings, one time prized, with time grow dim:
He changes not, nor varies, nor doth falter;
   And we are ever rich in having Him.

God's love abides, though others loves may perish,
   Though streams, whereat we drank, may sadly dry:
Yes, Though some love may fail we much did cherish,
   We still may find in Him a sure supply.

And — to God's care there surely is no ending!
   He who gave Christ can not withhold His care:
And we may know the joy of His attending
   And in the hour of need shall find Him there!
—J. Danson Smith

Honesty

HIDDEN MEANINGS

(Sometimes we really don't mean what we say or say what we mean.)

"WE HAD A FAIR CROWD LAST SUNDAY NIGHT"
 Had to count the pianist three times to make an even dozen.

"THE ENTHUSIASM OF OUR PEOPLE IS AMAZING"
 Before the service, people talk louder than the preacher can preach.

"TO TEACH THIS CLASS OF BOYS IS A REAL OPPORTUNITY"
 You will find out if you are a man or a mouse.

"WE NEED TO PREPARE OURSELVES FOR GREATER SACRIFICE"
 There'll be a special offering soon.

"THIS HAS BEEN THE GREATEST YEAR THE CHURCH HAS EVER KNOWN"
 When we met the budget by the skin of our teeth.

"EVERYBODY SHOULD HAVE TIMES OF QUIET"
 Please don't call me when I'm watching "Gunsmoke."

"I LOVE THAT KIND OF SERMON, PREACHER"
 First time in ages you have let us out on time.

"I BELIEVE CONSISTENT GIVING IS THE ANSWER"
 And I've been giving 25 cents since 1939, how's that for consistency . . .

"Finally, brethren, whatsoever things are true . . . honest . . . just . . . pure . . . lovely, whatsoever things are of good report. If there be any virtue, and if there be any praise, think on these things" (Phil. 4:8).

PLEASE BE VERY FRANK...

A minister's mail brought a request which read, "Will you please tell us all you can about Mr. 'A', his character, his habits, and his financial responsibilities?"

The minister's reply was, "I found his name on the roll when I came to serve this church. Neither he nor his family attend church. They say it is the only morning they can rest. His name is not recorded on our treasurer's books, so I can not tell anything about his financial responsibility. That is all I know."

Somehow the letter was revealed to Mr. 'A'. Was he ever burned up and did he tell the pastor! Among the things he said was, "Any minister worth the name should know that a man's relationship to the church and his financial contributions are of a confidential nature."

So the minister wrote a second letter. "All I know of the gentleman is of a confidential nature and he has explicitly requested that I do not tell the truth."

We like to give good references. Help make it easier for us. And then there is that matter of the final record which is beyond human evaluation. It's up to you.

When Johnny was six year old, he was with his father when they were caught speeding. His father handed the officer a five dollar bill with his driver's license and said, "It's O.K., son, everybody does it."

When he was eight he was permitted at a family council presided over by Uncle George, on the surest means to shave points off the income tax return. "It's O.K., Kid," his uncle said, "Everybody does it."

When he was 12 he broke his glasses on the way to school. His Aunt Francine persuaded the insurance company that they had been stolen and they collected $27. "It's O.K., Kid," she said, "Everybody does it."

When Johnny was sixteen he took his first summer job at a big supermarket. His assignment was to put the overripe tomatoes in the bottom of the boxes and the good ones on top where they would show. "It's O.K., Kid," the manager said, Everybody does it."

When he was 19, he was approached by an upperclassman who offered the test answers for $3. "It's O.K., Kid," he said, "Everybody does it."

Johnny was caught and sent home from college in disgrace. "How could you do this to your mother and me?" his father said. "You never learned anything like this at home!" His aunt and uncle were also shocked. "If there's one thing the adult world can't stand, it's a kid who cheats!"

Knowledge

WE KNOW SO LITTLE

The six-year-old who had succeeded in taking a simple toy apart and putting the pieces back together again as they were in the first place, declares with boyish enthusiasm, "Daddy, I know how to do everything!"

"If you want the real low-down on just any old thing, ask me" confidently advises the jaunty youth of twenty.

"If it's in my line, maybe I can tell you. I know my business from A to Z," says the man of thirty-five.

The field of human knowledge is so vast that even a specialist can hardly have more than a speaking acquaintance with the more important facts of his subject," admits the man of fifty.

"I have lived a good many years," confesses the man of seventy, "but I haven't learned much. What I know is so little; what I am ignorant of is so immense."

Our knowledge of nuclear energy has made us afraid of what we have learned.

If you have knowledge, let others light their candles at it.

"Knowledge cannot be stolen from us. It cannot be bought or sold. We may be poor, and the sheriff may come and sell our furniture, or drive away our cow, or take our pet lamb, and leave us homeless and penniless; but he cannot lay the law's hand upon the jewelry of our minds."
—Burritt

It's a great pity that things weren't so arranged that an empty head, like an empty stomach, wouldn't let its owner rest until he had put something in it.

> If a man knows not and knows not
> that he knows not — he is a fool.
> Shun him —
>
> If a man knows not and knows that
> he knows not — he is humble.
> Teach him —
>
> If a man knows but knows not that
> he knows — he is asleep
> Wake him up —
>
> But, if a man knows and knows that
> he knows — he is wise.
> Follow him.

Knowledge is proud that he knows so much; wisdom is humble that he knows no more.
—Cowper

An inward knowledge of God has solved all the paradoxes of His Word.

Human things must be known to be loved; but Divine things must be loved to be known.
—Pascal

Few minds wear out; more rust out.
—Bovee

Education without God is like a ship without a compass.

The stomach is the only part of man which can be fully satisfied. The yearning of man's brain for new knowledge and experience and for more pleasant and comfortable surroundings never can be completely met. It is an appetite which cannot be appeased.
—Thomas A. Edison

GUARDING THE GATES

The five senses, sight, smell, taste, hearing and feeling are our only means of acquiring knowledge. Psychologists tell us that there is nothing we receive through these gates of knowledge that is not forever indelibly impressed upon the brain or mind of every individual. Whatever we see, or hear, or touch, or taste, or smell will never be forgotten. We have difficulty bringing some of these to memory sometimes but they are always there in the subconscious mind to assist us or to plague us. It is no wonder that the Holy Spirit's teaching in the Bible warns us so strongly to beware of what we allow to go through these gates. THINK! Never permit anything to pass through one of these gates which you do not want to have haunt you in years to come. Guard the gates of wisdom.

FRUITS OF THE SPIRIT

Jesus said, "Learn of Me."

The Christians should allow others to light their candles from our knowledge.

It's good to have an open mind if you know what to let in.

Knowledge in truth is the great sun in the firmament. Life and power are scattered with all its beams.
—Daniel Webster

The degree of one's emotion varies inversely with one's knowledge of the facts — the less you know the hotter you get.
—Bertrand Russell

DID YOU KNOW?

Did you know that the Jewish child receives 335 hours of religious training each year; the Roman Catholic about 200 hours; while the average Protestant receives scarcely 30 hours?

A survey was given in Illinois to twelve Christian Churches ranging in average attendance from 50 to 250; 684 persons took the test. The questions were simple and factual truths known by most any primary student of the Bible. YET . . . 64 percent did not know what Book of the New Testament tells of the beginning of the church . . . 53 percent could not name five of Jesus' disciples . . . and 50 percent could not give the complete plan of salvation in its simplest form. The average grade was 55.3 percent.

Friend, every individual stands in desperate need of learning more of God's Word. There is no better place to learn about God's Word than in His House on His Day — the Lord's Day. It is a sad thing when people reach the place of feeling no need for this study.

The only commodity on earth that does not deteriorate with use is knowledge.

"Study to show thyself approved unto God; a workman that needeth not to be ashamed, rightly dividing the word of truth" (II Tim. 2:15).

CHRISTIAN ABC'S

Act instead of Argue
Build instead of Brag
Climb instead of Criticize
Dig instead of Depreciate
Encourage instead of Envy
Fight instead of Faint
Give instead of Grumble
Help instead of Harm
Invite instead of Ignore
Join instead of Jeer
Kneel instead of Kick
Love instead of Lampoon
Move instead of Mold
Nurture instead of Neglect
Obey instead of Obstruct
Pray instead of Pout
Quicken instead of Quit
Rescue instead of Ridicule
Shout instead of Shrink
Try instead of Tremble
Undergird instead of Undermine
Vindicate instead of Vilify
Witness instead of Wilt
EXterminate instead of EXcuse
Yield instead of Yell
Zip instead of Zig-zag.

Minds are like parachutes: They won't function unless open.

BILLY SUNDAY: I went to a theological book and crammed my brains with sentences long enough to make the jaw of a Greek professor squeak for a week. It didn't amount to shucks. So I went and loaded up the old gun with rough-on-rats, pecac, saltpeter, rock salt, dynamite and every other kind of explosive, and I pulled the trigger, and that Pharisee gang has been on the run every since.

Some people drink at the fountain of knowledge, other just gargle noisily.

Knowledge does not comprise all which is contained in the large term of education. The feelings are to be disciplined; the passions are to be restrained; true and worthy motives are to be inspired; a profound religious feeling is to be instilled, and pure morality inculcated under all circumstances. All this is comprised in Education.
—Daniel Webster

Knowledge humbles the great man, astonishes the common man and puffs up the little man.

I used to know all the answers — but my folks have been thinking up new questions.

BLESSINGS

America

AMERICA: READ THIS

Character, integrity, self-reliance — it is the loss of these American traits that is leaving us more impoverished than the outflow of gold.

As long as Americans earned what they were paid, produced more for more wages, saved for their own security, paid their bills and demanded that others do the same . . . there was no worry about gold, or the value of the dollar. The dollar was impregnable because American character was behind it.

But when the greedy something-for-nothing, the whining somebody-else-not-me selfishness has sapped American character, American strength goes out with it, as it always does.

Oliver North has been quoted as saying the government has the responsibility to promote the general welfare not to provide welfare to the general public.

A NOTED PREACHER OBSERVES

Would you not think that in such an hour, with the foundations crumbling, with humanity wallowing in blood and tears, churches would be crowded and men setting their houses in order and getting right with God? Far from it; revelry and not repentance is the spirit of the age. America is at play, not at prayer.

SHAMEFUL!

America spends 8 hours at movies to 1 at church; only 1 in 12 regularly attends church; 7 out of 8 quit by age 15; has 3 times as many liquor places as churches; gives over 3 times as much to alcoholism as to religion!

BUT WHAT ABOUT AMERICA?

Russia is not known for its religious emphasis; but instead for its teaching of atheism. The Russian cosmonaut stated in Seattle recently, "I circled the earth 13 times and I never saw God up there."

Today in Russia, only 6.2% of the people attend any church on any given Sunday. Most of these are older people, very few youth are interested in the church.

40 years ago in America on any given Sunday, 46% of the population was in some church. We still claim to be a Christian nation, and pray that God will be with us. YET TODAY ONLY 7.6% OF OUR POPULATION IS TO BE FOUND IN CHURCH on any given Lord's Day, according to one recent survey. This is slightly more than 1% ahead of Godless Russia.

America is rapidly going blind. Let us wake up and return to God.

—Author Unknown

THINK THIS ONE THROUGH... IN TEN YEARS

Church membership in the U.S. has increased 30% in the last ten years! BUT...

Illegitimacy has increased 300% in the same period of time.

Pornography is increasing four time faster than our population, approaching a 20 billion dollar a year figure!

Venereal disease has increased 72% in the past years! (In spite of miracle drugs).

For every dollar spent by our churches (all faiths and sects) we spend $12,000 on crime each year!

There are 175,000 more taverns in the U.S. than the combined total of all buildings dedicated to the worship of God!

Combine all of the money we give to all churches, synagogues, temples, etc., and we give eight times this amount each year to gamblers!

DeTocquerville once said, "America is great because she is good. If she ceases to be good she will cease to be great."

WHAT AMERICA NEEDS

- A leader like Moses, who refused to be called the son of Pharaoh's daughter, but was willing to go with God.
- Army generals like Joshua, who knew God and could pray and shout things to pass rather than blow them to pieces with atomic energy.
- A food administrator like Joseph, who knew God and had the answer to famine.
- Preachers like Peter, who would not be afraid to look people in the eye and say, "Repent or perish," and denounce their personal as well as national sins.
- Mothers like Hannah, who would pray for a child that she might give him to God, rather than women who are delinquent mothers of delinquent children.
- Children like Samuel, who would talk to God in the night hours.
- Physicians like Luke, who could care for physical needs and introduce their patients to Jesus Christ, who is a specialist in spiritual things.
- A God like Israel's, instead of a "dollar god," the "entertainment god," and the "auto god."
- A Saviour like Jesus, who could and would save from the uttermost to the uttermost.

Men came here (to America) in the first place not to be "free" to do what they want, but to be free to do what they "ought."

Americans used to shout, "Give me liberty!" Now they just leave off the last word.

Liberals in government are the ones who want to take our money and give it away — not their own.

The average American takes 19,689 steps daily — mostly in the wrong direction.

Freedom

COMMUNISM

>A stranger came to our town
>He was tall and dressed in black
>He had a briefcase in his hand
>And wore a derby hat.

He went about from house to house
And wrote down all our names.
Your homes, your schools, your churches
Must undergo a change.

>Your teachers and your preachers
>Have been removed he said
>Your democracy is gone, and
>Communism has come instead.

You'll move to public centers
To work in mines and farms
Your children will learn doctrines
And sleep in sheds and barns.

>Their love for homes and parents
>Will be frozen into hate
>They'll renounce their religion
>For the worship of the state.

Your girls will work in shops and hovels
Their faces drawn and thin
Their clothes are course and grimy
And they domicile with men.

>I awoke. T'was but a dream
>I'm glad it wasn't true.
>It's happened in other countries
>Will it come to me and you?

HOW DO YOU VOTE?

A sermonette by Dr. Kick Hillis says — "I saw them — tens of thousands of them. I interviewed many of these people. Though every story was different, each contained the same element of cost:"

"For my vote I gave up my parents."

"For mine I turned over everything I owned."

"For my vote I surrendered my entire family."

"It is better to be a beggar in Hong Kong than to be anything in Red China."

"I could not stand to have my children told there was no God."

"Our church was taken away and our Bible and hymn books confiscated. We were ordered not to meet together in worship. This made life so useless. I knew I couldn't live this way. I fled."

With courage, and a high cost they voted for the things they believed — for the Bible, Christ, His Church, Christian ideals and the freedom to worship. They put some of us to shame. How did you vote last Sunday? — LHF

WAKE UP, AMERICANS

In 1787 Edward Gibbon, the great English historian, completed his notable work, *The Decline and Fall of the Roman Empire.* Here is the way he accounted for the fall of the great Empire:

1. The rapid increase in divorce; the undermining of the dignity and sanctity of the home, which is the base of human society.

2. Higher and higher taxes, and the spending of public moneys for free bread and circuses for the benefit of the populace.

3. The mad craze for pleasure; sports becoming every year more exciting and more and more brutal.

4. The building of gigantic armaments when the real enemy was within, in the decadence of the people.

5. The decay of religion — faith fading into mere form, losing touch with life and becoming impotent to warn and guide the people.

IT DEPENDS ON YOU

The average age of the world's great civilizations has been 200 years. Those nations progressed through this sequence:
From bondage to spiritual faith.
From spiritual faith to great courage.
From courage to liberty.
From liberty to abundance.
From abundance to selfishness.
From selfishness to complacency.
From complacency to apathy.
From apathy to dependence.
From dependence back again to bondage.
In fourteen years the United States will be two hundred years old. This cycle is not inevitable.
"IT DEPENDS ON YOU."

THE FOUR FREEDOMS

We have freedom from want, and use it to eat junk, drink poisonous beverages, and wear outlandish clothing.

We have freedom of speech. We use it to tell dirty stories, to maliciously gossip about our neighbors and acquaintances, and to take God's name in vain.

We have freedom of the press, and with it we run moronic comic strips, conduct Hollywood gossip columns about our failure in marriage relationships, and detail the most vicious and villainous crimes imaginable.

We have freedom of worship, and use it as a freedom FROM worship, never going to God's house to give gratitude to Him for His many and wonderful blessings.

And because we misuse what we have been given, it should come as very little surprise when God takes them away!

If communism is so wonderful you would think they'd take down the iron curtains and put is some picture windows.

HOW CHRISTIAN IS OUR NATION? THINK

Now I sit me down in school
Where praying is against the rule.
For this great nation, under God,
Finds public mention of Him odd.

Any prayer a class recites
Now violates the Bill of Rights.
Any time my head I bow
Becomes a Federal matter now.

Teach us of stars, of pole and equator
But make no mention of their Creator.
Tell us of exports in Denmark and Sweden
But not one word on what Eve did in Eden.

The law is specific, the law is precise
Praying out loud is no longer nice.
Praying aloud in a public hall
Upsets believers in nothing at all.

In silence alone can we meditate
And if God should get the credit, great.
This rule, however, has a gimmick in it;
You've got to be finished in less than a minute.

So all I ask is a minute of quiet
If I feel like praying, then maybe I'll try it.
If not, O Lord, this plea I make:
Should I die in school, my soul You'll take.

Socialism in our nation will become top heavy. Those who demand a hand out will increase and vote for the cowardly politician who will promise it.

When God made the oyster he guaranteed his absolute economic and social security. He built the oyster a house, his shell, to shelter and protect him from his enemies. When hungry, the oyster simply opens his shell and food rushes in for him. He has freedom from want.

But when God made the eagle he declared: "The blue sky is the limit — build your own house." So the eagle built on the highest mountain. Storms threaten him every day. For food he flies through miles of rain and snow and wind.

The eagle, not the oyster, is the emblem of America.

It is no more reasonable to damn our economic system because freedom permits men to abuse their opportunities under the system, than it would be to charge the Church with responsibility for the sins of men who, in exercising that same freedom, refuse to abide by the teachings of the Church.

—Alfred P. Haake

It is taxation without representation when government uses our tax money to advertise lotteries and to promote gambling.
—Don Earl Boatman

People are not free when imprisoned by leaders who put up iron curtains and stone walls. Ignorance of truth is the stronghold of tyrants.

Friends

There is an old story about a rich man without friends who wanted to know why a certin poor man had so many. The faithful servant, who went into the market place and along the highways to find out, brought back this simple answer: "He has friends because he is one."

A minister was awakened at 6:30 by a prishioner with some freshly killed meat for the parson. The man thought it was a big joke to find the minister in bed and asked "Don't you ever work?" A few nights later at 11:00 p.m. the minister came by the farmer's house which was darkened. He rang the doorbell until the alarmed farmer came to the door, then asked, "Don't tell me you're in bed at this hour. Don't farmers ever work?" They remained the best of friends.

Take care that the face which looks out from your mirror in the morning is a pleasant face — you may not see it again all day, but others will.

SAY SO

Does a neighbor help a little,
 As along the way you go—
Help to make your burden lighter?
 Then why not tell him so?

Does a handclasp seem to lift you
 From the depth of grief and woe,
When an old friend shares your sorrow?
 Then why not tell him so?

Does your heavenly Father give you
 Many blessings here below?
Then on bended knees before Him,
 Frankly, gladly, tell Him so!

A friend is one to whom one may pour out all the contents of one's heart — chaff and grain together — knowing that the gentlest hands will sift it, keeping what is worthwhile.

If a man does not make new acquaintances as he advances through life, he will soon find himself left alone. A man, sir, should keep his friendship in constant repair.

Some friends remain faithful to us in misfortune, but only the loftiest will remain faithful after our errors and sins have come to light.

The only safe and sure way to destroy an enemy is to make him your friend.

YOUR BEST FRIEND

Love your enemy!
He is your truest friend.
He spurs you to accomplish
Your every worthy end.
Faithfully he scorns you,
Lest you become too proud
All your friends are numbered
But your enemies are a crowd.

Love your enemy!
No virtue could be won
Without his hateful help.
He is a benison.
So be faithful to him,
And never once forget
How much he does for you.
He is your best friend yet!
—Alice Josephine Wyatt

The reason a dog has so many friends is that he wags his tail instead of his tongue.

THE FRIEND WHO STANDS BY

When trouble comes your soul to try
You love the friend who just stands by.
Perhaps there's nothing he can do;
The thing is strictly up to you,
For there are troubles all your own
And paths the soul must tread alone;
Times when love can't smooth the road,
Nor friendship lift the heavy load.
But just to feel you have a friend
Who will stand by until the end,
Whose sympathy through all endures,
Whose warm handclasp is always yours,
It helps somehow to pull you through,
Although there's nothing he can do.
And so with fervent heart we cry
"God bless the friend who just stands by."
—C.W. Holmes

WHAT I CALL A FRIEND

One whose grip is a little tighter
One whose smile is a little brighter,
One whose deeds are a little whiter,
   That's what I call a friend.
One who'll lend as quick as borrow,
One who's the same today as tomorrow,
One who'll share your joy and sorrow,
   That's what I call a friend.
One whose thoughts are a little cleaner,
One whose mind is a little keener,
One who avoids those things that are meaner,
   That's what I call a friend.
One who's been fine when life seems rotten
One whose ideals you've not forgotten,
One who has given you more than he's gotten.
   That's what I call a friend.

AND YE SHALL FIND

If you would seek
  Along life's way
A friend to walk
  With you each day;
A friend to give
  You strength, and aid
You through the night
  When you're afraid;
If you would seek
  (And seek you must)
To find a friend
  In whom to trust
A friend to keep
  You from despair,
Someone you know
  Is always there,
Then seek no more,
  For here's the end
To your long search:
  Make God your Friend.

Too many cutting remarks can chop up the strongest friendship.

The most I can do for my friend is simply to be his friend. I have no wealth to bestow on him. If he knows that I am happy in loving him, he will want no other reward.

A friend is one who knows all about you and likes you just the same.

We spend a lifetime making true friends — and only seconds destroying them with thoughtless words.

A friend is one before whom I may think aloud.
—Ralph Waldo Emerson

A drunk behind the wheel is not your friend if you are in the car.

A friend steps in when the whole world steps out.

Opportunity

WASTED TIME

*The day slipped by and time was spent
And all the good things that I meant
To do were left undone because
I had no time to stop and pause,
But rushed about, went here and there,
Did this and that, was everywhere;
I had no time to kneel and pray
For that lost soul across the way;
I had no time to meditate
On worthwhile things.*

*No time to wait,
And so I wonder, after all,
When life is over and I'm called
To meet my Saviour in the sky
Where saints live on and never die,
If I can find one soul I've won
To Christ by some small deed I've done;
Or will I hang my head and whine,
"Forgive me, God, I had no time."*

I SHALL NOT PASS THIS WAY AGAIN

I shall not pass this way again,
   The thought is filled with sorrow
The good that I should do today,
   I may not do tomorrow.
If I this moment shall withhold,
   The help I should be giving,
Some soul may die, and I will lose
   The greatest joy of living.

Only the present hour is mine,
   I may not have another
In which to speak a kindly word,
   Or help a fallen brother.
The path of life leads straight ahead,
   We can retrace it never,
The daily record that we make
   Will stand unchanged forever.

To cheer and comfort other souls,
   And make the pathway brighter;
To lift the load from other hearts,
   And make their burden lighter,
This is the work we have to do,
   It must not be neglected,
We must improve each passing hour,
   Is of us all expected.

I shall not pass this way again,
   Oh, then with high endeavor,
May I my life and service give
   To Him who reigns forever.
Then will the failures of the past,
   No longer bring me sadness;
And His approving smile will fill
   My soul with joy and gladness.

DAYS

Each day is a storehouse given you
   Fresh every morn from God's hand;
Do you stop to think of this
   When at its door you stand?
Twenty-four empty, waiting hours,
   All ready for you to fill with
Worthwhile thoughts and worthwhile deeds
   And service, if you will.

You're given a chance to store
   Away treasures of love and joy,
And satisfaction of work well done
   That time cannot destroy.
So put your best into all your day
   With eyes opened wide to see, and
Eager hands stretched out to grasp
   Each opportunity.

   Yesterday is a cancelled check—
   Tomorrow is a promissory note—
   Today is the only asset you have.
   Spend it wisely.

THE HILL

Two little men stood looking at a hill,
   One was named "can't" and the other
   was named "will."
Can't said, "I never in the world can
   climb this hill."
So there he is at the bottom of it still.
Will said, "I'll get to the top because I will."
   And there he is now at the top of the hill;
At the bottom is "can't"; at the top is "will."

PUBLIC WORSHIP

Some suggestions on how to get the most out of church attendance and public worship:

1. GO GLADLY: "I was glad when they said unto me, Let us go into the house of the Lord" (Psalm 122:1).
2. WORSHIP REVERENTLY: "Oh, come let us worship and bow down; let us knell before the Lord our maker" (Psalm 95:6).
3. PRAY EARNESTLY: "Confess your faults one to another, that ye may be healed. The effectual fervent prayer of a righteous man availeth much" (James 5:16).
4. SING JOYFULLY: "O come, let us sing unto the Lord, let us make a joyful noise to the rock of our salvation. Let us come before His presence with thanksgiving, and make a joyful noise unto Him with psalms (Psalm 95:1,2).
5. GIVE FREELY: "Give unto the Lord the glory due unto His name; bring an offering, and come into His courts" (Psalm 96:8). "Freely ye have received, freely give" (Matt. 10:8).
6. LISTEN ATTENTIVELY: "Take heed what ye hear" (Mark 4:24). "Wherefore, my beloved brethren, let every man be swift to hear" (James 1:19). "Therefore, we ought to give the more earnest heed to things we have heard, lest at any time we should let them slip" (Heb. 2:1).
7. ACT UNITEDLY: "Behold, how good and how pleasant it is for bretheren to dwell together in unity (Psa. 133:1).
8. LIVE PEACEFULLY: "The Lord bless thee and keep thee: the Lord make His face to shine upon thee, and be gracious unto thee; the Lord lift up His countenance upon thee, and give thee peace" (Num. 6:24-26).
9. DO DUTIFULLY: "Be ye doers of the word, and not hearers only (James 1:22).

—Latonia Christian

So many are lost because in youth they are "too young"; in manhood, "to busy"; in maturity, "too worried"; when aged, "too old"; when sick, "too ill"; when dead, "too late." NOW is the acceptable time with God. Don't wait until it is too late!!

I KNOW SOMETHING GOOD ABOUT YOU

Wouldn't this old world be better
If the folks we meet would say,
"I know something good about you,"
And then treat us just that way.
Wouldn't it be fine and dandy
If each handclasp warm and true,
Carried with it this assurance;
"I know something good about you!"
Wouldn't things here be more pleasant
If the good that's in us all
Were the only things about us
That folks bothered to recall!!
Wouldn't life be lots more happy
If we'd prasie the good we see,
For there's such a lot of goodness
In the worst of you and me!
Wouldn't it be nice to practice
This fine way of thinking, too—
"You know something good about me,
I know something good about you!"

All great people have climbed up through difficulties. If their lives had been easy we would have never heard of them. In overcoming obstacles, one develops courage, strength, determination, and a ruggedness that may be needed for some great responsibility and opportunity farther up the road.

What greater calamity can fall upon a nation than the loss of worship?

—Emerson

If you don't have time to do the job right, where will you find the time to do it over?

WHAT DO YOU THINK?

If you think you are beaten, you are.
If you think you dare not, you don't
If you'd like to win, but you think you can't
It's almost certain you won't.

Life's battles don't always go
To the stronger or faster man;
But sooner or later the man who wins
Is the man who thinks he can.

Four things come not back — the spoken word, the sped arrow, the past life, and the neglected opportunity.

Recite your blessings and your face will respond with a smile, not a frown.

If God writes opportunity on one side of the door, He writes responsibility on the other side.

Blessings

There is a story of a small boy who was seen going along the road with his shoulders bent under the weight of a younger child. Someone commiserated with him, and the small boy replied, "He's not a heavy load; he's my little brother."

The pessimist says: "My cup is half empty." The optimist says: "My cup is half full." The Christian says: "My cup runneth over."

COUNT YOUR BLESSING

If Ol' Man Self Pity has got you
  Sit right down with pencil in hand,
List all the things your are grateful for
  They are like counting grains of sand.

Perhaps a new talent has come to you
  Or your work takes on new meaning,
Or maybe your day has become brighter
  By friendliness of people you are meeting.

Maybe you've taken a longed-for trip
  Or perhaps been restored to health,
Or been able to overcome loneliness
  Or even had unexpected wealth.

Whatever may be your blessings
  Just take time to jot them down,
You'll have a list to amaze you
  And surely chase away your frown.

As one's heart is filled with gratitude
  Every bit of Self Pity will depart,
There can never be a feeling of heaviness
  In a truly grateful heart.
  —Kathryn Ballenger

NEED MAKES THE DIFFERENCE

The rain causes the farmer to rejoice. His crops need it and it will help him to feed the multitudes. Those on a picinc complain that they can't go and enjoy their food.

Counting your hardships and miseries makes a deep rut and no one will want to be in it with you.

THE SHIP CAME IN

The sole survivor of a shipwreck was cast upon an uninhabited island. After a while he managed to build a rude hut in which he placed his "Little All" that he had saved from the sinking ship. He prayed to God for deliverance, and anxiously scanned the horizon each day to hail any ship that might pass. One day, upon returning from a hunt for food, he was horrified to find that his hut was in flames. All that he had was gone. To his limited vision, it was the very worst that could happen, and he cursed God. Yet, the very next day a ship arrived, "We saw your smoke signal," the captain said.

Sometimes our sorrows and troubles might just be smoke signals to bring a great help.

THE LAYMAN'S BEATITUDES

1. Blessed is the man whose calendar contains prayer meeting night.
2. Blessed is the man who does not remain away from the church because it drizzles.
3. Blessed is the man who can stay over an hour in a church service.
4. Blessed is the man who loves his Lord's work with his pocketbook as well as with his heart.
5. Blessed is the man who leaves the back pew for the late-comers.
6. Blessed is the man whose watch keeps church time as well as business time.
7. Blessed is the man who does not have a summer "layoff" from his religion.
8. Blessed is the man whose eyesight will stand as much reading of the Bible as of the Sunday Newspaper.

Man, like the bridge, was designed to carry the load of the moment, not the combined weight of a year at once.

—Wm. A. Ward

DAY BY DAY

Lord, give me strength for this day's task—
  From rising until setting sun
  In everything Thy will be done.
Not for tomorrow would I ask,
  At twilight hour, oh, may I say,
  "The Lord has been my guide today."

And if for me tomorrow dawn
  Upon this earth, I'll gladly say,
  "Thank God for another day."
And praise His name another morn.
  Thus day by day I'll work and pray
  Till dawns at least God's endless day.
    —Mary H. Willingham

They say school children are weak in mathmatics. If they can count to 50 they still couldn't count all their blessings.

TODAY

Today is ours — Let's live it.
And love is strong — Let's give it.
A song can help — Let's sing it.
And peace is dear — Let's bring it.
The past is gone — Don't rue it.
Our work is here — Let's do it.

The world is wrong — Let's right it.
If evil comes — Let's fight it.
The road is rough — Let's clear it.
The future vast — Don't fear it.
Is faith asleep? — Let's wake it.
Today is ours — Let's take it.

THE WEALTH I POSSESS

I've figured my blessings, I've counted my cares,
I've balanced the book of my daily affairs,
A column for credits, a column for debt,
A place for unkindness I cannot forget.

And yet there were pleasures along with the pain,
And seldom a loss but some little gain.
I find I have more than I have ever known,
Astonished to note all the wealth that I own.

I've figured my blessings but little, I fear;
My cares I have counted each day and each year.
Forgotten the pleasure, the pain I have kept,
Forever in mind every moment I wept.

The loss I remember, the sorrow recall,
The happiness hardly remember at all.
But now I have taken a balance at last,
The joys and griefs of the present and past.

I've figured my blessings, I've set them apart
In a book I am keeping, the book of my heart,
I need not set down all the troubles and care,
I find I already have it written there.

But I had forgotten the love that is mine—
It took a whole column, the hate but a line.
The joy already greater, the grief always less,
I'm really astonished the wealth I possess.

—Douglas Malloch

Don't shy away from difficulty, they are so often the very means by which we are proven to be worthy of God given responsibilities. Rejoice in the difficulty, knowing that God has counted you worthy of the test. "We are tried by fire."

THE PARABLE OF THE ANT

The ant was bearing a tremendous load. The piece of straw was several times its size. It seemed impossible that the ant could manuever with such weight on its back. Finally, it came to a narrow crack in the sun-parched soil. It was an insignificant crevasse — there were many around just like it. But the gap was too wide for the ant to cross. Pausing at the crack, in apparent reflection, the ant then removed the straw from its back and as if by previous plan, spanned the opening with the straw. Then, crossing over the bridge of straw, he once again picked up the burden and continued on his way.

He had made a bridge of his burden!

How like this should the Christian way be. How quick we are to label an obstruction as an impasse. How often we give up under the weight of continuous burdens. Should we not refresh our memories with the word of the Master, "Come unto me all ye who labor and are heavy laden, and I will give you rest?" Christ did not bear the cross — He used it.

THE BEST THINGS IN LIFE

The best and sweetest things in life are things you cannot buy;
The music of the birds at dawn, the rainbow in the sky.
The dazzling magic of the stars, the miracle of light.
The precious gifts of health and strength, of hearing, speech and sight.
The peace of mind that crowns a busy life of work well done.
A faith in God that deepens as you face the setting sun,
The boon of love, the joy of friendship. As years go by,
You find the greatest blessings are the things you cannot buy.
                                                —Patience Strong

Those whom God blesses, devils cannot curse.

We have the blessing of God's power through prayer.

THE UNBOUGHT GOOD

What would our land be worth to us,
  The land we sell and buy,
And fence about, and call our own,
  Without God's open sky
To hold the sunset's rose and gold,
  The white clouds floating high?

What would our fields bring forth for us
  Without the gifts He sends,
Without the sunshine and the rain
  On which our bread depends,
His little water-brooks to flow,
  His birds to be our friends?

Oh, as the land without the sky
  That ever bends above,
So barren and so desolate
  Our lives without His love;
The blessings that no gold can buy
  Our greatest riches prove.

Said one, "I planned an ultra-modern home."
  But a Hungarian woman whispered, "I have no home."
Said another, "I dreamed of a country place for luxurious weekends."
  But a refugee child kept saying, "I have no country."
I started to purchase a new kind of washing machine;
  When a woman said softly, "I have nothing to wash."
I wanted a quick-freezing unit for storing quantities of goods.
  But across the water came the cry, "I have no food."
I ordered a new car for the pleasure of my loved ones;
  Then an orphan murmured, "I have no loved ones."

The greatest sum in addition is to count your blessings.

TAX EXEMPT INVESTMENTS

A tax assessor came one day to a poor minister of the gospel to determine the amount of taxes the minister would pay.

"What property do you possess?" asked the assessor.

"I am very wealthy," replied the minister.

"List your possessions please," the assessor instructed.

The minister replied:

"First, I have everlasting life (John 3:16).

Second, I have a mansion in heaven (John 14:2).

Third, I have peace that passeth understanding (Phil.4:7).

Fourth, I have joy unspeakable (I Peter 1:8).

Fifth, I have divine love that never faileth (I Cor. 13:8).

Sixth, I have a faithful, pious wife (Proverbs 18:24).

Seventh, I have healthy, happy, obedient children (Exodus 20:12).

Eighth, I have true loyal friends (Proverbs 18:24).

Ninth, I have songs in the night (Psalms 42:8).

Tenth, I have a crown of life (James 1:12).

The tax assessor closed his book and said, "Truly you are a very rich man, but your property is not subject to taxation."

I thank God for the bitter things;
  They've been a "friend to grace,"
They've driven me from the paths of ease
  To storm the secret place.

I thank Him for the friends who failed
  To fill my heart's deep need;
They've driven me to the Savior's feet,
  Upon His love to feed.

I'm grateful too, through all life's way
  No one could satisfy,
And so I've found in God alone
  My rich, my full supply!

—Florence White Willett

"And we know that all things work together for good to them that love God, to them who are called according to his purpose" (Romans 8:28).

Miserable people see thorns, but those who want to count blessings see roses.

Some people make themselves miserable and those around by counting their miseries.

NATIONAL EVILS

War

EDITORIAL — LONDON PRESS — 1942

We have been a pleasure loving people honoring God's day picnicing and bathing. Now the shores are barred, no picnics and bathing.
We have preferred motor travel to the spritiual growth. Now there is a shortage of motor fuel.
We have ignored the ringing of church bells calling us to worship. Now no bells ring except to warn of invasion.
We have left the churches half empty when they should have been filled with worshippers. Now the churches are in ruins.
We would not listen to the ways of peace. Now we are forced to listen to the wails of war.
The money we would not give to the Lord's work is now taken from us in taxes and high prices.
The service God has asked of us is now conscripted for the country.
Lives we refused to live under God's directions are now under the nations control
Nights we would not spend watching unto prayer are now spent in anxious air raid precautions.

Wars are fought by boys, suffered by women, paid for by posterity, starvation by little children and usually started by old men who should know better.

Men will carry guns until they learn to carry crosses.

The cost of the war with Japan was $300,000,000,000. With that sum we could have sent $1,500,000 missionaries for 50 years.

MY WISH

*If I could have my wish today,
And only one,
This would I say:
That peace on earth,
Good will to men,
Might reign supreme,
And ne'er again
In all the ages yet to come
Would there be war.*
—Ruth Smeltzer

War is not the last resort, in the most cases it is the first resort. Dictators make it happen.

THE COST OF KILLING

Harold Osen, in the New York Daily News suggests that in primitive times the cost of killing was practically nothing. Even as late as the time of Julius Caesar (100-44 B.C.) it cost only 75 cents to kill an enemy soldier. During the time of Napoleon, the cost had arisen to almost $3,000. In the Civil War, the mortality expense was $5,000. The four years of World War I brought the cost up to $21,000 and in World War II the price amounted to $55,000. The cost of killing in the "Police action" in Korea reached the figure of $75,000 for each enemy soldier killed.

When will men sit at the feet of the Great Galilean and learn to "beat their swords into plowshares and their spears into pruning hooks"?

In contrast to the above, it has been suggested that it costs slightly less than $15 to convert a man and make him a Christian. Our way of murder and war is costly indeed, and it solves no problems. It only creates more. Christ's way of salvation is the only answer to the problems of nations and men — and it costs so little. Tragedy it is that we are not willing to pay what it costs.

The war that will end war will not be fought with guns.

❦

Worldliness

Commercialists advise us to:
1. Wake up with caffeine.
2. Keep going on nicotine.
3. Kill pain with aspirin.
4. Stay alive with Geritol.
5. Drown worries in alcohol.
6. Grow slender with Metrecal.
7. Adjust the stomach on Tums.
8. Lift your arches with steel.
9. Write examinations on Benzedrine.
10. Quiet tensions with tranquilizers.
11. Go to sleep on Barbiturates.
12. Start the new day with bubbling alkalizers.
13. Get rid of yesterdays's bad taste to make room for today's.

Religion should never try to "compete" for men's hearts and souls at the level of worldly appeal. In this realm, the church must always come off second best to the golf course, the race track, or the theater. Nor does architectural elegance of its building, the high income bracket of its members and the drama of its worship service necessarily make a church "great." The real power of a church, be it big or small, comes from the combined spiritual dedication of its members.

A noted educator once said: "The dance hall is the nursery of the divorce court, the training shop of prostitution, and the grad school of infamy."

NATIONAL EVILS

> *Mr. Worldly went to church*
> *He never missed a Sunday;*
> *Mr. Worldly went to hell*
> *For what he did on Monday.*

Christ put the church in the world, the Devil put the world in the Church.

Careful considerations:
1. Three-fourths of the fallen girls in America were ruined by the dance, according to the testimony of the dance experts.
2. The modern dance is the only place where the vilest of men can embrace the purest of girls in the closest familiarity with the approval of society.
3. The Roman Catholic confessional reveals the fact that nineteen out of twenty of their girls who go wrong attributed it to the dance.
4. The greatest attraction of the dance is the embrace and would be permitted in no other place of decent society.
5. Christians cannot dance and yet abstain from all the appearance of evil.
6. Dancing is the only amusement that depends solely on the mingling of sexes for its existence. Separate sexes and the dance would die.
7. If a man embraced his neighbor's wife as on the dance floor in other places, he would very likely get shot.
8. Thousands of men have used the dance as the surest and the best way to trap a girl.

A man always goes to the devil before he goes to the place prepared for the devil.

There is no greater mistake than to suppose that Christians can impress the world by agreeing with it.

When a person feels that his mind is getting broader, it is more likely that his conscience is stretching.

You cannot walk with God and run with the devil.

CORNBREAD HABIT

There is a man who has the "Cornbread Habit." He just has to have a piece of cornbread every 20 to 30 minutes. Every morning as soon as he awakens, the first thing he thinks about is his cornbread. He eats a piece before he dresses and sometimes, he eats another piece before going to work, with his pockets full of cornbread which he eats every few minutes all day.

On the way home he stops at the store for more cornbread, for fear that his wife has forgotten to get any. Once she did forget and he got so ill-tempered that he had to drive five miles before bedtime to get some. Otherwise, he would have been so irritable that he would have yelled at her and the kids.

This man attends church services, but the last thing he does before entering the church building is stand on the curb or step and eat another hunk of cornbread. Then he throws the crust and sack on the ground and goes in. Between classes and the Worship Services, he rushes outside and eats another piece of cornbread. And after the final Amen he quickly joins the other cornbread eaters on the sidewalk and the crumbs fly.

Isn't it peculiar that a man would get the cornbread habit?

DO YOU KNOW?

Heavy cigarette smokers died of heart disease at nearly twice the rate of those who had never smoked. The death rates from cancer of the lung were at least 5 times higher in the heavy cigarette-smoker group than in non-smokers.

Fun is sometimes the devil's substitute for real Christian joy!

Confirming the above item, studies in England, using the same technique with 60,000 British physicians as subjects, have reported practically identical results.

If a young male never smokes, his chances of acquiring cancer of the lung are 1 in 170-190; if he smokes a pack or more daily he has a 1 in 15-20 chance of developing lung cancer.

KEEP IT OUT

All the water in the world,
  However hard it tried,
Could never, never sink a ship
  Unless it got inside.

All the evil in the world,
  The blackest kind of sin,
Can never hurt you one least bit—
  Unless you let it in.

Every minute you are angry you lose sixty seconds of happiness.

Too many of us conduct our lives on the cafeteria plan — "self-service" only.

I had a little tea party
  This afternoon at three.
'Twas very small—
  Three guests in all—
Just I, Myself, and Me.

Myself ate all the sandwiches,
  While I drank up the tea;
'Twas also I who ate the pie,
  And passed the cake to me!

FROM SOJOURNERS TO SLAVES

"A new king that knew not Joseph." What a profound statement! It was the changing course of history.

One day the Hebrews were citizens. The next day they were slaves.

This could happen in America.

It did happen. A new history has been written.

A new Mrs. Murray that knew not God. Read it as it really is. What a change. One day in Maryland, religious freedom. The next day lawsuits.

One day children bowed their heads in prayers in the school cafeteria. The next day the gestapo says, "Eat your food, kid. Forget God and thanks for your meal."

Watch our freedoms go! We have not seen anything yet unless the Supreme Court bows to the Supreme God.

—Don Earl Boatman

Your temper is a valuable possession — don't lose it.

Life is too short for littleness.

—Disraeli

One of the weaknesses of our age is our apparent inability to distinguish our needs from our greeds.

Sin without sorrow is the soul's most serious sickness.

It is truly written, the bigger a man's head gets, the easier it is to fill his shoes.

Many an argument is sound — just sound.

NATIONAL EVILS

STATISTICS IN THE SEVENTIES

In the time it has taken you to open this book and read to this point on the page, three people in the United States — shoplifters — have broken the commandment, "Thou shalt not steal."

By the time you reach this point on the page, there have been four acts of vandalism against private or public property.

At this point . . . someone is being arrested for drunkenness.

At this point on the page, someone has burglarized a home.

Now a business establishment has been burglarized.

Now someone is being arrested for disorderly conduct.

If you are an average reader, then you will reach this point on the page one minute after you begin reading. Every minute someone's automobile is stolen.

Every minute and a half someone in the United States is arrested for assault.

Every two minutes someone is arrested for attempting to kill or commit serious injury to another human being.

Every two minutes someone is arrested for some other major violation of our liquor laws.

Every three minutes there is a gambling law violation arrest.

Every five minutes a human being is robbed by someone who threatens him with death or great bodily injury.

Every six minutes someone is arrested for a sex offense.

Every seven minutes someone is arrested for a criminal offense against family or children.

Every eight minutes an arrest is made for carrying a deadly weapon.

Every nine minutes someone is arrested for narcotic law violations.

Every eleven minutes someone is arrested for forgery or counterfeiting.

Every twelve minutes there is an arrest for prostitution or commercialized vice.

Every twenty minutes a woman is forcibly raped.

Every twenty five minutes someone is arrested for receiving, buying or possessing stolen property.

Every thirty five minutes there is an embezzlement.

Every fifty minutes . . . someone is murdered.

Last year 2,600,000 serious crimes were reported by the FBI, which represents an increase of thirteen percent over the previous year. The major crime rate is up fifty-eight percent over six years ago. The reported crime loss in the United States was $27,000,000,000 which does not include the astronomical sums necessary for maintenance of large police forces to protect us.

Since you began reading this article, one hundred and fifty shoplifters have stolen property; one hundred and seventy acts of vandalism have occurred; twenty-two people have been arrested for drunkenness; four homes and four business establishments have been burglarized; ten people have been arrested for disorderly conduct; four automobiles have been stolen; eleven people have been assaulted; seven people have attempted to kill or commit serious injury to another human being; three, arrested for drunken driving; and a person robbed by someone who threatened him with death. Within the next fifteen minutes — somewhere — a woman will be forcibly raped. Within the next forty-five minutes, someone will be murdered.

The clock ticks. And with each passing second, the jungle closes in tighter around us . . . blocking our view of heaven.

The above statistics were out of date before the ink was dry. Unless we stop sin, sin will stop our nation.

Sin is to be hated and repented of . . . not justified and practiced!

Secret sins won't stay secret!!!

Some sinners may have mended their ways, but the patches still show.

One does evil enough by doing nothing good.
—German proverb

THINGS YOU JUST CAN'T DO

Sow bad habits and reap good character.
Sow jealousy and hatred and reap love and friendship.
Sow dissipation and reap a healthy body.
Sow deception and reap confidence.
Sow cowardice and reap courage.
Sow neglect of the Bible and reap a well-guided life.

Sin has many tools, but the lie is the handle that fits them all.

THE DEVIL'S TOOL

Satan called in three of his lieutenants for a strategy session to stop the progress of a group of dedicated church members bringing people to God. . . . Rancor said, "Let's convince them that there is no God." The Chief laughed right in his face saying, "That will never do. Men somehow seem to sense that there is a God." . . . Then Bitterness said, "We'll just convince them that God doesn't really care about right and wrong." Satan admitted that the idea had merit, but he went on to explain that too many men realize that God does care . . . Finally, it was Malice's turn. "Let them believe that there is a God and that He cares about right and wrong. . . . But let's just keep whispering that there is no hurry." There was a big smile on Satan's face! Malice's advance in the organization below was assured.

Many a person who thinks he is "playing it smart" is playing right into the hands of the devil.

Burn the candle at both ends and you double the chances of getting your fingers burned.

SIN IN OUR NATION'S CAPITOL — 1989

Robberies in Washington rose from 1,072 in 1960 to 12,236 at the end of that decade, largely as a result of heroin, primarily a male addiction that caused an increase in one-parent families. Crack may be producing "no-parent children."

Drugs are both cause and effect of something unprecedented. The problem is social regression of a sort without precedent in urban history.

Industrialism and urbanization created many social problems, but also created economic growth and a social surplus for government to divert for the elimination of problems of material deprivation. However, what makes today's form of poverty-amidst-plenty so frustrating is that it cannot be solved or even appreciably dented by normal welfare-state transfer payments.

The intergenerational transmission of poverty is produced by the disintegration of family structure. In Washington, 68.3 percent of minority births are illegitimate (in Balitmore, 80 percent). In what is called a "typical elementary school" in Washington's Anacostia section, 90 percent of all pupils are from single-parent homes.

Today family disintegration is one of the principal correlates of poverty. In 1988, 24 percent of America's 63 million children lived with only one parent, double the 1970 percentage. Most single-parent households are headed by women, and such households have a poverty rate of 55 percent. The Bureau of the Census estimates that only 39 percent of children born in 1988 will live with both parents until their 18th birthday.

Family structure almost certainly now is, as Moynihan and many other suspect, "the principal conduit of class structure." That poses the most immense challenge ever to confront American social policy, a problem of unprecedented complexity.

The fact is that sin is the most unmanly thing in God's world. You never were made for sin and selfishness. You were made for love and obedience.

—J.G. Holland

NATIONAL DEBT

The course of history is changed like the bed of a mighty river. The water licks away at the bank of the weak side for years, then suddenly it breaks through and runs rampant on a new course. It didn't happen all at once.

The tide of communism, atheism, immorality and false religions all work away at the weakness of a nation, and then it breaks through to destroy everything in its way.

There is time. We can be citizens instead of slaves, but we had better act now. We can be saints or sots, but act now. We can be free men or fooled men, but act now.

We were citizens under our great presidents. Beware lest there be a new "king that knows not God."

—Don Earl Boatman

LAZINESS

Work and worship are two spokes in a wheel that cannot be broken without serious difficulty. A lazy man is never a worshipping man. A worshipping man is always an industrious man. The two go together.

The Scriptures teach — "If a man will not work let him not eat" (II Thess. 3:10). The New Testament church was very generous in its benevolent spirit, but it has no obligation to feed lazy bums. Laziness deserves no respect or consideration.

The socialistic government that carries along thousands of lazy people who will not work, costing the tax payers millions of dollars, is a crime against society. God forbids it. It is not fair to the industrious or to the lazy ones.

Industrious and religious people cannot forever hold a nation together. Laziness and selfishness are termites that eat away at foundations. The building crumbles before people are aware of the impending doom.

When things go wrong, don't go with them.

THE MOVIES

*They move our youth away from God
From Christian paths our father's trod
From honor, honesty and right
 To deeds that curse, corrupt and blight;
From beautiful, uplifting truth;
 To falsehood hurtful to our youth;
From morals fine and grand and clean
 To passions low and base and mean.*

*They move our youth to sin and crime,
 From sacred things and things sublime;
They move to nudity in dress
 And take much virtue girls possess;
They move from modesty in style,
 And lead to evil all the while
From traits that we delight to trust
 To lewdness and destructive lust.
Who named the movies named them well
 For fast they move our youth to hell.*

OVERCOMING EVIL

A sheepman in Indiana was troubled by his neighbor's dogs who were killing his sheep. Sheepmen usually counter that problem with law suits or barbed wire fences or even shotguns, but this man went to work on his neighbors with a better idea. To every neighbor's child he gave a lamb or two as pets; and in due time when all his neighbors had their own small flocks they began to tie up the dogs, and that put an end to the problem. So it goes all through the New Testament: "Be not overcome of evil, but overcome evil with good" (Romans 12:21). There are many ways of applying this verse to the practical problem of life.

—J. Wallace Hamilton

COSTLY COMMODITY

Sin is the most expensive thing possible.
It wastes money.
It wears the body into decay. But, bad as these things are, there are even worse behind; for it blights the intellect and withers the moral nature of man.
It wakens the will; it blunts the conscience; it hardens the heart.
It dries up all the finer feelings of the soul, so that ultimately all regard for truth and holiness is gone.
But worse yet: sin is an enslaving thing. It becomes the master of the man who indulges in it, and sets him to do the hardest drudgery. It hires him out, as it were to feed swine, leaving him to feed along with them.
That which was at first a joy becomes in the end a bondage.
That which was at first a pleasant companion becomes at length a cruel taskmaster; which compels him to make brick without straw, and sometimes even without clay.
Sin defiles, disfigures, debases, and blasts all it touches.
It is at once a state, guilt and a pollution.

The wages of sin is death, unless we quit the devil before pay day.

If all the thoughts we ever thought
  Were thrown upon a screen,
If all the deeds we ever did
  By all the world were seen,
If some loud speaker should blare forth
  All words we ever said,
I think we'd hang our heads in shame,
  And wish we all were dead.
From others we can hide some things
  We've thought and said and done,
But cannot hide them from the Lord
  He knows them every one.

WORDS FOR SINNERS

You don't have to go on strike to get an increase in the wages of sin.

Sin is first appealing, then apalling; first alluring, then alienating; first deceiving, then damning; it promises life and produces death; it is the most disappointing thing in the world.

INDIFFERENCE

Nothing that is good can be trusted to the lazy man. Place him in a new house and he will allow it to deteriorate and fall apart. Place him on guard and he will sleep in the hours of danger.

The working and worshipping man can always be trusted. He proves it over and over again. Before tranquilizers, grandpa had something to make him sleep. He called it work.

A glowing ember removed from the fire, first cools, then goes out. Likewise, a person who stays away from church. Go to church. Learn work and worship.

—Dalorl Braham

SERMON IN VERSE

I was angry with my friend;
I told my wrath, my wrath did end!
I was angry with my foe;
I told it not, my wrath did grow!

How wonderful if Christians put into practice the truth of this sentiment by William Blake. Christ said it this way: "If thy brother shall trespass against thee, go and tell him his fault between thee and him alone."

SOCIALISM A FAILURE

The war on poverty is a failure because it does not deal with the heart. We have supported the American Indian for generations but they are among the poorest of the poor. When a single mother without a husband keeps producing babies, she is simply adding to the welfare rolls. We now have third generations who have learned the art of living off the government. Socialism in Russia has proven to be a trap. Many people in America have found that they can not escape the governmental hand.

THE 23 CHANNEL

The television is my shepherd, My spiritual life doth want;
It maketh me to sit down and do nothing,
It leadeth me beside men of no faith,
It restoreth my desire for worldly pleasures,
It requireth all my spare time, and;
It keepeth me from doing the will of God, because:
It presenteth so much foolishness which I must see,
It increaseth my knowledge of nonsense, and;
It keepeth me from the study of the Word of God,
Ye, though I live to be a hundred, yet:
The viewing of my television shall have first place in my life,
   as long as it doth operate for,
It is my closeth companion,
It's sound and it's picture, they comfort me;
It presenteth foolishness and folly before me continually,
And, it keepeth me from surrendering my whole life unto God.
It anoints my mind with seeds of corruption, and
It fills my head with vanity, which profiteth me nothing;
My cup remains empty.
Surely, no good thing will come of my life, because;
I am devoted to my television,
Which leaveth me no time to serve God acceptably,
Thus, I will dwell in the house of confusion forever.

—Joseph Bakke

I AM A GAMBLER

Yes, I am a gambler. Oh, not the kind that frequents places behind closed doors in some secluded spot or in a back room of some night club or den of iniquity. I'm not that kind of gambler. Nor do I play the ponies or bet on sporting events. Such gambling as that is *peanuts* to the gambling I do.

You see, I gamble with souls at stake. I'm betting that I can live a life of indifference, a life of neglect of those things that are of God and still be saved.

I'm gambling with the souls of my children as the stake. I'm betting their souls by letting them miss Bible School and Church services. Although I neither live righteously nor influence them toward it, I am betting their souls on the hope that they will have wisdom enough to guide their own lives unto the Lord.

I'm betting that I can remain indifferent to the teaching of Christ on Liberality, that I can fail to give as prospered, and that Christ will bless me eternally, still. I'm betting I can have a 'don't care' attitude toward the lost about me and still please God.

Yes, I am gambling against impossible odds, with my soul and the souls of my children at stake, for you see, 'I AM A LUKEWARM CHRISTIAN.'

Sin is not hurtful because it is forbidden, but it is forbidden because it is hurtful.
—Franklin

You will never get ahead of anyone as long as you are trying to "get even with him."

Beware of the little sins; for a very small leak will sink a great ship.

If you are in the wrong place, the right place is empty.

Voluntary slavery to sin is some people's idea of personal liberty.

A STRIKING CONTRAST

Man calls sin an accident;
God calls it an abomination.
Man calls sin a blunder;
God calls it blindness.
Man calls sin a chance;
God calls it choice.
Man calls sin a defect;
God calls it a disease.
Man calls sin an error;
God calls it enmity.
Man calls sin an infirmity;
God calls it a fatality.
Man calls sin a luxury;
God calls it leprosy.
Man calls sin a liberty;
God calls it lawlessness.
Man calls sin a trifle;
God calls it a tragedy.
Man calls sin a mistake;
God calls it madness.
Man calls sin a weakness;
God calls it willfullness.

—Hugh Atkinson

"MAX JUKES" did not believe in Christianity, and he married a girl of like character. From studies made of 1026 descendents of this union, 300 died prematurely; 100 were sent to the penitentiary; 190 sold themselves to some vice, 100 were drunkards and the family cost the state of New York 1,100,000 dollars.

"JONATHON EDWARDS" was a Christian and believed in Christian training. He married a girl of like character. From this union they studied 729 descendents. Of this family, 200 were preachers; 65 were college professors; 13 were university presidents; 6 had written good books; 3 were U.S. Congressmen; and 1 was Vice-President of the United States. This family did not cost the state a single dollar.

TOBACCO

I have walked in summer's meadow
  When the sunbeams flashed and broke
But I never saw the cattle
  Or the sheep or horses smoke.
I have watched the world with wonder
  When the grass with dew was wet,
But I never saw a robin
  Puffing at a cigarette.
I have fished in many a river
  When the sucker crop was ripe,
But I never saw a catfish
  Puffing at a pipe.

Man is the only living creature
  That parades this vale of tears
Like a snorting tractor engine
  Puffing smoke from nose and ears.
If Dame Nature had intended
  When she first invented man
That he'd smoke, she would have built him
  On a widely different plan.
She'd have fixed him with a stovepipe
  And a damper and a grate
And he'd have a smoke consumer
  That was strictly up to date.

Covetousness is the basis for the gambling craze that is on the increase encouraged by state legislators.

A boy starts smoking to prove he is a man. Twenty years later he trys to stop for the same reason.

The wages of sin have never been reduced.

People who do not wish to "get involved" are usually quite selfish by nature. They know it will cost them to be committed to the Church.

These people remain uncommitted in other areas of living. when their marriage demands some sacrifice, they get divorced. When their boss demands some overtime, they quit their job. When a friend is in need, they would rather lose the friend.

These are the "selfish ones." These are the childish and immature. The world waits for their help. God waits, also. They stand for nothing and avail to nothing.

They flounder in melancholy and even hypochondria, and dissolve into old age and oblivion leaving no footprints on the sands of time.

"Whosoever will save his life shall lose it; and whosoever will lose his life for my sake shall find it" (Matthew 16:25).

Alcohol

PITY THE DRUNKARD

I pity him of weakened will
 Who yields to alcohol;
Whose life is marred and mind distraught;
 With loss of pride and all.

But God have mercy on the ones
 Who sell this "death" for gain
And bring damnation on mankind,
 And poverty and pain.

The greatest peril confronting this country is what is happening to our womanhood; women now surpass men as drunkards.
—Bishop Ralph Cushman

WE REPEALED PROHIBITION

But we did not repeal the heartaches and the despair that are in legalized liquor.

We did not repeal the crime and lawlessness that beer and whiskey always produce.

We did not repeal the habit forming and enshackling power of alcohol.

We did not repeal the law that passes on to the next generation the terrible physical effects of drinking by potential fathers and mothers.

We did not repeal the fact that liquor unleashes one's moral sense so that immorality and fast living result.

We did not repeal the fact that liquor steals a man's brains, lessens his efficiency, and lowers his income-producing powers.

We did not repeal the law that says the drunkard cannot inherit the Kingdom of God.

SONG OF THE RYE

It was made to be eaten,
And not to be 'drank';
To be threshed in a barn,
Not soaked in a tank.
I come as a blessing
When put through a mill;
And as a blight and a curse
When run through a still.

Make me up into loaves
And your children are fed;
But if into drink,
I'll starve them instead.
In bread, I'm a servant,
The eater shall rule;
In drink I am master,
The drinker a fool.

IT IS STRANGE

It is strange that alcoholism is the only disease where it is considered illogical and unethical to annihilate the cause. To prevent malaria, we kill the mosquito; to prevent a germ disease, we kill the germ; to destroy beverage alcohol, however, is considered an infringement of personal liberties.

—Janice Johnson

Ever notice that the man who drinks every now and then usually drinks more now than he did then?

I know of a man who was arrested in the state of Kansas for wrecking a tavern but I have never heard of anyone arresting a tavern for wrecking a man.

WHEREAS

WHEREAS, The use of intoxicating liquors as a beverage is productive of pauperism, degradation, and crime; and believing it is our duty to discourage that which produces more evil than good we therefore pledge ourselves to abstain from the use of intoxicating liquors as a beverage.

—Abraham Lincoln

Drinking costs Wisconsin 40 million yearly for: police, jail, dependent support, hospitals, tax loss, income loss, industrial accidents, and absenteeism!

Alcoholic joys are brief, the resulting are lasting.

Alcohol belongs in the radiator, not the driver.

NOBODY'S BUSINESS

It's nobody's business what I drink:
  I care not what my neighbors think,
Nor how many laws they choose to pass,
  I'll tell the world I'll have my glass.

So he drank, in spite of law or man,
  Then got into his old tin can,
Stepped on the gas and let her go,
  Down the highway, to and fro.

He took the curves at sixty miles,
  With bleary eyes and drunken smiles.
Not long 'till a car he tried to pass,
  Then a crash, a scream, and breaking glass!

The other car is upside down,
  About two miles from the nearest town.
The man is free, but his wife is caught,
  And he needs the help of that drunken sot.

Who sits in maudlin, drunken daze,
  And hears the scream and sees the blaze;
But he's too far gone to save a life
  By helping the car from off the wife.

The car is burned and a mother dies,
  While a husband weeps and a baby cries,
And a drunk sits by — and still some think
  It's nobody's business what they drink!

Small fry to father: "How come a soda will spoil my dinner and a martini will give you an appetite?"

SAFETY SLOGAN: He who drinks before he drives puts the quart before the hearse.

"BEER BELONGS" WHERE?

The brewers of America, those who traffic in the souls and bodies of men, women and children, have now launched an advertising campaign to sell Americans the vicious lie that "beer belongs." The brewers, however, do not want their beer where it really belongs.

It belongs in the stories of car wrecks that blight our highways.

It belongs in the morgue where the dead are laid out after the alcohol-provoked bar-room brawl.

It belongs in the penitentiary where it has sent so many otherwise good men.

It belongs on the bad-debt rolls where are found the names of men who spend all they have on the brewer's product while an innocent family goes without the necessities of life.

It belongs in the juvenile courts of the land where it sends the children of those who buy the product of the brewer's art.

It belongs in hell where it finally sends the soul of those who are foolish enough to believe they can drink the stuff and still serve the Lord.

If you value your soul, treasure your children, and are interested in your future welfare; beer does not belong in your home!

STATISTICS SOON OUT OF DATE

There are three times as many drinking places as there are churches in America.

There are two times as many young women serving as barmaids in America as there are enrolled in our colleges.

There are over ninety-five million people in the United States who drink.

Washington, D.C., is the "drinking capitol" of the world.

Americans spent around ten billion dollars for drink last year.

Every third teenager in America drinks.

In Nashua County, New York, a survey showed that ninety percent of all high schools students were drinking.

America now has seven million alcoholics.

MARIJUANA AND ALCOHOL

A chemist who is regarded as one of Cleveland's most knowledgeable persons on this subject said: "We have come to look on alcohol as a way of life. It is, in fact, a way of death. We recoil in horror and chastise those who smoke marijuana, but turn our heads when it comes to alcohol. Yet, alcohol — in fact it does more harm to a user and causes more grief to others — is a greater problem in our society than marijuana will ever be."

Another authority concluded: "The answer is not to make two wrongs by legalizing marijuana, but to begin attacking alcohol with the vigor we have exhibited in dealing with marijuana."

Riding on the freeway is like Russian roulette — you never know which driver is loaded.

To escape alcoholism is simple: Never take the drink just before the second one.

HOW COME?

A San Diego, California, beer firm and the Teamster's Union head are reported to be wrangling over whether the company's truck drivers may use the company's product with their lunch. The company says that 25 drivers may not drink beer and then drive the 8 ton trucks. The Union claims the company has no right to tell them what to have for lunch. The company hired a private detective who shadowed a couple of drivers that were suspected of violating the rule against drinking on the job. The detectives carried a camera hidden in a lunch box and took pictures of the drivers in a cafe drinking beer. The drivers were fired.

Ever hear of a shoe company (or you name the company — even the one you work for) firing employees for using the product manufactured by the company? Or could it be that the company is aware of the fact that there is a lot about their product that is never told about in the ads or on the T.V. set. How come?

NATIONAL EVILS

EVERYBODY GETS SOMETHING

From a certain amount of corn, the distiller gets four gallons of whiskey that retails for $16.80. Of this, the farmer gets 45¢, the government gets $4.40, the railroad gets 80¢, the manufacturer gets $1, the drayman gets 15¢, the retailer gets $7, the customer gets drunk, the children get rags, the politicians get votes and the back-sliding church members get mad at the preacher for mentioning it.

DRINK IS NO RESPECTOR OF PERSONS

Out of 30,000 alcoholics in Massachusetts, there were:
  600 former doctors
  300 former priests and ministers
  170 former dentists
  633 former lawyers
   17 former judges
  600 former businessmen
When they took their first drink they never expected to end up as drunkards on Skid Row. There are over 4 million alcoholics in the United States today.

THE DRUNKARD'S ONLY CONSOLATION

If you cannot absolutely refrain from drinking; then start a saloon in your own home. Be the only customer and you will have to buy a license. Give your wife $12 to buy a gallon of whiskey. There are 128 snorts in a gallon. Buy all your drinks from your wife at 40 cents a shot and in four days, when the gallon is gone, your wife will have $39.20 to put in the bank and buy another gallon of the stuff. If you live ten years and buy all your booze from your wife, and then die with the snakes in your boots, and your soul burns in hell, she will have $35,750 on deposit with which to bury you, bring up your children, buy a house and lot and marry a decent man and forget she ever saw you.

ONE THOUSAND BOYS WANTED

We are constantly losing our old customers, by the following means: 20 committed suicide last month; 120 are in jail; 18 are on the chain gang; 4 are condemned to die; 45 are on relief; 13 have been sent to asylums. The few left are on skid row and of little use to us. If we don't get new customers, we'll have to close our business. We don't care whose boy you are. Come early and stay late. Apply at:
BEER TAVERN OR LIQUOR STORE
ANY CITY...................................ANY STATE

CAN YOU UN-MIX MIXED-UP YOUTH?

I'm all mixed up; can you help me? My daddy says it's all right for the state to sell whiskey to raise money for our schools but he doesn't want me to drink it and help support the schools like he does. I don't know why because I am the one who goes to school to get the education. Why can't I help support the school? My teacher says it is not good to have legal whiskey to drink for it leads to crimes and it's bad for our mind and body. If it's good for our state to sell whiskey to educate us, why don't they fire our teacher for talking against something that is good for our education? If having whiskey is good for our education, why does Mama say our preacher is a good man? He doesn't help our school because he doesn't drink. Why does my daddy say that old man that passes our home is no good because he drinks a lot? Daddy has already said it was good for the state to sell it because the tax money went to the school. If nobody buys any whiskey, the state doesn't get any money. The old man helps our school more than anybody I know because he spends all his money for whiskey.

If it helps our schools for people to buy whiskey from our state liquor stores, why does the state put them in jail for drinking it? That is what it is sold for, isn't it? What I thought was wrong is good and what I thought was good is bad. I'm old enough to go to school, I'm old enough to know the truth.

CHARGED WITH MURDER

"Prisoner at the bar, have you anything to say why sentence of death should not be passed upon you?"

Not a whisper was heard anywhere, and the situation had become painfully oppressive, when the prisoner was seen to move, his head raised, his hand clinched, and the blood rushed into his dull, careworn face.

"I have! Your honor, you have asked me a question, and now I ask, as the last favor on earth, that you will not interrupt my answer until I am through.

"I stand here, before this bar, convicted of the willful murder of my wife. Truthful witnesses have testified to the fact that I was a loafer, a drunkard, a wretch, that I returned from one of my prolonged debaches and fired the fatal shot that killed the wife that I had sworn to love, cherish and protect.

"While I have no remembrance of committing the fatal deed, I have no right to condemn the verdict of the twelve good men who have acted as jury in this case, for the verdict is in accordance with the evidence.

"But may it please the court, I wish to show that I am not alone responsible for the murder of my wife."

The startling statement created a tremendous sensation. The judge leaned over the desk, the lawyers wheeled around and faced the prisoner, while the spectators could hardly suppress their intense excitement.

"I repeat, your honor, that I am not the only one guilty of the murder of my wife.

"The judge on this bench, the jury in the box, the lawyers within the bar, and most of the witnesses, including the pastor of the old church, are also guilty before Almighty God, and will have to stand with me before His Judgment Throne where we shall be righteously judged.

"If it had not been for the saloons of my town, I never would have become a drunkard, my wife would not have been murdered, I would not be here now, ready to be hurled into eternity! Had it not been for the inhuman traps, I would have been a sober man and an industrious workman, a tender father and a loving husband. But today my home is destroyed, my wife murdered, my little children — God bless and care for them! — cast out upon the mercy of the world! — whilst I am to be hung by the strong arm of the State!

"God knows I tried to reform, but as long as the open saloon was sin in my pathway, my weak, diseased, will-power was no match against the fearful, consuming agonizing appetitie for liquor. For one year our town was without a saloon. For one year my wife and children were happy and our little home was a paradise.

"I was one of those who signed remonstrances against re-opening of the saloons in our town. One-half of this jury, the prosecuting attorney on this case, and the judge who sits on this bench, all voted for the saloons! By their votes and influence the saloons were re-opened, and they made me what I am"!

The Judge made a motion as if to stop further speech, when the prisoner hastily said:

"No! No! your honor, do not close my lips. I am nearly through.

"In my drunken, frenzied, irresponsible condition I have murdered one, but you have deliberately voted for the saloons which have murdered thousands, and they are in full operation today with your consent.

"You legalized the saloons and made me a drunkard and a murderer, and you are guilty with me before God for the murder of my wife.

"Your honor, I am done. I am now ready to receive my sentence and be led forth to the place of execution. You will close by asking the Lord to have mercy on my soul. I will close by solemnly asking God to open your blind eyes to your own individual responsibility, so that you will cease to give your support to this dreadful traffic."

The new deal of Roosevelt included voting for alcohol. The days that have followed have revealed that alcohol, beer and wine are part of a dirty deal against sobriety.

It isn't the wet roads that are dangerous. It is the "wet" driver.

NATIONAL EVILS

AIN'T IT THE TRUTH

A town, not long ago, was about to vote dry. The wife of the liquor seller, the only saloon in town, said, in tones of almost despair to her Negro wash-woman, "If this town goes dry, I won't be able to pay you to do our washing. I don't know how we will be able to live ourselves." The generous-hearted colored woman answered sympathetically, "Don't you worry about it. If your husband has to shut up his liquor place, my husband won't be able to get drunk and we'll have plenty and you can do our washing."

VERDICT OF THE WORLD'S RELIGIONS

The man who accustoms himself to intoxicants is sure to become accustomed to look upon iniquity and immorality as the proper thing.
—Talmud (Jewish)

The man who gives himself to drinking intoxicating liquors he even in this world digs up his own root.
—Buddha

O ye who believe, verily wine and divining are only an abomination of Satan's work, avoid these that happily ye may prosper.
—Koran (Mohammedan)

"Have a drink?"
"No thanks! I don't like it!" In 20 years of liking it, I lost 15 jobs, 2 good wives, got held up and robbed once, got in jail 5 times, spent $250 for a "cure," lost hundreds and hundreds of dollars from time out from work with hangovers — couldn't work — too sick, and a judge let me know through my present wife that the next drunk will get me 6 months straight time — no buying out. I just don't like it anymore. Some fun wasn't it?"

Tongue

"I've gossiped about my neighbor," said the woman to her minister. "One day I saw her stagger across the yard, so I told a few friends that she had been drunk. Now I find that her staggering was caused by a leg injury. How can I undo this gossip I started?" The minister excused himself for a moment, returned with a pillow and asked the woman to follow him to the side porch. He took the knife, cut a hole in the pillow and emptied the feathers over the railing. A small breeze soon scattered tiny feathers all about the yard, among shrubs, flowers, even up in the trees. A few feathers floated across the street heading for unknown destinations. The minister turned to the woman. "Will you go out now and gather every one of the feathers?"

The woman looked stunned. "Why that would be impossible!"

"Exactly," replied the minister sorrowfully. "So it is with your gossip."

FOR A KIND TONGUE

Enable me, our Father, to realize that words once spoken, like coins in circulation, pass from person to person along an uncharted course. Grant me the insight so to speak that any words of mine may be repeated without giving hurt. Help me not to criticize but rather to stress the things that are pure, lovely, and of good report. Make my habit of thought gentle and eager to pass along news of kindness and work well done. May my words build, never destroy, faith and confidence. To this end I pray that Thou wilt lead me in the ways of understanding. Amen.

He who thinks by the inch and talks by the yard ought to be moved by the foot.

Do not be angry that you cannot make others as you wish them to be since you cannot make yourself as you wish to be.

When a little bird tells you something, don't repeat it until you find out whether or not the little bird is a cuckoo.

GOSSIP

Somebody told to somebody else
  A story that they had heard;
And somebody changed the tale a bit
  And often added a word.
But somebody's heart was touched with pain
  As the gossips had their fun.
And little they knew as they went their way
  Of the harm their word had done.
How carefully we should guard our tongues
  As we live from day to day,
Because we can make or mar a life,
  With the careless words we say.
  —Hilda Butler Farr

Gossip is the "A-bomb" of the soul; its radioactive influence poisons anyone it touches. Homes and hearts have been broken by its evildoers. Lives have lost their lustre by the tarnishing power of gossip.
  —Dick Blanchard

Never encourage gossipers; they will talk about you too.

It isn't the things that go in one ear and out the other that hurts as much as the things that go in one ear and get all mixed up before slipping out the mouth.

JACK'S IN JAIL

"Jack Lee is in jail," said Mrs. M. to Mrs. A. as she met her on the street. "Well, who'd have thought it!" said Mrs. A. "But I'm not surprised when I reflect; I'll bet that's what that group of men I just passed on the street were talking about." "They just now caught him," said Mrs. M., "For I saw the sheriff taking him up the court house steps just now." "What did they put him in jail for?" asked Mrs. A. "Oh, I don't know," answered Mrs. M., "But I wouldn't be surprised if it wasn't for writing a hot check." "My, my, what a dreadful thing to do," said Mrs. A. as she walked on down the street.

"Did you know that Jack Lee is in jail this very minute?" asked Mrs. A. as she met Mrs. R. further down the street.
"My gracious no!" answered Mrs. R. "What on earth for?" "Oh, I don't know — something about a check," answered Mrs. A., "Probably forgery." "Well, I'm not surprised," said Mrs. R. as she walked off. "I've always been a little skeptical of him anyway."

Jack Lee is in jail," said Mrs. R. to Mrs. N. when she met her as she was entering her front gate. "What, well, I never have been too sure of him. Poor Mrs. Lee, to think she should be married to a man like that. I was afraid when she married him that she would be sorry. I'm not surprised at all, but are you quite sure?" "Oh, I imagine he's already sentenced by now. Probably got a year and a day. Serves him right, though, anyone who would forge a check deserves it."

"Only think of Jack Lee," said Mrs. N. to Mrs. W. as she walked up to her in the department store. "What about him?" said Mrs. W. apparently more inclined to think of the new hat she was looking at. "In the penitentiary, that's all. He got a year and a day for forgery." "I thought he was a great favorite," said Mrs. W. "Ah, but we've all seen a great change lately," said Mrs. N. "When did you notice it?" "I don't know that it was spoken of until this morning but anyone might have seen it long ago."

At that moment the sheriff and Jack Lee walked down the court house steps. The new deputy badge that had been pinned on Jack's shirt was apparent to all. . . .

NATIONAL EVILS

WHY DO WE LISTEN?

*Why do we even listen
  To rumors that we hear,
When just the smallest inquiry
  May prove them insincere?*

*Why do we swallow gossip as
  The very gospel truth,
Without a certain knowledge of
  Our grown-ups and our youth?*

*The reason is, that people are
  More ready to condemn,
Than try to understand the ones
  Who want to work with them.*

*We are prepared to criticize
  Reluctant to forgive
And we ignore our own mistakes
  As swiftly as we live.*

*So why not slow our pace a bit
  And take another glance?
It may be we instead of they
  Who need another chance.*

You have become a mature person when keeping a secret gives you more satisfaction than passing it along.

If someone were to pay you for every kind word you ever spoke about people, and collected the same amount for every unkind word, would you be rich or poor?

It's smart to pick your friends, but not to pieces.

There's only one corner of the universe you can be certain of improving, and that's your own self. So you have to begin there, not outside, not on other people. That comes afterward, when you've worked on your own corner.
—Aldous Huxley

If you want to be miserable, think much about yourself: about what you want, what you like, what respect people ought to pay you, and what people think of you.

DID YOU EVER

Did you ever step outside of yourself?
To watch yourself pass by,
To try to see how you look to yourself
When no one else was nigh?
Did you see the faults that others see
When they look with the critical eye?
Or were you so blinded by love of self
You saw only perfection pass by?

WATCH YOUR WORDS

Guard well thy words,
  Set seal upon thy tongue;
No greater hero hath in
  This old world ever sung
Than he whose lips refrain
  From saying words unkind;
The gentle word and sweet,
  Bespeaks the wisest mind.
—Bertha Hornung

Talk is cheap because the supply is greater than the demand.

A gossip is someone who puts two and two together and gets WHEE!

Beware of a half truth; you may have gotten hold of the wrong half.

The tongue weighs practically nothing. Yet it is surprising how few people are able to hold it.

Many a married couple is like a team of horses — separated by a tongue.

SPECIAL DAYS

Thanksgiving

Thanksgiving is one of the great traditional American holidays, and yet it did not originate in America. About 3,000 years before it was observed in this country, God spoke to Moses in the days when the great host of Israelite slaves had just escaped from Egypt. They were having their first experience in the wilderness of Sinai. The original proclamation from God is reported in the 23rd chapter of Exodus, 16th verse: "Thou shalt keep the feast of harvest, the first fruits of in-gathering, which is in the end of the year, when thou hast gathered in thy labors out of the field."

When Thanksgiving Day comes, there will be many homes that will have tables overloaded with much food, but no real love and happiness in the home.

Proverbs 15:17 says: "Better is a dinner of herbs where love is, than a stalled ox and hatred therewith." A humble meal with love is far better than a feast on a fatted calf with hatred in the home.

In the sermon on the Mount, Jesus asked one of the most profoundly simple questions of His ministry — simple because its answer is so obvious, profound because its implications are so far-reaching. Addressing the disciples, Jesus asked, "Is not life more than meat, and the body more than raiment?"

Of course, many things such as friendship, health, integrity, faith and peace with God are greater than food and clothing. But multitudes of people live as if food and clothing were all that mattered.

As we get around the table this Thanksgiving for the most of us there will be a full table. The real question that remains is will there be full lives at the table?

—Tom Bennett

Giving thanks is a course from which we never graduate.

MONTHLY STATEMENT
(If God Should Bill Us)

Due to God, your Father in Heaven and Round About — For Services rendered during one month.

30 days of care and supervision, air, light, sunshine, and rain.
240 hours of restful recreative sleep.
720 hours of physical upkeep of heart, lungs, senses, digestion, locomotion.
90 very satisfying meals.
1 competent mind to analyze and judge, a memory to retain, a will to act.
A family that loves you, rejoices and sorrows with you.
A host of friends who believe in you and overlook your oddities and mistakes.
Neighbors, near and far, who band together to build a better community.
Skies and seasons that bring beauty and grandeur, parks and gardens.
A church that is free and strong, affording you worship, guidance, solace and fellowship.
Love from a God of justice, compassion and forgiveness, whose plans and purposes were spelled out by His Son, and whose Spirit abides with you.

Be thankful for the little things
A baby's smile, a blue bird's songs
A little home, where love abides
Where you can rest at eventide.
Be thankful for the rose that blooms
And sheds abroad its sweet perfume,
A little kindness here and there,
And happiness that you can share.
Be thankful for the friends so true
And skies above that are so blue
And for our blessings all the way
That we enjoy from day to day.

I GIVE THEE HUMBLE THANKS

For all the gifts that Thou dost send,
For every kind and loyal friend,
For prompt supply of all my need,
For all that's good in word and deed,
For gift of health along life's way,
For strength to work from day to day,
I give Thee humble thanks.

For ready hands to help and cheer,
For list'ning ears Thy voice to hear,
For yielded tongue Thy love to talk,
For willing feet Thy paths to walk,
For open eyes Thy Word to read,
For loving heart Thy will to heed,
I give Thee humble thanks.

For Christ who came from heav'n above,
For the Cross and His redeeming love,
For His mighty power to seek and save,
For His glorious triumph o'er the grave,
For the lovely mansions in the sky
For His blessed coming bye and bye,
I give Thee humble thanks.

—Author Unknown

Payment in full can be made by giving your gratitude, loyalty and obedience — if you wish, use this easy payment plan:
   A cup of cold water (just mention my name) given to a thirsty person in need will be applied to this account.
   Good deeds, pleasant gestures, friendly attitudes gladly received and credited

—Carl R. Brown

A thankful heart is a basic lesson to be learned. An ungrateful child can not be reached with a lesson on good things in life.

SPECIAL DAYS

HAPPY THANKSGIVING

The Johnsons had two turkeys
They sent one down the street
To Widow Brown who worked so hard
Her family's bills to meet.

Now Widow Brown had one small hen
So, when the turkey came,
She had her children take the hen
To Miss Carr, old and lame.

Miss Carr so glad to get the hen
Was stirring up a cake;
"A half of this," she said, "To John,
A blind man, near, I'll take."

"My, how I like a bit of cake" —
Old John was filled with joy—
"I have two apples, one shall go
To that poor Conner boy."

Now, if you want a happy time
Thanksgiving Day, this year,
Just do as all these people did—
Pass on some of your cheer.
—Etta F. Gilbert

The man who forgets to be thankful has fallen asleep in life.
—R.L. Stevenson

When we look at what we want and then compare that with what we have, we shall be unhappy. When we think of what we deserve, then of what we have, we shall thank God.

A THOUGHT FOR THANKSGIVING

If one should give me a dish of sand and tell me there were particles of iron in it, I might look for them with my eyes, and search for them with my clumsy fingers, and be unable to detect them. But let me take a magnet and sweep through it, and how it would draw to itself the almost invisible particles by the mere power of attraction.

The unthankful heart, like my finger in the sand, discovers no mercies; but let the thankful heart sweep thru the day, and as the magnet finds the iron, so it will find in every hour some heavenly blessings; only the iron in God's sand is gold!

—Henry Ward Beecher

Christmas

A PRAYER

Forgive us Lord our Christmases
  When your birthday we have spent
Upon our own desires,
  And selfish pleasures bent.
Forgive the times we've pondered long
  On what we would receive
Heeding not your gift of love
  For all who would believe
And when we pray, "Forgive us Lord
  Our trespasses" add too—
  When we've forgotten you.

The Christian spirit is the Christmas spirit, extended through the whole year. It is the attitude toward every person, the atmosphere of every act.

—Dr. E. Stanley Jones

The Christian can share in many ways during this season: by sending an appropriate Christmas card (not a picture of Santa and his reindeer), by singing carols of Christ's birth, by praying for peace on earth, by giving our largest gift to God, by showing our joy in Christ, and by sharing the Good Tidings.

Share Christmas! Help others to know the real meaning of Christmas — "Joy to the World! The Lord is come."

—Roger Stearns

THE MEANING OF CHRISTMAS

To God the Father It Meant Giving His Son . . .
"For God so loved the world that He gave His only begotten Son, that whosoever believeth in Him should not perish, but have everlasting life" (John 3:16).

To God the Son It Meant Leaving Heaven's Glory to Become a Servant Obedient Unto Death . . .
"Christ Jesus, who, existing in the form of God, counted not the being on an equality with God a thing to be grasped, but emptied Himself, taking the form of a servant, being made in the likeness of men; and, being found in fashion as a man, He humbled Himself, becoming obedient unto death, yet, the death of the cross" (Phil. 2:5-8, R.V.).

To the World It Means that God Has Provided a Saviour . . .
"I bring you good tidings of great joy, which shall be to all people. For unto you is born this day in the city of David, a Saviour, which is Christ the Lord" (Luke 2:10-11). Christmas hails the birth of Him who was born to die — to die in the sinner's stead, to purchase the redemption of his soul. "All we like sheep have gone astray; we have turned every one to his own way, and the Lord hath laid upon Him the iniquity of us all" (Isaiah 53:6).

To You It Means that God Offers You Eternal Life as a Gift . . .
"The wages of sin is death; but the gift of God is eternal life through Jesus Christ our Lord" (Rom. 6:23). "To as many as received Him, to them gave He power to become the sons of God, even to them that believe on His name" (John 1:12).

THE INN THAT MISSED ITS CHANCE
(The Landlord Speaks — A.D. 28)

What could be done?
The inn was full of folks:
His honor, Marcus Lucius, and his scribes
Who made the census; honorable men
From farthest Galilee, come hitherward
To be enrolled; high ladies and their lords;
The rich, the rabbis, such a noble throng
As Bethlehem had never seen before
And may not see again . . .
Of course, if I had known them, who they were,
And who was He that should be born that night . . .
Had I known,
I would have turned the whole inn upside down,
His honor, Marcus Lucius, and the rest,
And sent them all to the stables.
So you have seen him, stranger, and perhaps
Again may see Him? Prithee say for me
I did not know; and if he comes again,
As he will surely come, with retinue,
And banners, and an army — tell him my Lord
That all my inn is his to make amends.
Alas, alas! to miss a chance like that!
This inn that might be chief among them all—
The birthplace of the Messiah—
Had I known!
—Amos R. Wells

Although I wish you joy all year,
Each hour of each day,
I wish you joy at Christmas
In the most special way.

I wish you joy at Christmas,
May this special day renew.
The true meaning of His birth
To loved ones and to you.

LAMENT OF THE INNKEEPER

The innkeeper counted his shekels;
  His business was excellent that day;
He could not be bothered with peasants.
  And so he had turned them away.
He could not afford them a lodging,
  A place which some nobel might fill;
He motioned them off to the stable,
  A bit of a cave in the hill.
But later he sat in the courtyard,
  This innkeeper weary with years,
And gathered the children about him
  And mingled his story with tears:
"I could have found room for the Christ
    child;
  I could have given my own:
I might have been blessed by His presence
  I might have — if only I'd known.
If only I'd watched for His coming
  And heeded the prophets of old,
If only I'd sheltered those peasants
  And not been so greedy for gold!
I know that my God has forgiven
  For now in His love I can sing,
But always — I'll always remember
  I might have been host to the King!"

—Mary Helen Anderson

OTHERS

Someone has well said: "The message of Easter is 'Think of Heaven,' the message of July Fourth is 'Think of our nation,' the message of Thanksgiving is 'Think of your blessings,' the message of New Year's Day is 'Think of the passing of time,' but the message of Christmas is 'Think of others,'" God was thinking of others when he sent Jesus to become the world's Redeemer, and all who have the true Christmas spirit think in terms of others.

CHRISTMAS BELLS

*I heard the bells on Christmas Day
Their old familiar carols play,
  And wild and sweet
  The words repeat
Of peace on earth, good will to men.*

*And thought how, as the day had come,
The belfries of all Christendom
  Had rolled along
  The unbroken song
Of peace on earth, good will to men.*

*And in despair I bowed my head;
"There is no peace on earth," I said;
  "For hate is strong,
  And mocks the song
Of peace on earth, good-will to men!"*

*Then pealed the bells more loud and deep:
"God is not dead; nor doth He sleep;
  The wrong shall fail,
  The right prevail,
With peace on earth, good will to men."*

*Till, ringing, singing on its way
The world revolved from day to day,
  A voice, a chime,
  A chant sublime,
Of peace on earth, good will to men.*

—Longfellow

Is the Christ at the *top* of your gift list? Have you given him your life? And of your means?

If you can keep Christmas for a day, why not keep it always?

JESUS IN HISTORY

Jesus is a historical person. There is a lot of myth and folklore about Christmas, but Christ is real. There is more evidence that Jesus lived than there is that George Washington did.

He came for a purpose. That purpose was to save us from sins. It is difficult to find a sinner today. Alcoholism is called a disease. Adultery is called situation ethics. Drunkeness is called social drinking. Law is considered an infringement upon my rights. Cheating is approved because everyone is doing it.

Society operates on the basis that if we can break the law often enough that it sets aside the law and makes law the offender.

Jesus came to save from sin, not to be worshipped in a manger. We need to realize that sin is an offense to God. We are not sinners because we happen occasionally to feel guilty; nor are we virtuous because we sometimes feel complacent about not being so bad as some we could name. God's existence and our moral condition are objective facts, like the chemical composition of salt. Natural man would much like to have it otherwise, and to believe that his consciousness, not God creates reality. This, of course, is the ultimate rebellion, the essence of pride.

Jesus can not save the proud, the arrogant, and the rebellious one. We must confess sin before we can be saved from it.

—Don Earl Boatman

ON CHRISTMAS DAY

On Christmas Day the Child was born,
On Christmas Day in the morning;
He trod the long way, lone and lorn,
He wore the bitter crown of thorn,
His hands and feet and heart were torn,
He died at last the Death of Scorn,
But through His coming Death was slain,
That you and I might live again.
For this the Child of the Maid was born,
On Christmas Day in the morning.

CHRISTMAS

The coming of Jesus to the world was a new attempt of God to win man back to the way of righteousness.

Everybody loves a kitten, but many of those same people hate cats. Baby Jesus is lovable. Everybody celebrates Christmas and the babe in the manger. Many of those same people hate the grown up Jesus. He is the kitten grown into a cat.

You may like kittens and hate cats, but do not despise Jesus like that. Jesus is God's grace. Jesus is the love of God demonstrated.

Why do people like kittens and hate cats? Kittens are cute and demand very little. Their mother feeds them, but grown cats demand something of us. They have to be fed. They meow and complain.

Baby Jesus did not preach repentance. The mature Jesus did. Baby Jesus did not condemn sin. The Christ on the cross did.

While men love baby Jesus and hate Jesus, they will die in their sins.

Christ is not a threat to those who accept His message. He is a threat to those who do not want to change their lives. Even one of those on the Cross spoke out against Jesus. One of the men wanted a fresh start. He wanted to see Jesus in His kingdom.

You can have a new start. It must begin with acceptance of the Christ of the Cross. Worshipping a baby in a manger will not do it.

—Don Earl Boatman

Fourth of July

THE CHRISTIAN'S RESPONSIBILITY TO GOVERNMENT

The Christian makes government need a minimum. Christians are not sent to penetentiaries for stealing, killing and cheating. There are no courts and policemen necessary for the Christian. The law is for the lawless. The policemen are for the wicked. The

F.B.I. is for the traitors, the kidnappers, the thieves. The juvenile delinquents are not produced in the Christian homes. The scriptures teach honor to the government and Christians teach the scriptures.

Disrespect or law costs the tax payer billions of dollars.

Disrespect eventually breaks down the law enforcement. When public opinion takes the side of the criminal, the government is in real trouble. Courts uphold the written law, and when the lawless write the law the courts become powerless to combat the criminals.

The proper place to start curbing crime isn't in the electric chair, but in the high chair. Costs for crime are increasing.

When a gun toting youth on a rampage kills a man, it costs the state (that is us) about $125,000 to send him through the courts to the electric chair. If he is given a life term it may cost us $250,000.

This is the cost of one church building in which hundreds of young men are taught the sacredness of life and respect for law. Our choice is penetentiaries or churches.

In the churches we build men. In the penetentiaries and jails we try to mend them.

—Don Earl Boatman

BORN TO MAKE MEN FREE

Jesus in his teachings never condemned slavery and yet His followers eliminate it. He taught positively that God loves all men. The man who loves God can not at the same time keep his fellow man in bondage.

Jesus did condemn bondage to sin and bondage to religious traditions. The Pharisees would kill if their religious authority were jeopardized.

Christianity casts off the shackles of bondage, gives man a clean mind, a controlled body and a purpose that is holy.

This America needs, if we would be free, politically and religiously.

—Don Earl Boatman

New Year's

RECIPE FOR A HAPPY NEW YEAR

I WILL:

Like Paul — forget those things which are behind and press forward.
Like David — lift up mine eyes unto the hills from whence cometh my help.
Like Abraham — trust implicitly in my God.
Like Enoch — walk in daily fellowship with my Heavenly Father.
Like Jehosaphat — prepare my heart to seek the Lord.
Like Moses — choose rather to suffer than to enjoy the pleasures of sin for a season.
Like Daniel — commune with God at all times and in all places.
Like Job — be patient under all circumstances.
Like Caleb & Joshua — refuse to be discouraged because of superior numbers.
Like Joseph — turn my back on all seductive advances.
Like Gideon — advance, even though my friends are few.
Like Aaron & Hur — uphold the hands of my minister and the leaders of the church with my prayers and support.
Like Andrew — strive to lead my brother to Christ.
Like Stephen — manifest a forgiving spirit toward all who seek my hurt.
Like Jesus — go about doing good.

A GOOD NEW YEAR'S RESOLUTION:

During the coming year I will go nowhere I can't take Jesus Christ.
I will say nothing I would not want Him to hear.
I will do nothing I would not want Him to know about.
I will be the best example to others that I possibly can, for His sake.

I RESOLVE

Not to speak unless I have something to say,
To think well before I speak
To be sympathetic — not apathetic — listener.
To regard every incident that touches my life as worthy of deepest consideration and courtesy.
To remember at all times that the kind word is invariably the right word.
To be generous with my smiles, and never to bear a dour visage.
To try to develop calmness and poise under trying conditions.
To spend a part of each day in solitude, meditation, and prayer.

A NEW YEAR

A disciple is a learner and a doer. It is true in every realm. The Communists have disciples. They are making great strides against the church which has membership rolls but too few zealous disciples.

Some church members are like Uncle Zeb's rooster. He said that his rooster was the sleepiest and laziest rooster in the world. Uncle Zeb said his rooster never crowed at sunrise; he just waited until other roosters crowed, and then he would nod his head.

Three out of every four persons in your town will stay home from church today, but will nod their head that it is good to have churches in town. We need a new year in church attendance.

The power that supresses churches is apathy, indifference, laziness, on the part of the church members.

The Communists great enemy is the disciple of the Lord. Church members who do nothing, give nothing to the church, are giving everything to the enemy. They are giving their influence. If we are not active for God, we are on the side of the enemy.

Make a New Year resolution to keep. Resolve to be a real Christian.

—Don Earl Boatman

Nobody can really guarantee the future. The best we can do is size up the chances, calculate the risks involved, estimate our ability to deal with them, and then make our plans with confidence.

Life has but two ends, and one end has been used. Take care of the other end.

—Holmes

THE CLOCK

The clock of life is wound but once,
And no man has the power
To tell just when the hands will stop,
At late or early hour.
To lose one's wealth is sad indeed.
To lose one's health is more.
To lose one's soul is such a loss
That no man can restore.

NOW

I can not change my yesterdays,
  For they are past and gone,
With all their sorrows and their joys,
  Their faults and victories won.

I can not see my days to come,
  They are in other hands;
No anxious though of mine can check
  Or speed life's trickling sands.

So, why grieve o'er my yesterdays,
  Or brood on coming years?
Better to labor, laugh and love
  Each day as it appears.

—Winifred M. New

SPECIAL DAYS

In the New Year your every word, thought and deed will be recorded. God's bookkeeper makes no mistakes.

RESOLUTIONS FOR GOOD CHRISTIANS

1. I resolve to attend every service of the church, barring illness.
2. I resolve to be in Bible School every Lord's Day.
3. I resolve to be in church every Lord's Day.
4. I resolve to attend the evening service every Lord's Day
5. I resolve to attend Bible Study every Wednesday.
6. I resolve to make better use of my talents in this New Year.
7. I resolve to give more time to the church work in this New Year.
8. I resolve to give more money to the Lord's work in this New Year.
9. I resolve to pray every day.
10. I resolve to read the Bible every day.

I AM RESOLVED

To put more T-H-I-N-K into my thinking
Like the needle that points to the pole;
To put more D-O into my doing,
So that nearer I'll come to my goal.
To put more W-O-R-K into my loving.
A love that is not tainted by self.
To put more G-I-V-E into my giving.
Gifts alive with the soul of myself.
To put more P-R-A-Y into my praying.
And thus let Him help bear my loads.
To put more T-E-A-C-H into my teaching,
And show the world the love-lighted road.
To put more S-I-N-G into my singing,
Songs that are filled with passions of soul,
To put more M-A-N into manhood,
And let the Master have full control.

Have you as yet in this first month of this New Year joined the crowds of people who have made a RESOLUTION to make RESTITUTION and bring about RESTORATION in all matters of their life? Or are you still among the few who with RESERVATION and near total RESIGNATION are bringing about a complete REJECTION of the faith-life they are to live that the Christ and His Church might be magnified and glorified? If so, begin this Lord's Day with your family and "MAKE CERTAIN OF HEAVEN IN THIS NEW YEAR"!

> ANOTHER YEAR — is but another call from God
> To do some deed undone and duty we forgot;
> To think some wider thought of man and good,
> To see and love with kindlier eyes and warmer heart,
> Until, acquainted more with him and keener eyed
> To sense the need of man, we serve
> With larger sacrifice and readier hand our kind.

I have never heard anything about the "resolutions" of the Apostles, but I have heard a great deal about the Acts of the Apostles.

—Horace Mann

PAUL'S RESOLUTIONS

1. I resolve to be enthusiastic (Phil. 4:4).
2. I resolve to better equipped (I Tim. 3:17).
3. I resolve to be enlightened (I Tim. 4:13).
4. I resolve to be encouraging (Prov. 15:13, 17-22).
5. I resolve to be an example (I Tim. 4:12).
6. I resolve to be evangelistic (Rom. 1:14-16).

Translate resolutions into definite deeds or you will forget them.

Realizing that I cannot hope to achieve these objectives by my own strength, I will rely upon Christ, for "I can do all things through Christ which strengtheneth me" (Phil. 4:13).

Perhaps the most valuable result of all education is the ability to make yourself do the thing you have to do, when it ought to be done, as it ought to be done, whether you like to do it or not.

Easter

EASTER DAWN

*Just before the Easter dawning,
It was mankind's darkest hour;
Then the sun in all its splendor,
Rose majestic in its power.*

*In a garden white robed lilies
Grew around an empty tomb,
Spreading their sweet blossoms near it,
In a springtime's Easter bloom.*

*Thus, among the stately lilies,
Dressed in garments shining bright;
Stood the Risen Lord in triumph,
Victor over death's dark night.*

*At His feet we bow before Him,
For death's stone is rolled away;
And we sing glad hallelujahs
On this glorious Easter Day.*

—E. Erickson

PALM SUNDAY

His coming made the great afraid;
They feared a Man so meek:
Since common people round Him stayed,
And joyed to hear Him speak.

Of Him the rich and proud had heard.
They thought Him Herod's foe.
To bitter rage their hearts were stirred
To see Him welcomed so.

The poor with palm leaves strewed His way
And greeted Him with song.
Where'er He went that Sabbath day,
They followed Him along.

Of Him the humble had no doubt.
The wise misunderstood
The gentle Man who went about
The cities doing good.
—Edgar Guest

There are many famous rocks and stones but the most famous one was rolled away at the tomb of Jesus.

How vain is our faith if the Christ be not risen;
How dark is the tomb if the Lord is still there;
How heavy our burden of grief and transgression,
How deep our despair!

Oh, justified faith in a finished salvation!
Oh, sure resurrection that comforts our woes!
Oh, glorious light in the valley of shadow,
Because Jesus arose.

WHAT THEN?

When the great plants of our cities
  Have turned out their last finished work;
When our merchants have sold their last yard of silk
  And dismissed the last tired clerk;
When our banks have raked in their last dollar
  And paid the last dividend;
When the Judge of the earth says, "Close for the night,"
  And asks for a balance—
    WHAT THEN?

When the choir has sung its last anthem,
  And the preacher has made his last prayer;
When the people have heard their last sermon,
  And the sound has died out on the air;
When the Bible lies closed on the altar,
  And the pews are all empty of men,
When each one stands facing his record,
  And the great book is opened—
    WHAT THEN?

When the actors have played their last drama,
  And the mimic has made his last fun;
When the film has flashed its last picture,
  And the billboard displayed its last run;
When the crowds, seeking pleasure, have vanished,
  And gone out in the darkness again;
When the trumpet of ages is sounded,
  And we stand up before Him—
    WHAT THEN?

When the bugle's call sinks into silence,
  And the long marching columns stand still;
When the captain repeats his last order,
  And they've captured the last fort and hill;
When the flag has been hauled from the masthead,
  And wounded afield checked in,
And the world that rejected its Saviour
  Is asked for a reason—
    WHAT THEN?

THE BEST OF OUT OF MY TREASURE

PALM SUNDAY

Thy King has come
Unlike the mighty one of old,
Unlike the rivals for his power today,
In meekness, riding on an ass, alone.
Let this, his mind, be in you all
Seek out no reputation, nor seek gold;
Search out instead the true humility
And follow in the dust-stirred road
The donkey's tracks toward Golgotha,
The God-planned route that leads to life
Through, not by-passing, the Cross, the tomb.

The best news ever heard came out of the graveyard. A great difference between Mohammed and Christ is that Mohammed is still in the grave.

Perhaps it was in the woodland
Where He went with heart of woe,
That the Master dreamed of a lily
With golden heart aglow.
Perhaps when His kind gaze faltered
Deep in the heart of man,
The vision of something perfect
As an Easter lily began.
The winter is over, and Sorrow,
Borne on the wind's cold breath,
Is list in the lovely Springtime
That gives the life to Death;
And the beautiful Easter lily,
Stands chaste and divinely tall,
The pure white dream of the Master
Who blesses and loves us all.

—Anne Campbell

THE RADIANCE OF EASTER

Like dawn after a moonless night, like springtime after the snows of winter, like clear understanding after the fog of confusion, and like comfort after fear, comes the radiance of Easter to bring us joy.

For Easter, with its reality of the risen Christ, is the triumphant answer to suffering and death, to our questions of what lies beyond this life. It is the golden key to the meaning of life for now - for eternity.

"He is not here, for He is risen" (Matt. 28:6).

WHAT EASTER IS

Easter is the singing of happy birds once more;
Easter is the ringing of bells from shore to shore;
Easter is the budding of trees that did not die;
Easter is the scudding of white clouds across the sky;
But more than just the sprouting of seed and bulblet brave,
Easter ends the doubting of life beyond the grave;
Easter is the snowing of hope and faith on men;
Easter is the knowing that we shall live again!
—Enola Chamberlin

The empty tomb proves Christianity, but the empty pew does not.